PLAY DIRECTING IN THE SCHOOL

A drama director's survival guide

DAVID GROTE

MERIWETHER PUBLISHING LTD
Colorado Springs, Colorado

Meriwether Publishing Ltd., Publisher
P.O. Box 7710
Colorado Springs, CO 80933

Editor: Arthur L. Zapel
Typesetting: Sharon E. Garlock
Cover design: Tom Myers

Library of Congress Cataloging-in-Publication Data

Grote, David.
    Play directing in the school : a drama director's survival guide /
  by David Grote. -- 1st ed.
      p.   cm.
    ISBN 1-56603-036-3 (pbk.)
    1. Amateur theater--Production and direction. 2. College and
  school drama.   I. Title.
  PN3178.P7G76   1997
  792' .0222--dc21   97-31802
                                                 CIP

1   2   3   4   5   6   7   8   99   98   97

CONTENTS

INTRODUCTION

Play directing can be an art, but like all real art, it is built on a solid foundation of craft. The craft can lead to the art, but the art itself can never compensate for lack of craft. So the director must be a craftsman first.

Fortunately, craft can be learned. Like all crafts, directing is best learned by doing. Experience is the best teacher.

Unfortunately, experience is also the slowest teacher. We get so caught up in our immediate problems that we haven't time to reflect, to consolidate, to theorize, and to revise.

This book is my attempt to organize what I have learned from some thirty years experience so that it can be used by other directors. Although the advice and procedures described can work at almost any level, the discussion is framed in the context of the school. I chose this framework for several reasons. First, this is the hardest place to direct a play. In a school, the director is not only a senior partner in a joint creative process but is also a teacher. You must not only stimulate creativity but also teach the participants how to use that creativity. In particular, you must work with actors who don't yet know how to act. You have a very small talent pool from which to choose. You have far more limited personnel resources than almost any other type of theatrical production. In most cases, in addition to directing the play, you must also be your own producer, designer, and technical staff.

Secondly, directors in a school situation have usually had very little training or preparation. You are always hired for some other reason and assigned (or allowed) to direct plays as an afterthought.

Because of this, most people in the professional theatrical world automatically assume that directors in the schools are incompetent. Many are, perhaps. But then so are many of the directors cluttering up the major stages of the world. Unfortunately, many competent teacher/directors share this opinion of themselves. They convince themselves that, since their actors are students and their budgets are small and no one in the local community cares about Art and Culture, there is no way they could put on good shows even if they learned to be the greatest play directors in history.

Which is my third reason for writing this book. There is no inherent reason why school play productions must be done badly. They can be done well, often very well indeed, if they are directed well. Good play direction is defined by the play, not the budget or the building in which the play is performed.

1

There are, of course, a lot of other books about play directing, but these tend to fall into two groups. One group is textbooks, which tend to be so theoretical or generalized that they end up actually telling the potential director nothing that can actually be used in rehearsal. The other group is made up of theories and reminiscences of famous directors. These are certainly interesting, but they offer very little practical help, because they work only with the best actors in the best professional situations.

Books aimed specifically at directors of amateurs tend to be about "How to Put on a Play." For the most part, they concentrate on quick and easy ways to do scenery, costumes, props, and publicity. They can help the practicing director, but they still aren't really about actually directing a play.

This book tries to cover the actual process of directing a play, described not as theory but as a step-by-step sequence. It begins with the selection of the play and then follows each step of the rehearsal process. It gives considerable attention to some very fundamental, and often ignored, aspects of the craft of staging a play. For inexperienced teachers, it is also a detailed examination of the unique problems of the secondary school situation, with some theory and much practical advice about ways to get the most from student actors during preparation and rehearsal. For experienced teachers and directors, it is, I hope, also a stimulus and a reminder and a source of additional ideas or insights that could help lead to better productions.

Occasionally, the advice included in this book will sound dogmatic. If so, I can only apologize. Nothing in here is determined by theory. Everything is based on things I learned from that hardest of all teachers, experience. If I warn you against certain "mistakes," it's because I have already made that mistake, in some cases more than once. One of the reasons for writing such a book is to help other people avoid the problems of reinventing the wheel. Not everything I advise will work in every situation, but I advise them in the hopes of saving other directors from the pain of making mistakes they don't need to make.

That said, the book will, I hope, speak for itself. But there is one last point I would like to add. Remember, whenever and wherever you are directing a play, at that time and place, you are the theater. In America, we think of the theater as Broadway, the regional theaters, maybe summer stock, and perhaps, very far away, the Royal Shakespeare Company. But most Americans have never seen a professional production of a play. If they have seen a play at all, it was almost certainly at a school. If it wasn't at a school, it was at a church or a community theater, which also use amateur actors and in which the directors face exactly the same kinds of problems as the director in the school. Almost all of our professional actors began in an amateur production as a teenager. It makes a difference whether you do a good job or a bad job. In many cases, it makes a much greater difference than it does on Broadway, for people who don't like their first exposure to theater rarely have a second. You are a real director, and you are an important director, wherever you are. So there's no reason why you shouldn't also be a good director.

CHAPTER ONE
SELECTING THE SCRIPT

Play directing begins with the play itself. One of the most important decisions you will make in the complete directing process is your choice of the play.

Before any decisions can be made, you must get to know the available material. Unfortunately, and at the same time fortunately, you can never know all the material available. There are about 400 years of material in English alone, not to mention the centuries of material from continental Europe and Asia nor the emerging theaters of Africa and Latin America. In addition, every year hundreds of new plays will be published.

We start out doing the plays we know, which are usually just the plays we've already acted in or seen someone else do, or perhaps were assigned for readings in college. A lot of people think that shows our ignorance, but in fact that's the way the professionals do things, too. Very few people at any level of theater actually read plays — they leave that to their agents or managers or assistants. Even so, you need to find time and money to read.

There are so many factors involved in choosing a playscript that you need to have lots of options. This is especially true in schools, where specific needs or problems can require something other than "standard" entertainment. Which means reading lots of plays you've never heard of.

Most of this material is not suitable to your needs, but there are also many good plays that are. The only way to find them is to read. Read every play you can get your hands on. Unfortunately, this will turn into an expensive habit because you will have to buy most of these scripts. Libraries have some plays, but they usually put the drama section very low among their purchasing priorities. Major publishers and leasing agents do not send out free perusal copies to high school teachers (if they did, who would be left to buy them?).

But whatever the cost might be, you simply cannot expect to do the job well if you select your plays only from the handful of plays "everybody knows."

I must stress *reading* the playscripts. Over the years, I have run into a distressing number of teachers who select plays for production by their titles or their catalog descriptions without ever reading them. Catalog descriptions are ads and like any other ads are designed to make the product as attractive as possible. No publishers purposely lie, but the play you get may not be at all what you had in mind when you ordered it. Always order individual copies first and read them before actually scheduling even the simplest production. And always re-read plays you read years ago or saw other people do before you decide to put them into production — you may have forgotten something terribly important about such shows.

Even more importantly, do not stop reading when you find a play you like. There are any number of reasons for selecting a play for production. You should consider all of them before you make your final decision. It is a good idea to keep and update a list of shows that are "possibles." Make a list. Whenever you read a play you like, put it on your list. Keep reading and keep adding to the list. You never know when you will need a particular kind of play. Without this kind of list, it's very easy to forget a good show that you read years ago but which would be perfect now.

THE SEVEN QUESTIONS

When it's time to select a play, pull out your list of possible scripts and ask yourself seven basic questions about each of them:

---

1. Do you like it?

2. Can you do it?

3. Can you afford it?

4. Can you find the performers?

5. Is it hard enough?

6. Can you get away with it?

7. Do you want your group to be associated with it?

In the course of your analysis, you will usually find that fifteen to eighteen of every twenty of the shows on your list will be eliminated by one or more of these questions. That's why you need a list. When you find a script that successfully meets all these criteria, then you've found a show you should do.

1. Do you like it?

This seems an obvious question, but it is often overlooked by directors who work in school, churches, and similar programs. Students will tell you what they want to act in. Other teachers will tell you what they would like to see, either for personal interest or more often to fit in with their curriculum. Principals, ministers, and other administrators will make very specific suggestions, especially if previous shows lost money or led to community complaints. Sooner or later, you will try to guess what you think your audience would want to come to see. All of these factors may be considered, but you must remember that you are the one who actually does the work.

Choose a Play You Can Live With, Enjoyably

You will give every spare moment of your life for at least three months to this show. You have to study it, plan it, interpret it, design it, rehearse it, explain it, and defend it. You have to look at it every day, when it's bad as well as when it's good. You have to listen to those lines and watch that stage business over and over for weeks on end. While you are doing this, for all practical purposes you will lose your personal life. If you are married, your spouse will start to complain that you are never home to fix meals, stop the leaky faucets, or help with the children. Your children will start to make jokes about the stranger at the breakfast table. You will not have time to drop in on friends, to play a little softball, to even go to a movie. To give up so much, you must get something personal in return. If that return is boredom, the work is not worth it.

No matter how many people offer suggestions, no one else is going to direct the play. No one else has to live with the decisions made, the standards set, or the example given to the young people you work with. There is enough pain and agony in this work when everything is perfect. There is simply no point in making it worse by doing something you don't enjoy, no matter how much pressure or obligation you may feel. Nothing can be gained for yourself, your program, or your audience in such a situation.

Remember, too, that there are many ways to "like" a play. There are any number of plays that you might enjoy watching — once. But in rehearsal, you are going to watch it several dozen times. If you are willing to do that, then the play is worth considering further.

2. Can you do it?

This is a harder question, because it requires a valid self-examination. Do you have the experience, the intelligence, the imagination, and the skill to deal with the script, to translate it to your actors, and to solve the technical problems of the production? If you think you can do that, then go ahead.

Some people overestimate their abilities, of course, and take on more than they can handle. But this usually involves technical problems, not directing problems. As we'll discuss later, you shouldn't try to do *War and Peace* if you don't have the physical and financial resources. But these are different from personal directing resources. Most school directors in my experience err in the wrong direction when they ask themselves this question. When faced with a "difficult" script and an "easy" one, they choose the easy one because they lack faith in their ability to "do more." Their own low self-esteem intimidates them. They feel they must do "high-school" plays because they aren't good enough to do "classics" or "Broadway" material. For some people, this is true, but for most it is not. Almost everyone who directs a play in a school or church group has a college degree, which is more than can be said for many professionals and many of the people in Hollywood. So chances are, you are smart enough to understand most plays.

We often forget what makes a good play good. We've all spent so much time in college literature classes that we've come to believe that real literature is something no one can understand without a Ph.D. This is simply not true, and it's especially not true in the theater. Every successful play (which includes the very finest) must be comprehensible in one viewing, because that's all the audience gets. What makes good plays good is that you can find more there if you choose to give it a second viewing. On first viewing, a merely adequate play and a very good one will look about the same, if done well. This can be seen each night on TV — a show that is interesting and entertaining on first viewing will usually be dull and flat when you see the rerun. Professionals spend most of their time trying to make poor material look better than it is. They get away with it, for the most part, because they are experienced professionals. The young people in your casts are not. They need all the help from the script that they can get.

Genuinely Good Plays Have a Lot of Depth and Strength

This helps both the director and the actors. A play's apparent difficulty is often its strength.

Good material has a way of helping the actors and directors, as long as they trust the material. I once surprised a convention meeting by suggesting that it was better for high school actors to play Chekhov than children's theater, because children's theater was much harder to do. I exaggerated to make a point. Nevertheless, the idea is fundamentally sound — it *is* easier to direct and to act when the material gives you real characters and interesting action. When the script offers nothing but cardboard characters and illogical action, it will demand the greatest skill and imagination to disguise.

Our Town *Is a Uniquely Difficult Play to Produce*

Teacher/directors often let technical problems dominate their concerns. Their fear of scenery gets them in over their heads in other areas. It would be a difficult point to prove, but my experience suggests that *Our*

Town, for example, is more often done because it has no scenery than because the director really understands, admires, and can deal with the material. That was why I staged it the first time I did it, and what I learned during the process of messing it up the first time made me do it again just as soon as I felt mature enough to try. *Our Town* is one of the most complex, inventive, and difficult plays in American theater. It has no plot in the normal sense of the word, it has two and one-half acts of exposition and one-half act of climax, with no tension or suspense in between. It has no conflicts as we usually understand dramatic conflict — everyone loves everyone else, and there isn't anything remotely resembling an argument, much less a fight, in the complete play. The stage action deals with unimportant things done thousands of times in our lives by practically everyone, so that characters never really seem to "do" anything. How are you going to make all this come alive and be as interesting as it could and should be? How are you going to make all this seem interesting to the audience, particularly an audience raised on car chases and three-second sound bites? How are you going to help your actors fill in all the important spaces between the lines?

Our Town is a great play, and this is no attempt to talk you out of doing it. But it illustrates quite clearly how a show that looks like it could be easy to stage because of its simple scenery can in fact be a very difficult show to direct in other areas. You must consider more than mere technical difficulty.

At the same time, it is important to remember that you need not always solve technical problems in the same way they were solved in New York. There are often much simpler, easier, and cheaper ways to do things, and to do them well, than the way New York designers did them. Remember, a New York designer who does things simply and cheaply and so effectively that the scenery goes unnoticed is a designer who soon will be out of work precisely because no one noticed the scenery. Simplicity, frugality, and dramatic effectiveness have very little importance in the professional theater, where complexity, expense, and attention-grabbing effects are what bring good reviews and new jobs to a designer. A little imagination can go a long way in this area, so don't be afraid to use the imagination that you have.

But there will still be shows that are too complicated or too technically involved for your experience at this time. If, after careful thought, you decide that you're just not ready for this yet, then the show will have to wait until you feel that you are.

3. Can you afford it?

This is purely a matter of economics. There is x amount of money on hand, plus y amount that you think you will take in from ticket sales, with z the amount the show will cost. If z is more than x+y, you need to find another show. Of course, the problem is: How can I estimate x, y, and z correctly?

In general, x is determined in one of three ways. In some organizations, part or all of the drama budget comes from some centralized fund. In schools, this is often called a Student Activity Fund, or some similar name. The fund collects a fee from students, or even takes money from the basic budget of the school. Then that money is split up among various school activities, from sports to clubs, in varying amounts. If any profits are made by any of the various groups, the money is added to the central fund to be split up later. In church groups, the money usually comes from a fund set aside for Youth Activities. In community youth groups, it often comes from the Parks or Public Service funds. Wherever it comes from, you start the year with a specific amount of money on hand, which you may or may not be expected to recover in ticket sales.

In many ways, this is the most practical system, because it is stable — you know what your budget is for the year. Its only real problem is that the amount given to your particular budget is determined more by organizational politics than by your need. The people who decide how much money to give you rarely understand what you need the money for.

A Word of Warning About Budgeting Politics

Unless you are in a very unusual organization, fiscal responsibility is often punished. Although you will usually be asked to submit a request, you must never request only what you need. Administrators demonstrate their fiscal responsibility not by controlling expenses but by cutting budget requests. A principal who cuts your requests by twenty percent is seen by the school board as a much more responsible administrator than one who gives you exactly what you need and sees that it is spent well. If you budget carefully and decide that you must have $1,500 or the program will die, and then request $1,500, your program will die. Because you will receive $1,200. If you need $1,500, you must always ask for $2,000 or $2,500. Everybody knows this, and everybody overestimates; it's a bureaucratic game played in every organization in the world. And it's terribly frustrating, because it punishes honesty and rewards hypocrisy. But it is the way the world works, and you must learn to play by the same rules as everyone else. If you're new in the program, ask around quietly to find out what the going rate of overestimation is. Most people know, although not everyone will tell you the truth about it.

Spend All the Money You Receive

If you receive $1,500, it is wise and practical to spend all $1,500. This is not hard to do, since there are always long-term investments, such as extra makeup, lighting instruments, or tools, that are needed. The important thing is that you do it whenever you have the chance. Do not ever give back the money you didn't spend. If you do, next time around they will give you less. You may think you have been frugal and responsible. They interpret this to mean that you overstate your requests more than everyone else, so they will cut your budget request even more than they cut everyone else's. In far too many cases, if they give you $1,500 and you spend $1,750, they'll take money away from other programs to give you $1,750. Personally, I find that reprehensible, and I would never recommend such behavior. But take a look at your school and see who and what is rewarded: It will be a very rare school that does not encourage teachers to lie in budget requests and to overspend wherever possible and that does not reward them whenever they do so. If you are in such a school, you would be a fool not to do as everyone else does.

Financing With "Seed Money"

Another major method of financing is "seed money." Some group will give you money to be used as a start-up fund for fund-raising performances, with profits expected to go back to the original group. In schools, the most traditional form has been the Senior Play, which is expected to raise money for Senior activities. This is a difficult situation. You have no control over the funds you begin with, you get no rewards when you are successful, and you get all the blame if the show doesn't make very much money. If this is the situation, it is better to decline the responsibility. Walk away. Let the people who want the money do the work and take the flak.

Be Completely Self-Supporting in Financing Your Theater Program

You have your own ticket sales and maybe a fund raiser or two, but the school or church itself provides no additional financial support (except for the use of the building). If you made money on previous shows, you have some money on hand to apply to the next production. By the same token, if you lose money on one production, it could wipe out a surplus you have built up over several years. This is actually not a bad situation, because you control all your budget yourself, and the profits from one big hit can sustain you through several years of shows that barely break even or lose a little. This in turn gives you a lot of flexibility in the kinds of plays you can select and the ways you can schedule them. But it can also lead to intense pressure to be "commercial," for fear of incurring a large loss when you have no funds to fall back on.

There Is No Best Method of Financing a Production.

Each group will have significant variations within any of these three basic methods of finance. The most important thing is that you understand exactly what the financial situation is before you begin play selection.

As for the money to be gained from ticket sales, there is no simple way to predict this. Attendance at plays in school or church groups, and with it your potential income, is determined by almost everything under the sun except the choice of play itself.

The following factors must be considered:

Size of organization — large schools have more students, more parents, and more friends, and thus more potential audience, than small schools. On the other hand, at small schools, everyone knows everyone else, and a much greater percentage of students attend all school activities.

Size of town — if the town has only one high school, everyone in town feels obligated to "support" activities at the school, and audiences will be drawn from the entire community. But once the town has a second high school, community audiences will disappear from both schools. Audiences will drop until they include only relatives and friends of cast members, while the community at large — those people with children in other schools or with no children at all — will no longer automatically support school activities. This is especially obvious at productions by church groups. You may be able to expect almost all the members of your church to show up, but don't expect anyone from the church down the street.

Geography — if the community is fairly isolated, attendance goes up; if you are near to or in a city with an active night life, attendance will decline.

Ticket prices — if tickets cost too much, people won't come. On the other hand, if they are too cheap, people will assume the show must not be worth much and will stay home.

Factors for Predicting Attendance

The one consistent factor in attendance is cast size. The larger the cast, the larger the audience. In my experience, once my largest program was established, I could predict within twenty-five people what my attendance would be for every single show before the season began. For a nonmusical play, I simply multiplied the number of people in the cast by fifteen to twenty; for a musical, I multiplied the number in the cast by thirty. Good word-of-mouth might push the ratio a bit higher, while casting decisions or bad word-of-mouth might drop it down a bit, but beginning with my second year at the school, that ratio never varied in any significant manner. Given the other factors above, the formula for your school could be higher or lower — I have visited some schools for which the formula runs around fifty to sixty audience members per cast member, and I have seen some schools that are lucky to draw ten people per cast member. Rarely will you find that any other factors will change your formula once you are established. I drew at exactly the same ratio for the musical *Company* as I did for *Anything Goes*, and at the same ratio for the nonmusical tragedy *The House of Bernarda Alba* as I did for the famous comedy *You Can't Take It With You*.

Some schools do bad shows and draw well; others do good shows and can't draw flies; still others do good shows and play to large audiences. But the odd thing is that this never seems to change, no matter what the show is. "Famous" plays do not draw any better or any worse than shows no one has ever heard of. The reason for that is quite simple — very few people in most communities have ever heard of any plays, period. If the play has been turned into a movie, people might recognize the title. Even so, this won't help your attendance much — people who liked the movie might come to see it as a play, but then again they might choose to stay at home and watch the video instead.

Factors for Predicting Expenses

Finally, you must predict what the show will cost to produce. This, too, is all but impossible to do with any accuracy, because there are so many variables involved. Certain costs are fixed: Royalty, for example, will be fixed in the play catalog (or in the case of musicals, by negotiation with the agency) and will not change no matter what other decisions you make. You will also have to buy scripts and can easily predict what that will cost. Publicity costs are also predictable with accuracy — call up any printer and ask what fifty or one hundred posters will cost, and then you will know whether you want fifty or one hundred posters, or perhaps no posters at all.

Most other expenses are unpredictable. Ten different organizations will spend ten different amounts on scenery and costumes for the same show, because they will do the scenery and costumes in ten different ways, on ten different stages in ten different communities. Unfortunately, only experience can help you learn to estimate this. If you are a genuine beginner, then start with a play with limited scenery and costume demands, or, if you have a large budget, do a show for which you can rent scenery and costumes. For anything in between, you will be operating blind.

The best method, because it is the most practical method, is to ask if you can possibly produce the show on the amount of money you expect to have. There are ways to stage almost any show effectively on relatively small budgets, as long as you are willing to live with a show that looks like you did it on a small budget. This doesn't mean the show will look tacky, for there are ways to use your money effectively. It does mean that you can't expect to produce on $150 what it took New York $500,000 to produce. You must be willing to try to stage shows in different ways.

If there is any likelihood you can pay for the production, then you should keep the show on your list. If it is clear that you haven't the money at this time, better to eliminate the show now than destroy your future.

4. Can you find the performers?

There are several different aspects to this question.

First, it is a consideration of simple numbers. Will you have access to enough bodies to fill all the roles? In any program, there will be a certain number of people who will always show up for auditions. But you need not depend only on these. You can increase this number by publicity, by sending the regular students you have out to find recruits among their friends, and sometimes just by stopping students in the hallway and asking them to audition. There will still be limits, most of them depending on the size of the school, the time of year, and the status of the program in previous years. But there are far more potentially talented performers in your school or in your church than most people realize, if you spend the time and energy to find them.

Second, it is a consideration of specific roles. Some plays just require bodies, while others require bodies with very specific skills. This is the one area in which "good" plays can become more difficult than "bad" ones. You can't do *Hamlet* if you don't have a number of males who can read, speak without mumbling, say sentences of more than six words in length, and do a little fencing as well. You can't do *Kiss Me Kate* if you don't have half a dozen very good singers. No matter how much you admire the material, your students must reach the practical skill level required to deal with the physical requirements of the material before you can do it well. You will naturally teach them in rehearsal, and in the process increase their skill levels, but there are limits on what is possible within any specific rehearsal period.

The dangers at this point are twofold: You may become so concerned about one role — Joan, for example, in *Saint Joan* — that you fail to recognize the real difficulty of the show. You will often have two or three girls who could play Joan reasonably well, but rarely will you have enough boys to play the Dauphin, the Inquisitor, and the six or more other very demanding male roles in that play. At the same time, it is tempting to precast the show or select a show specifically to show off a particular student. This is disastrous. If other students feel you precast roles, they will quit auditioning. Anyway, you can be sure that if you pick *Saint Joan* to showcase Sally, Sally will get pneumonia during the first week of rehearsals or decide at the last moment to audition for the cheerleaders instead of the play.

A Method for Estimating the Availability of a Cast

Ask yourself this: "If I had to cast this show from only students I have used before, could I do it?" If the answer is yes, then chances are good you will find a good cast, even when some of those students who were in the last show or who are in your acting class don't show up at auditions. Most of the time, I recommend that people live a little dangerously (but only a little). At my first school, my first play was *Thieves' Carnival*, which takes about twice as many men as women. When we got to auditions, I cast every boy who showed up, and I still had two roles unfilled. The yearbook photographer had come to take pictures, but I made him read. He in turn said that if he had to do this, so would his buddy waiting in the car. That's how we found our last actor. The photographer turned out to be excellent. We couldn't keep him away from any other shows the rest of his high school career, and he eventually became a collegiate drama major. His buddy eventually played Big Daddy in a college production of *Cat on a Hot Tin Roof*. Neither would have ever gotten started if I had picked a show to fit only the boys I knew would show up. At my next school, after casting a show with four male roles from only five male auditioners, I decided to take the bull by the horn and find some boys. For our next production, I selected *The Front Page,* which needs seventeen males. We twisted arms, stroked egos, and cajoled boys throughout the school, but we eventually found all the boys we needed. More importantly, once they were involved, almost all of them came back for future shows.

You won't always be this lucky, of course, but you have to take chances. Every show you do is a gamble, no matter how small the cast or how sure you are of certain individuals. Estimate your human resources carefully, but remember there is no sure thing when dealing with people, especially with young people. Sometimes it backfires: After so many successful gambles, I selected a very demanding show because I felt absolutely secure that I had not one but five different girls who could play the critical principal role well. Not one of the five showed up at auditions, leaving me with a makeshift cast and a barely adequate production. Don't do *A Chorus Line* if you have no dancers, but don't automatically reject a show just because you can't guarantee that a suitable performer will audition.

5. Is it hard enough?

Most people ask this question backwards, asking if the material is easy enough for their students rather than hard enough to challenge them.

You get better at a craft by gradually increasing the difficulty of the work undertaken. You learn by studying the things you do not yet know. If you know that you could direct the show in your sleep, and that your probable actors could play the roles without effort, then you have no business doing the play. No one will learn anything, and the time you spend will be wasted.

This is important, even if you're not in an actual school situation. Any time you do a play, it is a potential learning experience for everyone. One of the reasons churches and community youth groups have play production programs is to help the young people learn about life, about themselves, and about other people. You don't have to be teaching "acting" or "theater" to consider what you will teach in the course of the production. Make every show a challenge in some way.

Plays That Look Easy Often Turn Out to Be Difficult

You should be aware of a curious psychological quirk among student actors. Whenever work looks easy, teenagers tend to do it poorly. You can see this in almost any class: If you give students a month to write a book report in English class, almost no one will start reading the book until the day before the report is due. (This is, of course, not limited to teenagers; most adults will also put off any serious work until the last possible moment — when do you usually do your taxes?) If an assignment looks easy, half the class will forget to do it at all. The same thing happens in a play that looks easy: The cast will play around and doodle through rehearsals until the last possible minute before applying themselves just enough to get by. The result will almost always be a slipshod performance. But if the material is clearly difficult, they will start work from the very beginning and work hard all the way through because they will be afraid of not making it by the time the show opens.

Of course, what is easy for one will be very hard for another. The best way to maintain a level of difficulty is to maintain variety. Never do two similar shows back to back. Follow a light romantic comedy with something realistic and emotionally intense, follow a realistic play with a more stylized or physical show, follow a show full of young characters with one full of more mature roles, and so on. Keep the plays and roles varied, and then both you and the students will always have new challenges to meet and to learn from.

Also, be very careful how you define difficulty. As we have seen in other sections of this chapter, shows may be difficult in some areas and very easy in others. In the same way, roles may look difficult and be very easy to play. For example, despite the first impression, the easiest role to play in *The Miracle Worker* is Helen — as long as the actress is short and doesn't look directly at anyone, audience sympathies and the play itself will make her look terrific. But Annie is a different question. She must look mature, use a forbidding exterior to mask a very fragile interior, and do all this while hiding her eyes behind dark glasses which prevent the audience from seeing her expressions. Thus, the role that will demand your best actress will be Annie, not Helen. Similarly, almost any teenaged girl with minimal expression can play Anne Frank — the hard roles in that play are those six adults around her. They have not only a far greater emotional range to play but must also project physical maturity as well.

Always remember that you are a teacher as well as a director, in school or out, and that you have a responsibility to stretch your performers. If you can cast the show with people who can play all the roles simply by doing what they've always done, then you shouldn't be doing that show, any more than you should be doing it if there is no hope that you can ever find a competent cast.

6. Can you get away with it?

This is, without doubt, the single most confusing and frustrating aspect of play selection. In most schools, the director is not the final arbiter of play selection. The principal or someone selected by the principal may have the right to veto any play that they regard as unsuitable for your students to do. This unsuitability is determined by a number of rules, sometimes clearly laid out and expressed, sometimes merely implied. Unfortunately, these rules seem to have nothing to do with either the theater or with the reality of student life or interests.

These rules will also vary from school to school, even within districts or communities. In general, your actors will not be allowed to say certain words, in particular the F word and "God" or "damn." No one will be allowed to smoke on-stage (originally because it was thought to be sinful and now because it is thought to be unhealthy), and many schools will not allow characters to pretend to be drinking alcoholic drinks. Almost anything to do with sex will be forbidden. And it will rarely matter whether you are in a small town or a large city — similar rules will be in effect in both.

The problem for the teacher/director is that such rules seem to have no rational foundation. When the language you hear in school hallways from fifteen-year-old girls is much more vulgar and profane than I heard in a year in Vietnam, how can we forbid an actor to say, "damn"? When more than a quarter of all teenaged girls are pregnant at least once before they graduate from high school, how can we pretend that in moments of passion adults never do more than hold hands?

Even odder, how is it that some plays can violate these rules and never

17

face any complaint from administrator or public? *Grease,* for example, has become a staple of high schools across the country, and to the best of my knowledge, not a single case of suppression or audience complaint has ever been noted. This, in spite of the fact that the plot is almost completely focused on the assault on Sandy's virginity. No one complains about *Harvey,* in which the hero is an alcoholic, nor about *Arsenic and Old Lace,* which features two sweet little old ladies who poison old men with homemade liquor. Few complain about *My Fair Lady,* where Higgins scatters "damns" about the stage with impunity, or about *South Pacific,* which requires a very clear sexual consummation.

The fact of life is that restrictions on your play choice have almost nothing to do with morality or logic and almost everything to do with public relations. Each rule you have to deal with was developed and instituted as a result of complaints from some local pressure group. That's why every school has a different set of rules.

In general, most complaints come from religious pressure groups. But in recent years, other groups have taken note, and now you are likely to find someone who will object to almost any play selected. And the complaints may be completely without logic: I know of at least one teacher who was forced to drop *Godspell* from her schedule and ordered to put on a more "Christian" play — *Fiddler on the Roof.*

Churches Sometimes Are Able to Do More Daring Plays Than Schools

Ironically, church groups often deal with more controversial subject matter. For one thing, most people in the organization already share an understanding of the "rules." There are no competing moral codes; you all already agree about most things, or you wouldn't all be in the same church. But church groups sometimes are willing to be more daring, because they want to use drama to examine specific social or moral issues. In schools, no matter what the administrators might claim about their mission to train students for "the real world," all they really want is to go for a few days without the phone ringing.

Don't Argue Endlessly About Play Selection

There isn't any rational solution to this problem, because the problem itself is irrational. My best useful advice is: Don't take on your principal head-on. If he or she says you can't do a play, make your case in a logical manner and then, if he or she isn't persuaded, find another play. If he or she says something must be changed, change it. If changing it would destroy the play, find another play. You have to live with this principal all the time, and if he or she thinks you have to be watched constantly, then you will be watched constantly. If you are seen as reasonable and understanding, you will be left alone more often than not and left to do what you want to do without interference.

At the same time, remember that no rules are cut in marble: Most people don't know anything about any plays, so that if you do something they've never heard of, you may be able to deal with subject matter that would not be possible in better-known material. As we have seen, there are some perfectly acceptable plays that include almost every activity or word that is supposed to be forbidden in most cases. As a matter of experience, most people who in fact complain about your material are people who have neither seen nor read that material; they just "know" that something is wrong with it. No one complains about the high school staples like *Harvey,* because everyone "knows" they are all right simply because everyone does them. Yet you would be swamped with complaints the moment you said the word *Hair,* no matter how innocuous the material is or could be made to be with very little effort, simply because millions of people who have never seen it still "know" all about it. If no one in the community "knows" the play you pick is "dirty," the chances are good that potential complainers will not bother to come see the show and therefore will never complain about it. In many other cases, you can make changes without damaging the material — you can offer characters coffee rather than martinis, cut the cigarettes completely, or delete an expletive or two here and there without damaging most material.

This is another area in which doing "classics" is actually an advantage. It might be hard to get approval for teenage sex in, for example, *Blue Denim.* But it is a rare principal who would refuse permission for *Romeo and Juliet,* despite the very same teenage sex. No one wants to be in the papers as the principal who banned Shakespeare. And it's a rare member of the community who would complain about Shakespeare, for the same reason.

7. Do you want your group to be associated with it?

Many, if not most, teacher/directors get so distracted by the nonsense associated with the most vocal pressure groups that they forget that parental and community objections are sometimes valid. When you try to select a play, you are also deciding the image of your program. Every play projects a message to the performers, to other students, and to the community at large. You have to understand what image you want to project, and then select plays that will in fact project that image.

Theater in the schools should be educational, and it should be relevant to the lives of the students. But there comes a time when the recognition of certain realities of life may in fact be seen as condonement or encouragement of those aspects of life. The school represents society as a whole to its students. It also serves as the only public authority figure in the lives of most teenagers. What it accepts or says it will accept is a potent influence on student lives, whether they wish to admit it or not. To some degree, actions in the school plays will be seen as admirable, or at least acceptable, actions simply because they are a part of the school play.

In the same way, your material in some way represents the educational image and policy of the school itself, no matter how much support you may or may not receive from your principal. If the show you present has no artistic merit or provides no challenge to performers or audience, you may be sending a message that not only your program but also the school as a whole has no commitment to education and no standards.

Similarly, the show may take positions on social issues that are inconsistent with your understanding of the school's mission in your community. To pick a popular example, *Grease* is an energetic and entertaining musical. But its message is that real life doesn't begin until you drop out of school and lose your virginity. Most adults watching a professional production can see that message as little more than a pleasant fantasy, since questions for them about school and virginity have long since been settled. But to high school students, these are very real issues. It seems to me that at a time when the drop-out rate is so high and a degree is so essential to employment, this is not a message that schools should be encouraging students to believe. Despite its many other attractions, that message makes *Grease* a very dubious choice for schools. Similarly, I would be happy to do *Godspell* just about anywhere *except* in a public school, precisely because I think it is so effective. While I may agree with its content personally, I don't think a public school in a pluralistic religious community is the proper organization to underwrite and support such a production. You may disagree. But the point is, you should think about it before you decide to do the play. After it is on-stage is too late.

Consider How Play Selection Affects Your Total Program

Sooner or later, you will have to decide where you want your program to go and what kind of a program you want it to be. If this is really your first play, it may take a while before you get there, but even the first play should be aimed where you want to go. A cute little "mellerdrammer," for example, may get kids on stage and people in the audience, and may even be fun to do, but is it the kind of show you want to be associated with? Basically, you must ask, "Can I go out in public and look people I respect in the eye when I tell them what play I have selected?" If you can't, then you shouldn't be doing this play.

In essence, you have to ask: "Why am I doing, not just this play, but any play at all?" I've phrased the discussion as a problem for the school teacher, but it holds true in any organization, at any level. If your only goal is to make a buck, then you aim for the lowest common denominator, like most of Hollywood and television. If your goal is just to keep the kids occupied during the summer, which is the real goal of many church groups, then you will spend very little time agonizing about this question. If your goal is to provide a moral, positive, life-enhancing way to occupy the young people, then you need to agonize about the question a lot.

Consider Your Own Social and Moral Standards

What kind of message does the play project about life in general? How does the play treat minority groups, for example, and how does it treat women, to point to two obvious and important issues each teacher must be willing to take clear positions on? If you think *The Taming of the Shrew* demeans women, then don't do *The Taming of the Shrew*, no matter what other arguments you may find in its favor. How does it jibe with your own moral standards? After all, it will have your name on it.

There is a tendency in contemporary schools to look for a play with a message about some current problem. As this book is being written, these tend to be about "women's issues," drugs, racial tolerance, or sexual restraint. While these are all important issues, you should be very careful in this area. It is always valid to use drama to teach, but remember, drama is also drama. If you only want to preach, few people will come. Keep your own goals and attitudes in mind, but always look for good drama first.

But you should also be very careful because such "message" plays can be very dangerous and damaging for the students who act in them. You must always consider what the play will ask individual students to do. The director in school and church groups operates in a unique environment, in which the actors must live off-stage with the same people who make up their primary audience. We may think we know the actors on TV or in professional plays, but we will never meet them in real life. So it doesn't matter what you may think Madonna, for example, is "really" like — her world and yours do not intersect in any way. But for teenaged actors (and adult actors in community or church productions as well), the play performance is a part of their real world. What they do on-stage tonight will be mentioned in class and in the halls tomorrow. You know they are "just acting," and the audience knows they are just acting. Yet somehow very few people in the audience are really sophisticated enough to clearly separate the performer from the role. There will always be the suspicion that the actor was chosen for the role because he or she was "really" like that.

Be Aware That the Lives of Teens Can Be Seriously Affected

If Susie kisses Jimmy, people will make jokes about both of them for weeks; generally, these will be good-natured jokes, and no harm will come of it. But if Jack kisses Jimmy, the jokes will cease to be good-natured, and it will not be forgotten. Similarly, if Susie plays a prostitute who takes Jimmy upstairs and starts undressing, the joking may also start to turn sour very quickly. And the better the students act, the worse it will get for them off-stage, precisely because it will be more convincing. Teenagers as a group are not nice people; they are at a very difficult period in life, and their insecurity turns to viciousness almost without warning. You have to consider this when you consider what you will ask your actors to do, for you will also be asking them to face their audience twice, in the theater and then later in the school at large. You can't trust their own judgment in such matters. They love to play fantasies. Very "nice" girls will all but demand to play prostitutes, for example, because they think it will be fun. Others will agree to do almost anything on-stage if it means getting a big part. You have to think for them in such matters. Some plays may have to be rejected in the best interest of the performers.

This is the biggest problem with plays designed to "raise consciousness" about some current issue. You may find a wonderful script about racial tolerance, but the kid who plays the racist bigot stands a good chance of being beaten up in the school yard for things he says on-stage. The girl who describes her abortion may find that she is known as the school slut. The character who comes out of the closet on the stage is also a real boy who has to survive in the showers after gym class. Think twice. And then think one more time. Such plays work best when played by outsiders, people the students don't already know.

At the same time, one of the most important values of the theater program is that it allows the student actors for a while to play adults and to deal with adult problems in a very genuine way. Learning a role requires far more commitment and understanding than writing an essay in class. The preparation of a role in which the student must learn to act as a parent, for example, is extremely educational and beneficial to all concerned. The rehearsal of mature material can in fact help the student mature. Thus there are very strong reasons for doing material that is as adult and mature as possible within your performance context.

There are advantages and disadvantages. Consider both carefully. You have to question every play and every role for potential problems.

***

After you have asked and answered these seven questions, you will have eliminated most of the plays from your possibles list. From the ones remaining, pick the show you most want to do.

If none remains, start reading again. A play that is unsuitable now will still be unsuitable when you get it in front of an audience. Never produce a show just because you can't think of another one.

PLEASING THE AUDIENCE

At this point, someone will be asking, "Don't we have to pick plays that audiences will like?"

Although it sounds a bit odd, audience is not all that important in your play selection, for one very simple reason. Audiences for plays with amateur actors generally do not come to see a play — they come to see the performers in the play. Thus, you must clearly distinguish between a play that will draw them in and a play that will entertain them once they are there — that is, you must separate advertising from entertaining.

The overwhelming majority of your audience will have no feelings, good or bad, about your show before they see it. Most of your audience simply knows nothing about the theater. They may recognize a few names, but only if they are names that have appeared on movies or TV shows. *The Fantasticks* is the longest-running play in New York theater history, but that will mean almost nothing to your attendance if you do *The Fantasticks*. Whatever you pick, if you do a good advertising campaign and have a good cast, you will draw just as well as if you do nothing but Tony Award winners.

Much more important is how the people in the audience feel about the show after they have seen it. Most of us get confused in this area when we say that what we do has be "entertaining." Of course it should. But entertainment is not a negative term. Most people equate "entertaining" with "childish," but they are two very different concepts. Many shows we pick because they are "just" entertainment turn out not to be even that. Any good theater must be entertaining — that is, it must get the audience's attention and hold that attention and engage the audience's mind for as long as the play is on the stage. Some shows are *only* entertaining, while others are entertaining *and* challenging, or entertaining *and* artistic, or entertaining *and* meaningful. But if they are not entertaining first, then they aren't good theater. *The Miracle Worker*, for example, is extremely entertaining, while it is also extremely serious in content; so is *Hamlet*, for that matter, or *Our Town* or *Saint Joan*. If they weren't entertaining to begin with, no one but scholars and killjoys would ever have become interested in their philosophical messages as well.

Unlike professional theater, your audience is guaranteed.

In one very real sense, in a school or a church group you are in a paradise — your audience is almost a sure thing (for good or bad), no matter what you choose to do. Unlike a professional theater, you don't have to find a way to convince people they will like the show before they will come to see it. All you have to do is produce a show that is so good they will like it once they have seen it. That isn't easy, but it is half the job a professional company must do. If you pick good material and do it well, the audience will be entertained by what you do.

After a while, in fact, the audience will come to share your standards. If you have given them plays that are entertaining and stimulating, they will find themselves vaguely disappointed by a show that is only entertaining.

When most people say their audience wants entertainment, they are in reality insulting their audience. In my experience, you can't have a successful program with that kind of attitude. Network television thinks that way, and you can see the results any evening on your TV set. Everything there tries desperately to be entertaining, and almost nothing actually entertains anyone. For the most part, it only succeeds in being background noise for the other parts of our lives, something we watch out of the corner of our eye in the vague hope that any minute now something interesting will come along at last.

Your audience is smarter than that and more lively than that. Television and mega-hit movies are openly aimed at twelve-year-olds. Even with an audience composed almost completely of high school students, the average mental age is several years higher than that. One nice thing about your audience is that it doesn't have many preconceptions about the theater. You can do just about anything, and they will think that's the way it is supposed to be. If you do it well, they will be interested and they will be entertained. If you do not insult their intelligence, if you start with good material and do it well, they will respond and participate in ways that will often surprise you.

The critical factor is doing your material well. Even the most simple-minded entertainment is not entertaining when done poorly. Done well, the most complex and demanding material is immensely entertaining.

CHAPTER TWO
ANALYZING THE SCRIPT

You can expect to stage a script well only if you understand what is written in the script.

It takes a long time to fully analyze a play, far longer than the average playgoer could ever imagine. But you must take the time to do this properly. You cannot be a good director without it. As a director, you must understand far more about the script than anyone else (except perhaps the writer). You have to understand both the detail and the whole. You should understand not just what every word means, but also why that word rather than another was used, and why each word and event occurs in one particular place rather than another. At the same time, you should understand how all these millions of choices come together into some unified whole, which you must design (or supervise design for) and stage. If your analysis is inadequate, the production will be inadequate. If your analysis is incomplete, you will have a difficult and unfocused rehearsal period.

Directors who work with young or amateur actors often try to tell themselves that detailed analysis is wasted effort. After all, they say, since the cast and the audience are primarily teenagers, they won't understand the "subtle" points. That is simply not true. The most difficult thing to remember in the age of academic literary studies is that every "complex" or "subtle" play of the past was written for an audience that did not take college courses in literature. Shakespeare's plays were written for and successful with people whose education and manners would make your student audiences look like the graduate faculty at Harvard. Yet they obviously understood what they were watching, or Shakespeare would not have retired a wealthy man. Audiences can grasp far more by watching and listening than we give them credit for. The fact that most of your audience would not be able to write a coherent dissertation about the play does not mean they can't grasp what is in it. Besides, if no one will understand it, why are you doing it to begin with?

While it is true that your audience won't spend the intermission discussing the development of nature metaphors in Act I, they will notice the effects of those metaphors. Or rather, they will notice the effects if you have made them. You can only make them if you noticed them in the script and understood their relation to the rest of the script. Everything in a play is there for a reason. To ignore anything is to defeat the reason for doing the play to begin with. You have to stage the play you have selected. If you are doing *The Miracle Worker*, you not only have an obligation to do what Gibson wrote, but you also can't possibly stage it without coming to grips with *everything* that he wrote in that script. Everything in a play affects everything else. To dismiss something out of hand because it is too subtle or complex is to destroy the play.

Detailed Analysis Is Essential

Before you begin detailed analysis, however, in the front of the production book, write yourself a brief note describing why you picked this script and what you like about it. It is easy in rehearsals to lose sight of this point, because you will be working with details. As a result, plays often change until they become unrecognizable, and the director and actors never notice because they are so closely involved. Every week or so, refer back to this note and remind yourself why you picked this particular play to work on.

Now you are ready to begin a careful analysis. This will require many different readings, and definitely should take several days, or more likely weeks, given a director/teacher's other duties. Although we don't have the space to describe the methods you can use to make and then test the accuracy of this analysis,* we can describe what a complete analysis involves. Before you are ready to design, cast, or begin rehearsals for a play, you should understand all the following points.

PLOT

What is the action of the play?

What events (most often acts of individual characters) actually lead to and cause other events? To what end do they lead? What precisely causes them to begin? The important factor here is a cause and effect relationship between events. Many of the things that happen on-stage in your script are not part of the action or plot, but serve other purposes. Many events in the action actually occur off-stage or in the past before the first scene in the play. But each of these events, after the first one, causes another event to happen, which in turn causes another, and so on until the end of the action. Similarly, each event after the first one is a reaction to, an effect of, a previous event.

Sometimes these cause and effect relationships will be unrealistic, or even unbelievable, but that is not at issue at this point. The important point is that they exist. These are fundamental to every other part of the analysis and to the audience's understanding of the performance. No one can under-

---

*I have described a much more detailed method for analyzing playscripts in *Script Analysis* (Wadsworth, 1985), and I cannot recommend it too highly.

stand what is going on without an understanding of this sequence of events and of the way each event leads to the next. You can't possibly make these clear to the audience without a clear understanding of them yourself.

How does each event of the action affect the relationship among the characters concerned?

Each event in the action occurs in a situation, and then when it has occurred, it changes the situation. What precisely is the situation at any time in the course of the action?

SETTING

Where and when does this action occur?

Although obviously related to scenery, this is not a question about scenery. A complete answer requires thinking on several different levels:

- Where and when do the events that are seen on-stage occur? Indoors or out? Which rooms? Whose rooms in whose home or building? Time of day? Time of year? Time in relation to previous scenes?

- Where and when do (did) the events in the action occur? Those seen on-stage, of course, occur in the same places as already noted. But what about those occurring off-stage and only mentioned or described on-stage? When and where precisely did they occur?

- As precisely as possible, what is the historical context in which these events occur? What place and what country are we in? What year precisely?

Some of this information is given on the cast list page and in the printed stage directions, but much of it is not. Sometimes, it may be very difficult to determine.

CHARACTERS

In which events of the action does each character participate?

Who and what actually carries the plot?

In which activities on-stage does each character participate?

Who is on-stage at any given time? Who knows what from firsthand observation?

What is each character's goal?

What do the characters seem to want to accomplish? This is not always easy or obvious, as you will know if you have done any acting at all. Characters don't always tell the truth about themselves, assuming that they even know the truth. Thus, it is sometimes easier and more productive to ask: What does each character actually accomplish? and then to accept that as the individual character's goal.

What conflicts arise from these goals?

With whom (or sometimes what) does each character come in conflict, and what exactly are the points of conflict between them?

At each individual event in the action involving a particular character, what is the character's immediate objective?

Even when a character may understand his or her goal, no one always thinks only of that. At the same time, when conflicts arise, these conflicts keep the character from reaching his or her own goal. Thus, the goal must be temporarily modified each time the situation changes. Sometimes these modifications are just conscious maneuvering, especially when the character, like Iago in *Othello* or Annie Sullivan in *The Miracle Worker*, knows clearly what he or she wants to accomplish (to destroy Othello, to teach Helen). Thus, they try different approaches in search of one that works, each of which is a separate, distinct objective. But when characters are not completely aware of their goal, they often appear to be changing directions completely. This occurs because they think they want one thing, but when faced with opposition, discover that they will accept or perhaps really want something else entirely. Helen Keller originally thinks she wants immediate gratification, but part way through the play recognizes that she wants to learn, which is a greater gratification. Hence, their objectives may change significantly each time the situation changes.

Is the character's objective the same as what the audience is led to believe?

Sometimes, the audience understands more about the situation than the character does. Hence, the character may try to accomplish one thing while the audience believes he is trying to accomplish something else entirely. This usually happens when a character says he is trying to help but, in fact, hurts, as, for example, when in *The Miracle Worker* Mrs. Keller wants to let Helen eat from her plate.

Sometimes the audience may misunderstand because the writer has kept some information secret. For example, until about half-way through Act II of *The Mousetrap*, the audience is led to believe that the policeman wants to solve the crime. This does not change the character's real objective, which you must help the actor to play. But as the director you have to recognize the difference between what the actor/character wants and what the audience is supposed to think the character wants. Then you must find ways to make sure that difference is sustained as long as the writer indicates. *The Mousetrap* is over just as soon as the audience realizes who the killer is, so you have to keep that secret to the last possible moment, even though you know already. If you don't do that, there will be no play.

What choices does each character make in each situation?

This will be extremely valuable in both your understanding of the nature of each character and your work with the actors. Consciously or unconsciously, each character makes a number of choices in the course of the play. Each choice somehow contributes to the action and each choice grows out of the character's objective. To understand these choices, ask: What precisely are the options available to the character in each situation? Which one is actually chosen? Which ones are rejected, and why?

What appearance does each character project?

This includes physical appearance; that is, what does each character look and sound like? Does this change over the course of the play? This question deals with things like age, clothing, general looks, size and weight, etc. It also includes the appearance of personality. People associate certain attitudes and character types with certain outward appearances, so what kind of a person does each character look like, no matter what they might be inside? Also, within each situation, what emotions are visible to others, no matter what the character may feel inside? There is information about this in the stage directions, of course, but there is far more information about it in the way all the characters describe and react to each other. Don't ignore that information.

What is the character really like?

What does the character feel at any given moment? How does he or she think? How would you describe their personality? In many plays, characters will be exactly the same inside as they appear to be on the outside. But in many others, the character will "really" be quite different from what he or she appears to be. Iago, for example, really is a villain, but in all his relations with Othello he appears to be a regular, friendly, and absolutely trustworthy fellow. In most cases, this polarity is not so intense or extreme, but such polarity exists with many characters.

What exactly does each character say and do at any given moment?

What does each word mean? What does each sentence mean? What does each speech mean? Precisely. You must understand every word. If there is one word you don't understand, you can guarantee that will be the one the actor will ask you to explain in rehearsal. More importantly, you must know because you need to know where to aim the actors, even if they don't ask.

What activities are called for in the script? This includes stage directions, of course, but it also includes activities implied in the lines themselves.

What does each character know?

How does each character relate to the other characters, and why? That is, what do they each know about what is going on? What do they know about each other? What do they know about the world in general? How smart or how dumb, how educated, how involved in general affairs are they? Does this knowledge change as the play progresses?

This also includes things the characters know unconsciously. For example, what is their cultural context, what kind of family did they come from, what country and time and social class are they a part of, and so on?

And finally, at each moment of the play, what do the characters know about themselves? Do they understand what they are doing, or why they are doing it?

One important point to remember as you deal with this question is that you, and the actors involved, know more than the characters or the audience. That is, you already know the ending. Hence, you know what is only hinted at, or perhaps even disguised, in the beginning scenes. In order to make a good performance, you have to understand what lies beneath the surface and use it to help the actors build their characterizations. But what the actors know and what the characters know are two different things. Your analysis must clearly distinguish between the two.

STRUCTURE

In what order are the events of the action revealed to the audience?

A play has a beginning and an end, but the beginning on-stage is not necessarily the same as the beginning of the action. *The Diary of Anne Frank*, for example, begins on-stage after the ending of the action and then goes back to the beginning; *Our Town* shows us the wedding day before showing us the beginning of the romance, and so on. Most plays tend to begin in the middle of things, so that much of the first scene is devoted to listening to characters tell us what has gone on in the past, before the lights went up. We call this exposition, but it actually occurs in the middle of the real action, not at its beginning. Often, important information about the action is kept a secret from the audience in order to promote a mystery, so that events that occurred long before the play began are not told to the audience until very late in the play.

The critical point is that the action of the play and the activity on-stage are almost never identical. The playwright always rearranges the story in some way, to produce an effect on the audience. If you intend to produce that effect, you have to understand the difference between the sequence of the plot and the sequence in which it is revealed to the audience.

How completely and when are the nature of individual characters revealed to the audience?

Some characters are what they appear to be from the very beginning, others change or appear to change in the course of the play, and still others are suddenly revealed to be different from what they had seemed to be. When, precisely, do these changes occur in the script? Remember that you know the "real" nature of each character because you've already been all the way to the end; what you want to know here is when some or all of this knowledge is actually given to the audience.

How does this affect the way the audience stays interested in the play?

This is generally called the structure, and is often broken into five basic steps: exposition, development or rising action, crisis, climax, and denouement. It is important to remember that you are talking about the arrangement of information for the audience, not the information itself. The precise structure may vary from play to play. In general, the early portions of the play will be devoted to background information, the middle portions of the play to revealing the various steps of the action, the crisis to clarifying the principal conflict or conflicts, the climax to resolving those conflicts, and the denouement to wrapping up loose ends and bringing the play to a close. The crisis occurs somewhere between half and two-thirds of the way through the play, and the climax comes very close to the ending.

EFFECT

What basic attitude to the action is encouraged?

In simplest terms, is the audience expected to laugh or to cry? Most plays lie somewhere between the extremes, and almost all will include a few opportunities to laugh. But each play invites a particular response from a particular, intended audience. What seems to be the intended response from this one? Does this vary? Are people supposed to laugh at the beginning and then not to do so later?

What kinds of suspense, if any, are encouraged?

One of the reasons information is not given to the audience in the same sequence as the action occurs in historical time is that the playwright wants to set up little (or big) mysteries that the audience will stay around to see solved. This is, of course, essential to "mystery" plays, like *The Mousetrap*, but it also occurs in many other kinds of plays. For example, in *The Odd Couple*, Neil Simon puts the world's biggest slob with the world's neatest man. Automatically, we are encouraged to ask ourselves, "How can they ever get along?" Once we ask that question, then we want to stay around to see how this arrangement could possibly work. How can a teacher possibly reach a girl who can't see and can't hear and doesn't want to be taught? How can a set of people possibly live undetected for years in an attic? When will other people realize what Iago is doing, and what he is really like? These are all forms of suspense that the playwright uses to get an audience interested and to keep it interested. All that suspense is determined by the order in which information that the director and cast already know is given to the audience.

With which characters is the audience encouraged to identify?

One fundamental way in which the audience "feels" something about a play is that it cares what happens to the characters. This is generally called identification, but you will also hear terms like empathy, sympathy, understanding, involvement, or attraction. In some shows, the audience may be encouraged to identify with one character only. In others the playwright may encourage identification with all of the characters, in still others with only a few. In some, the audience identification may change as they learn more about the various characters and the situation.

I cannot overstress how important this is to the success of a production. Nor can I overstress how it is usually ignored in directing classes and in most play analysis in the classroom. You must understand with whom the audience is expected to identify so that you can stage it to give them a real theatrical experience. This question dominates all questions of casting, of design, of staging individual scenes. This is how an audience really experiences a play. Once they identify with someone in the play, they begin to feel something about the play. At that point, and only at that point, have you really staged a play, rather than just put on a show. How could, for example, *The Diary of Anne Frank* function if it were not that most of us, male or female, somehow identify with the feelings of Anne? With that identification, Anne and her family are real people, just like us, and thus can't be the evil threat to humanity that the Nazis claim them to be. Without it, they are merely criminals hiding from the law. How could *Our Town* possibly keep an audience awake if they didn't somehow identify with Emily? How could we cheer for Oscar and Felix in *The Odd Couple* at the same time as we laugh at their situation, if we didn't, even if only a little, see some parts of ourselves in each of them?

There are a number of ways the audience is encouraged to identify, and not all will be used in all scripts. Some of these include:

Information — the more we know about a character, the more we understand about them, and the more possibility there is that we will come to accept what they do and to care about them.

Attractiveness — the more attractive the things that the characters do, the more we are likely to care about them. This may involve simple physical attractiveness. It may involve an interesting, pleasant personality. Sometimes, it may involve something dark and forbidden but still attractive precisely because of its wickedness.

Representativeness — the more people are "just like us," the more we are likely to identify with them. This is often given by playwrights not as information about characters but about setting: The audience recognizes the set as something like a room people like us might have, and so we are predisposed to believe that the characters we see in that room, wearing clothes such as we might wear, are in fact people like us.

Idealization — characters who are not like us but rather like our ideal selves tend to draw audience identification.

Status — audiences tend to identify with the weak and with the underdog. No one knows why — in real life, almost everyone sides with the strong. But on-stage, we almost always side with the weak.

Opposition — sometimes even unlikeable characters can draw our identification because they are opposed by or are opposed to even more unlikeable characters or forces. Othello does terrible things to a really nice woman, but we are encouraged to empathize with him because he is tricked into those terrible things by Iago, who is even worse.

Whatever methods or combination of methods may be used in each particular play, you must be aware of it before you start casting and rehearsals. Remember, also, that not every identification occurs with the same intensity. We are asked to identify with Anne Frank in a far more intense manner than we are asked to identify with Oscar Madison. *The Odd Couple* would be ruined if we, in fact, identified as intensely as we do with Anne Frank, for then we wouldn't find the scenes nearly so funny.

STYLE

What is the play's theme(s)?

At last, something we've heard mentioned in a literature class. What topics does the play deal with? What points, if any, does it make? What ideas or concepts does it illustrate or dramatize? What moral, if any, does it draw?

A play may have several themes of equal importance. It may have a single theme. It may have a dominant theme with several related, but comparatively less important, minor themes. Some themes may be very important or profound, others may be trivial or commonplace, and some may be important or profound but treated in a trivial or commonplace manner. But a theme will always be there. It would be impossible to develop a dramatic conflict without having some idea involved. The ideas expressed through the dramatic conflicts of your play's action constitute the themes of the work. The play may or may not make a point or draw a moral, but it will nonetheless always have a theme.

This should give you little or no difficulty. Finding themes is one thing we're trained to do by all our schooling. The important thing to remember is that it is only one of many factors a director should consider.

What is the play's tone?

This is usually placed along a continuum from the farcical to the tragic. Almost no plays are completely farcical, or completely tragic. Most combine elements of humor and seriousness in many different ways.

Remember, however, to try to answer this question only after you have completed all the preceding analysis. The biggest single mistake directors make in their analyses is deciding what kind of play they have before they have studied it. Knowing that the play is a farce, for example, they then find only the farcical aspects and miss many other parts of the play. As a result, they turn out very dull productions.

What is the play's style?

Perhaps no term is more misunderstood and misused in the contemporary theater than style. We learn names for various styles and pigeonhole various plays and various periods in categories that have nothing whatever to do with the material in the scripts. Then in planning and rehearsal we devote all our attention to producing the correct Shakespearean Style or Restoration Style or Surrealist Style rather than to producing the specific style of the specific play under analysis. The terminology for style tends to encourage us to see only that which we want to see. Don't make any decisions about style until after you have completed all the previous analyses.

Style can generally be understood to lie along a continuum running from the absolutely realistic to the completely artificial. The problem is that some plays may realistically depict a milieu that seems artificial to us: *The School for Scandal,* for example, depicts a world whose manners seem artificial to us, but those manners were commonplace in their specific time and place. It may better be thought of as a realistic play about artificial people, than as an artificial play in an artificial style. Similarly, *Our Town* depicts very realistic people and actions, but in a very artificial style that uses narration, pantomime, flashbacks, the talking dead, and so on. Hence, it has an artificial style with a realistic content, more realistic than many "naturalistic" plays. Be very careful how you talk about this, so that you can make such important distinctions. Once directors have determined a style for the play, they tend to force an equivalent style on all the contents of the play, which may not, in fact, be valid.

Remember, too, that almost every period in theatrical history has claimed to want to "hold the mirror up to nature." That is, practically everyone wrote with realistic intent. The differences have to do with the definition of reality at the time and the stage technology available to indicate that reality.

PRACTICAL MATTERS

What practical requirements does the script make for performance?

For example, how many scenes with how many different sets of scenery? What is needed in each set? How many entrances? What pieces of furniture? What specific props?

Be sure you consider exactly what the script demands as a whole, not merely what is listed in the stage directions. Some scripts have minimal directions, and you will have to determine such requirements without their aid. Other scripts, particularly those first done on Broadway, come with very detailed descriptions of the set, much of which you can and often should ignore or modify for your own stage.

What clothing will the characters require?

For example, what specific items are identified in the dialog? How many changes are necessary? How does the play's setting, particularly period, affect these?

What other technical effects are essential?

For example, are specific sounds heard off-stage that affect what happens on-stage? Are there specific lighting demands, such as changes in time, practical lighting instruments in the sets and props, fireplaces that are lit, etc.? Are there unusual makeup requirements beyond age and characterization, such as duplication of historical figures or animals or unrealistic appearances, such as ghosts or symbolic figures?

* * *

35

A complete analysis of your script requires detailed answers to all of these questions. Only when you have completed such an analysis are you ready to begin planning for production and rehearsal.

CHAPTER THREE
PREPARING FOR PRODUCTION

Once you have decided on your script and analyzed your script, there are still a number of important things to do before you begin rehearsing.

Now, you must think about practicalities.

SCHEDULE

In order to produce the play you have selected, you must schedule three things: your facility, performance rights, and your overall production process.

Scheduling the Facility

The very first thing you must do is to secure a firm reservation for your production on the school calendar. This is not nearly as easy as it sounds.

You will need not just a date. If you intend to do more than one performance, as most groups do, you will in fact need an entire weekend. In addition, this date must be far enough in the future to give you time for six to eight weeks of rehearsal (depending on the difficulty of the show and whether you rehearse four or five times each week), plus another three to four weeks to finish designs, to order materials, and to schedule auditions.

In most schools, only one group is allowed to have a school activity on any one date. This is a sensible rule, even when competing groups will not be using the same facilities. You would not want to have the play performing at the same time as a football or basketball game or a school dance. They would take away part of your audience and perhaps even part of your potential cast.

Unfortunately, once you eliminate the dates of major games and dances, less than a dozen genuinely free weekends will remain in the school year. Holidays make it even harder to find a date. In the fall semester, Thanksgiving sits there like a black hole. You cannot perform the show the week after Thanksgiving, because your cast will forget everything they know during the five nights off for that holiday. But two weeks after Thanksgiving is the start of Christmas programs as well as the beginning of basketball.

In some schools, finals now start in mid-December as well, as districts try to get the semester over before the long Christmas break. If you are fortunate, football will be over before the weekend before Thanksgiving, but even so, every group in the school will want to get that weekend if possible. In the spring, there is spring break, an entire week in which actors can forget everything they ever knew. So you have to perform before the break, or several weeks after. Now that most holidays are on Monday, it is all but impossible to get either actors or audiences to come on Fridays or Saturdays before those Monday holidays. Throw in midterms, finals, proms, and assorted conflicts unique to each school district, and there really are only three or four weekends available in the entire year. Every group in the school will be trying to schedule things on those weekends. So get on the school's master schedule as soon as you can.

Control Performing Space Before Opening Night

You must schedule absolute control of your performing space for at least one full week, and preferably two, before your opening night. If you open on a Thursday, that means from the Thursday before at an absolute minimum. This is essential — you simply cannot stage the play without it, as we will see later. Most people, including school administrators, do not understand this requirement. They think that a play is just a slightly more complicated concert or assembly, and they can't understand why you can't set up on the morning before the show, just like the awards assembly. Thus, you will find that people will think nothing of scheduling a concert on Tuesday before your Thursday opening, or a special assembly for all biology classes to see the snake lecturer on that same Thursday during the day.

This becomes especially complicated in those schools where the stage is in the same space with some other facility, such as the cafeteria or the gym or a flexible-space lecture hall. But you must be adamant. You may negotiate freely, and you should compromise with others as much as practical in all the weeks of rehearsal. But only during the weeks of regular rehearsal. You can rehearse many other places than on the stage. The tech rehearsals and dress rehearsals of that final week have to be on the real stage. Once you put your scenery and lights up, they can not be taken down, no matter how temporary the break might seem. To expect you to do otherwise is exactly the same as telling the swim team to practice on the basketball court.

Remember, this requires a full week. If you are doing a show in a worthwhile manner, you must place scenery, organize props and costumes, and focus lighting. It takes hours to do each of these things, even under the best of conditions. Many groups actually have to build the scenery on the stage, because they have no other construction space, and this only makes it worse. You have classes during the day, and students cannot stay to help you at 3:00 pm. Thus, you must have the stage space during the weekend before the show as well as during the final week.

Put your foot down. This is what they call a bottom-line issue. You have to have the stage to put up your scenery and lighting, and you cannot move scenery on and off the stage daily during that the final week merely for the convenience of others. If there is no stage available for the last week, then tell them — no show. Believe me, it's that important. And also believe me, if you don't make an issue of it from the very beginning, no administrator will think it important enough to even remember, much less worry about.

Lock in Your Reservation of the Stage

I must stress this point because it is such a consistent problem. Almost all schools are operated to reward the disorganized. You will find that anyone and everyone will be given the stage at the last minute, although you have had your reservation on the schedule for a year, unless you are willing to fight to the bitter end. They'll all say, "Well, you can't have the stage all the time," which is true. But the fact of the situation is that they didn't plan their own work well enough to realize they would need the stage in time to reserve it as you did. Unless your administrator believes you will fight like a wildcat, the administrator will punish you for being organized and give the stage away. Get on the calendar, get as much time as you can on stage, but most importantly, get your tech and dress rehearsal time absolutely protected. Get it on paper, and get it signed and sealed by every possible administrator, so that there is no question whatsoever about your schedule.

If you're working in a church group, particularly where the program is new, you will often have similar problems. The play will usually be staged in a hall where many other groups usually meet. You have to make it clear to all concerned that, during that last week at least, the regulars will need to meet in some other room.

Clearing the Rights

Once your date is safely scheduled, you must get permission to perform the play you have selected. Most plays written in the twentieth century are under copyright, which means performance rights are owned and controlled by the author or his or her agents. To legally present a copyrighted play, you must pay a fee, called royalty. For professional productions, this fee is negotiated individually as a percentage of the ticket sales. Most amateur groups, however, pay a fixed fee for each performance of the work that stays the same no matter how much (or how little) money you make. This fee is usually clearly stated in the catalog of the company from which you ordered scripts. If for some reason you are doing a play not yet handled by one of the agencies, you will need to contact the author or agent and negotiate rights, but this will rarely happen unless you are doing the premier production of a new play.

To obtain permission for your performance, simply write the agency a letter in which you clearly identify your organization, the play and its author, and the date(s) on which you intend to perform (use school or church letterhead). Be sure to clearly state that you are an amateur organization. In most cases, this can be combined with your letter ordering scripts. But be sure to specifically request performance rights; ordering scripts does not automatically give you rights to produce the play.

Generally, any play in the catalogs will be available for production by amateurs anywhere in the USA. However, there are times when permission may be denied. Usually, this happens when a play has been optioned for a movie production or for adaptation into a musical, or when a national tour of a major revival is scheduled. Occasionally, the agency will withhold rights because some other organization in your vicinity has permission to do the show. And sometimes plays will be listed in catalogs before rights become available, as when a show is nearing the end of its Broadway run. Most of the time, however, you will probably be given permission automatically by return mail.

Royalties are paid in advance.

Almost every agency will send you a bill for royalty to be paid *before* the show opens. Royalty must almost always be paid in advance, because you are purchasing the right to perform. This means you cannot wait until you have sold your tickets to pay this. However, since you are working in a school and probably paying for all your orders with purchase orders, this should be no problem — after all, most of your scenery and costume materials must also be paid for before the show opens. The only time this may be a genuine difficulty is when you are doing a musical, for musical royalties and rentals usually must be paid in full before they will even ship you the scripts.

A final note: Pay the royalty! It is unethical and illegal not to pay royalty for those shows in copyright. You will meet people who tell you they don't pay royalties, and thus save $100 or so from their production budget. Such people have become more common with the advent of the photocopier. Sooner or later, they do get caught. When they do, they have to pay not only the royalty but a stiff fine. And, to no one's surprise, the school will not pay the fine out of gratitude for all the money you saved the school by not paying the royalty originally. Pay the royalty.

Think of the example you set your students. How can we teach honesty if we begin by cheating and stealing on the very first step? Besides, if playwrights make no money, they quit writing plays. Then where will your drama program be? (Believe me, speaking as a sometime playwright, major productions are few and far between — even very famous writers have spells when they need that hundred dollars from your show to pay the bills.)

If, for some reason, the agency says you cannot have the rights to the play, find another play. You have no legal choice. To go ahead and produce it anyway is theft, legally and morally.

Scheduling the Production

Once the production is on the school calendar and the performance rights have been arranged, you can make your Master Calendar for the production. This is primarily for your own benefit, although students may see it and use it. On the Master Calendar (see Fig. 3.1 on page 42), note the dates of the following deadlines and events:

__ Order scripts

__ Expected receipt of scripts

__ Production meetings with designers and/or staff

__ Designs completed

__ Order costume rentals or materials

__ Order scenery materials or rentals

__ Auditions announced

__ Auditions

__ Rehearsal (est. dates and times)

__ Technical construction work days

__ Photo sessions

__ Publicity releases

__ Tickets ordered

__ Ticket sale begins

__ Expected receipt of rental items

__ Expected receipt of borrowed items

__ Scenery, lights, etc., begin installation on-stage

__ Tech rehearsals

__ Dress rehearsals

__ Performance dates

__ Strike

__ Cleanup and return work days

__ Due dates for rental returns

Sample Production Schedule

Sunday	Monday	Tuesday	Wednesday	Thursday	Friday	Saturday
Sep 22	Sep 23 Order Scenery Supplies	Sep 24	Sep 25	Sep 26	Sep 27 3:00 PM Production Meeting	Sep 28
			Announcements Auditions			
Sep 29	Sep 30 7:00 PM Auditions	Oct 1 3:30 PM Auditions	Oct 2 7:00 PM Callbacks	Oct 3 7:00 PM First Cast Meeting	Oct 4 3:00 PM Production Meeting Final Designs	Oct 5
Oct 6	Oct 7	Oct 8	Oct 9	Oct 10	Oct 11 3:00 PM Production Meeting	Oct 12
			7:00 PM - 10:00 PM Rehearsals			
Oct 13	Oct 14	Oct 15	Oct 16	Oct 17	Oct 18 3:00 PM Production Meeting	Oct 19
			7:00 PM - 10:00 PM Rehearsals			
Oct 20	Oct 21	Oct 22	Oct 23	Oct 24	Oct 25 3:00 PM Production Meeting	Oct 26
			7:00 PM - 10:00 PM Rehearsals			
Oct 27	Oct 28	Oct 29	Oct 30 Photos	Oct 31	Nov 1 3:00 PM Production Meeting	Nov 2
			7:00 PM - 10:00 PM Rehearsals			
Nov 3	Nov 4 Publicity Mailed	Nov 5	Nov 6	Nov 7	Nov 8 3:00 PM Production Meeting	Nov 9 Scenery On-stage
			7:00 PM - 10:00 PM Rehearsals			
Nov 10	Nov 11 Add Props	Nov 12	Nov 13	Nov 14 Program to Office	Nov 15 3:00 PM Production Meeting	Nov 16 10:00 AM Light/Sound Set
			7:00 PM - 10:00 PM Rehearsals			
Nov 17	Nov 18 7:30 PM Dress Rehearsals	Nov 19 7:30 PM Dress Rehearsals	Nov 20 7:30 PM Dress Rehearsals	Nov 21 7:30 PM Opening Night	Nov 22 7:30 PM Performance	Nov 23 7:30 PM Performance 10:30 PM Strike & Party
Nov 24	Nov 25	Nov 26	Nov 27	Nov 28	Nov 29	Nov 30
Dec 1	Dec 2	Dec 3	Dec 4	Dec 5	Dec 6	Dec 7
Dec 8	Dec 9	Dec 10	Dec 11	Dec 12	Dec 13	Dec 14

Fig. 3.1

These will vary in every production, depending on the demands of time and place. Most of them are discussed in more detail in the course of this book. In general, these various deadlines will occur approximately in that order.

Whenever anything must be ordered, such as costume rentals, remember that it takes time to process and to physically fill the order and it takes time to ship it. Always note on your schedule the deadline by which you must have placed the order so as to be sure it arrives when you need it. Otherwise, you will spend more than your total budget on long-distance phone calls and express shipping charges.

When you order scripts, always order extras. Order one script for each character in the play. Then order one extra for every eight actors, because at least that many will be lost during the course of rehearsals. Order two more for yourself, to make the production book, plus one for the stage manager/assistant director to use when they don't have the production book. Add one more for each designer involved. If you intend to allow students to read the script before auditions, add at least three more to replace the copies that will be lost during that period. Order scripts; **do not make photocopies.** That's illegal, in every instance. But in a practical sense, it is also counterproductive. Photocopied scripts are hard to handle during rehearsals. They flop around, they fall apart continually, they get out of order, and so on. Spend the five dollars and get real scripts that your actors can use.

PRODUCTION BOOK

As you prepare your analysis and then later as you work in rehearsals, you will need to keep a record of your decisions. This is done in a single copy of the script that is called the production book.

The production book is the bible for your particular production. It contains the script, of course, but it also contains all your blocking and other stage directions, all cuts and changes, all schedules, master lists for costumes, props, and scenery, and all light, sound, and other technical cues. In professional productions, the stage manager will keep a separate production book, also called the prompt book, which he or she prepares by noting down what the director says. In schools or churches, where you usually have to train the stage manager, it's often easier to just give the stage manager your production book partway through the rehearsals and let them be responsible for it from that point.

This is the one time printed scripts are less than helpful. Most scripts are printed with minimal margins. There is room for the actors to scrawl a bit of blocking, but that's about all. The director and the stage manager need gigantic margins. So you will usually need to make a special production book. The best way to make your production book is to use a loose-leaf binder and plain, unlined binder paper. Cut apart two copies of the script. Then glue one page to a page of binder paper, leaving a wide margin on the right hand side. Put these into your binder. Then, as you read, you will always have a blank page to the left, and the script on the right. Make analytical comments and notes on the left page. Record blocking and directions in the margin at the right. Most scripts will be smaller than a typed page, so there will be room at the top and bottom of the page for drawings to help you keep track of the cast while blocking the scenes.

In my books, I also leave a small margin to the left of the dialog page. I write all technical cues on that side of the page, so that they are separated completely from the actors' directions written on the right.

Schedules, additional notes, technical cue sheets, costume lists, etc., can all be added to the binder as needed.

The rule for your production book is always: When in doubt, write it down or put it in. Keep the book neat and legible, of course. But it is of no value to you if it doesn't include the information you need when you need it. Students forget blocking and directions, so be sure these are written down, no matter how sure you are that you will remember it. This is especially important when you start to make changes, as you always will in any rehearsal. But you also need to write down your analytical notes. You never know when they might come in handy in rehearsal.

LEARNING YOUR STAGE SPACE

While there are certain basic principles of blocking a show, which we will examine in detail later, every stage has peculiar characteristics that affect the way you think about blocking. Thus, before you begin to plan blocking, you must be familiar with the stage on which the show will be staged. If you have never worked on the stage before, then you must quickly familiarize yourself with the stage space.

It takes many years to learn a particular stage. It may seem mystical to the inexperienced, but each stage has its own personality. Each has its own eccentricities that will force you to do things in ways you would prefer not to try and at the same time allow you to do other things that would not work on other stages. As a school director, you have the opportunity to spend time to really learn your stage, which is a good thing — there are no more eccentric stages in the world than those built in schools. But for the beginner, or the experienced hand facing a new stage space, there are some simple procedures you can use to minimize the problems of preparing a show for any particular stage.

First, simply go into the theater space and get a general feel for the space. What kind of a stage is it? There are three basic types of stages in use today. Most common is the *proscenium* (Fig 3.2 on page 46). This is what most people think of when they hear the word stage: a raised platform at one end of a hall, with the audience arranged in rows facing the platform. The name comes from the opening — the *proscenium arch* — which is "pro" (in front of) the "scenium" (scenery). In many cases, you may find a proscenium stage without the arch, a simple platform at the end of an assembly hall (or the altar areas of a church, for example). This makes entrances and exits difficult but in other respects is the same as a "regular" proscenium stage.

The second type is usually called a *thrust stage*, (Fig. 3.3 on page 46) because it thrusts out into the audience. This usually has a small proscenium at the back for scenery and entrances, but at least some of the audience can sit to the sides of the actors.

The third major type is the *arena*, or *in-the-round*. (Fig 3.4 on page 46) In this, the audience can, in theory, sit on all sides of the actors. Most arena stages favor one side, and many directors choose to convert them to three-sided thrust stages. They are especially common in schools for the "second" stage, something more intimate than the main, large auditorium.

Walk around on-stage and in the audience area for a few minutes without any specific goals or questions. Just try to get a feel for the size and the general atmosphere.

Then, make a detailed examination of the space. Go back onto the stage and take some measurements. How wide is the stage opening? How deep from the curtain line to your last stage drape? How deep from the apron, if any, to the curtain line? Even more important for detailed blocking, how long is the diagonal from the UR and UL entrance areas to DC? (If you are unfamiliar with this terminology, see Chapter 4 before going any further.) Walk through these so you understand what this distance means in steps, not just in feet and inches. This measurement will be a very practical limit on how you plan stage activity later.

Look out at the audience area from the stage. How is it likely to feel to the actors? Is it comfortable or intimidating, intimate or cavernous? Will the audience seem close to the stage or far away? Will a small crowd look like a group or a set of scattered, isolated individuals?

Fig. 3.2: A Typical Proscenium Stage

Fig. 3.3: A Typical Thrust Stage

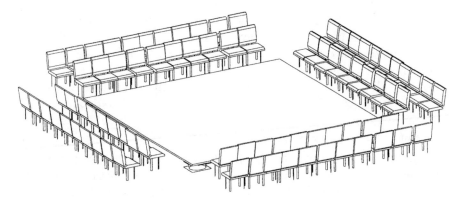

Fig. 3.4: A Typical Arena Stage

Sampling the Sight and Sound of the Stage

For this part of the familiarization process, you will need a second person, so bring a friend or one of your students. Leave them on-stage and go out into the audience areas. Take a seat at random and have them walk around on stage at random. Notice how close or how far they seem as they move up and downstage. This will vary enormously from house to house, but also from seat to seat in one house. Talk to them about anything, as long as it is casual. Listen to how the sound changes as they move around. (You want them to speak casually so that you hear acoustics at their weakest.) Then move to a different seat and repeat the process until you have sampled the sight and sound from each general area of the house.

The results of this experiment will often surprise you, for theaters do not operate logically. In the space in which I worked longest, we had an acoustical dead spot in the fourth and fifth row center, normally the most coveted seats for any performance — sound just reflected off the ceiling and bounced right over those seats. Another school in our district was supposedly built from the same plans, yet their dead spot was along the sides of the seating area. In a different school, the stage was so high in relation to the front row that people sitting there could not see below the actors' knees, and if the actors moved to about stage center, only the tops of their heads could be seen by this part of the audience.

You won't be able to eliminate any problems like these, but you can make attempts to adjust to them. If you know there are dead spots, you can devote extra attention to vocal projection in rehearsal. If you know vision is obstructed, you can arrange the set to keep the actors more visible, or you can compensate for such obstructions in your blocking patterns.

Establishing Sight Lines

Once you have completed these general observations, you should make some very specific measurements. Sit at the last seat in the first row and have your partner walk across the stage near the back of the stage. Mark the spot where they appear and then on the other side of the stage, mark where they disappear from view. Then move to the last seat at the other side of the same row and repeat the process. You have just established the sight-lines for your stage, which in fact determine the actual size of the stage (Fig. 3.5 on page 48). No matter how large your stage seems, anything placed outside these lines will not be seen by at least some portion of your audience. On most school stages, you will find that you have just eliminated about half of the stage. By the same token, you will also have indicated a kind of no-man's land, where actors may be visible to part of the audience but not to all. You must also keep this in mind as you plan your scenery and your blocking, particularly for entrances and exits.

Fig. 3.5: Sightlines on a Typical Proscenium Stage
The shaded area indicates the part of the stage visible to all of the audience seating.

Block Off Limited Vision Seats

In most school or church stages, very little of the stage is fully visible to all seats. You really have only two practical options. First, you may stage the show so that all "important" scenes happen in that tiny, visible area. Second, you may block off some or all of the seats with limited vision. Which you choose depends mostly on number of tickets you are likely to sell. Most groups can afford to lose the seats down on the sides, except perhaps for musicals (when of course you also need the extra stage space for the chorus), so blocking off seats is generally the best solution.

Measure these sightlines carefully and keep them with your production book so that you have them to refer to at any rehearsal. This is fundamental information.

Next, make a careful study of the building and equipment, noting not only what is available but also ways in which it may be adapted. For example: One of the easiest ways to expand a small stage is to add platforms in front of the apron. Can you do this here? Is there room between the stage and the first seats? If they are added, can you focus light on them? Can people sitting close to them see over the edges to the rest of the stage?

Lighting Considerations

Most lighting equipment on school stages is installed to light things like the band and choir concert, which is not at all the kind of lighting you need for a play. Take nothing for granted. How many instruments are on hand, how many plugs to plug them into, and where precisely are the lighting positions? In particular, are there positions that light the downstage areas? This will be critical in determining how close to the edge of the apron you can move the actors. How many dimmers do you have? This will determine the number of isolated areas you can have, which will in turn affect the way you block some crucial scenes.

Can the audience be rearranged? Can you move chairs around? Can you block off some seats, add others?

How high can you build platforms before the tops of actor's heads begin to disappear from view?

Questions for Total Stage Planning

How much room is off-stage on each side? Is this clear space or, more commonly, do important doors empty directly into it? Can scenery be stored there for multiset shows, and if so, how much? How many people can stand in the wings at one time, as they will need to when waiting for an entrance or making a sudden exit? This is especially critical on arena stages, where all entrances and exits are made from the aisles. Where are the real entrances to the room? Where can groups of actors wait to enter yet be out of sight of the audience? Where will props and scenery be stored? If in the hall, as they usually are, how big are the doorways they must be carried through?

Can any of the stage furnishings be shifted? Can light bars or teasers be raised or lowered to modify the sightlines or the lighting angles? Can drapery be moved to improve sightlines or masking problems, or removed completely if necessary?

Do you have fly space over the stage? If so, how high is it? Can you fly full scenery pieces, or is it, more typically, only limited fly space? How is the rigging arranged? How many people will you need on the crew to operate the rigging?

How quickly do your curtains operate? If hand pulled, how fast or how slow can they go? If mechanically controlled, at what tempo? Is this variable?

When you have answers to such questions, you have enough information about the stage to go to work. You won't know everything, of course. As I said earlier, every stage has its quirks. This is why you need to rehearse as often as practical on the stage itself, so that you can discover those quirks before it is too late to do anything about them. But you do have enough now to make serious plans about the blocking.

DESIGN

Few parts of your preparation have more effect on your blocking and rehearsals than the design for scenery, costumes, lights, and other related factors. Thus, the director always is a major participant in the design process. (For some directors in contemporary professional or collegiate theater, it often seems that design is the only part of the process in which they participate.) Nowhere is this participation more close than in the schools and similar groups, where the director is the designer as well.

49

Since there are numerous works available that explain modern design principles and practices, I won't attempt to deal with them all here. However, there are a few very important points you must keep in mind as a director that are glossed over or ignored in books focused on design and construction.

Ground Plan

Once you have familiarized yourself with the stage, then you are ready to prepare your ground plan. Even if you have a designer, you as director must have clear and final say on the nature of the ground plan, for no other single decision will have so much effect on the way you stage and direct the production.

The ground plan is simply a map of the floor showing the placement of scenery, furniture, and any large props. But it is far from a simple proposition.

The ground plan is neither obvious nor automatic. Every stage is different. Even if you use a script that comes with a ground plan in the back, the ground plan may not work on your stage. And even if it does fit on your stage, it still may not be a very useful ground plan.

You can't just copy it from the back of the script. You must plan it very carefully in terms of both the general flow of the show and specific business within the show. A change in the placement of an entrance way or of a sofa, the addition or the removal of a piece of furniture — any of these could have reverberations that will alter the whole shape of the show. At least half of your direction will be predetermined by the decisions you make about your ground plan. So consider this carefully.

An accurate scale drawing can be helpful.

Before you finalize your ground plan, be sure to make at least one accurate scale drawing. This is the only way you can ensure that your plan is practical. You must be sure that the furniture will fit on-stage, that there will be room between the furniture for the people who have to walk there, that entrances and exits will be big enough, and so on. Only a scale drawing will tell you this. This is one area in which computer graphics can actually be helpful. There are a number of cheap "home design" programs available now that quickly convert a ground plan into a 3-D visualization, often with a "walk-thru" option that lets you view the design from different angles and distances. Most use very standardized furniture and most can't cope with platforms or odd angles, so they are not much help to the actual design process. However, they do tell you enough to let you experiment with and clarify a ground plan.

Once you have the scale drawing, double-check everything. Especially tricky are period shows, where men wear swords or women have much bigger skirts than in modern-dress plays, each of which requires much wider spaces between furniture. Also think about anything people have to move around. For example, if a girl faints and someone has to carry her off stage, is the doorway wide enough to get her through without bumping her head? If the scene changes, can you get new furniture on-stage through the doorways? Once the scenery is built, it can't be rebuilt. Think about these situations before you finalize the ground plan.

Making a Physical Statement

The ground plan, however, is not prepared in isolation. It must be planned in relation to the scenery as a whole. And the scenery in turn is only a part of the complete design for the show. The design communicates information to the audience. It is the director's function in the design process to coordinate the work in all the design areas so that the information they communicate will contribute to, rather than interfere with, the rest of the production. Like the ground plan, much of this information will operate on the audience at a subconscious level.

This information is derived from your analysis of the script. Some people get confused about this, because no script will ever tell you exactly how to stage the play. Each designer and director must decide how the specific production will look on a particular stage, with a particular budget, and based on a particular understanding of the play. This does not mean that the script has no information about the design. The script tells you what you need to communicate through the design; you decide what means are most suitable for your particular situation.

Design elements must provide:

Place — Where are the characters in each scene? Where are the characters geographically? In what country or part of the country? What culture? Scenery tells part of this, of course, particularly in relation to each scene, but often costumes and props are even more important.

Time — At what time does each scene take place in relation to the clock? In what era do they occur? Costumes and lighting tend to be the major carriers of this kind of information.

Character Position — Where do the characters fit in their society? Are they rich or poor, important or insignificant, respected or detested? What specific social position or profession do they hold, if any? This is one of the areas in which schools have significant difficulties, usually because of limited budgets. It's relatively easy to build a set of walls, but it is not

51

nearly so easy to dress the rest of the stage with furnishings that complete the look required. Period plays, for example, require antiques.

Character Life — What kind of life do the characters lead? How do they feel about themselves? Are they essentially happy or depressed, neat or sloppy, active or sedentary, dynamic or retiring? These things can be told by almost any portion of the design, but it requires considerable care in selection of detail.

Tone and Mood — What general feeling is the audience expected to have about a moment, a scene, or the play as a whole? Lighting and sound play critical factors in this, but major impact is also made by the scenery and by the costumes seen together as a group.

Points to Remember

There are several additional points to remember about the various design aspects of any play production.

Detailed realism is not usually the answer, even for "realistic" plays. Much more valuable and effective for most shows is a form of "selective realism" built around one or two telling details. *You Can't Take It With You,* for example, depends on a sense of clutter, so on a proscenium stage you would probably want walls and doors and furniture and lots of props. The various settings for *The Importance of Being Earnest,* however, have no such requirements — all the information required for them might be given by one or two pieces of furniture, a free-standing arbor, and so on. This is especially important in multiset shows, but the principle applies in many other cases. If one or two small pieces can give the same information as a complete setting, to save time and money then build only the smaller pieces.

All design issues are complicated by the question of audience knowledge. For example, Malvolio in Shakespeare's *Twelfth Night* is "cross-gartered." Historically, that was nothing more than an odd way of tying the garters for his stockings. It apparently brought down the house for the Elizabethans, but it means nothing to us today. Most modern audiences wouldn't recognize a garter, crossed or otherwise. Hence, in most productions, the director and costume designer give Malvolio completely new stockings in some funny color or pattern, or even give him a completely new costume for that scene, so that he will be as funny-looking to us as he was to Shakespeare's original audience. To do the scene realistically would be accurate, but it would not give any useful information about the scene or the character to the audience.

The difficulty arises when we extend this practice to the point at which we believe the audience is stupid and thus can't be trusted to understand what they see and hear. The design imparts information about the play, but should never exclude any of that information.

Nor is realism always necessary. Design can and often should be stylized to some degree. That is, some portion of it should be exaggerated or emphasized in order to increase the clarity of the information it imparts.

However, when you stylize, remember that the design is supposed to establish a context in which the play can happen. It is not supposed to reveal everything in the play. This problem is more pronounced in the collegiate and professional theaters, where there are full-time designers and much larger budgets than in high schools. In schools, the problem more often arises in costuming than in scenery.

The best example of what I mean here can be seen in the old-fashioned melodrama, where the villain dresses in black and the hero always wears a white hat. The problem with this approach is: If the villain looks like a villain from the very beginning, what kind of suspense can you have about him or her? Villains in real life don't dress like villains — they dress like other people of their time, place, and class. If anything, they go out of their way to dress like good guys so they can trick more people with their villainy. If there is any doubt about how much interpretation to give to the audience, always design first for place, time, and social position, and let the actors do the rest.

Every Costume Gives a Message to the Audience

Be very careful that you don't give the wrong costume signals unintentionally. I once saw a collegiate *Our Town* "modernized" to the 1940s. The rationale for this change made intellectual sense: The forties are to audiences of the early eighties (which is when I saw this) what the turn of the century was to Wilder's original audience in the thirties. Unfortunately, in a perfectly accurate 1942 tailored red and black suit, Emily looked more like the Spider Woman about to attack Basil Rathbone than she did a small-town girl dressed for her funeral. It was awfully hard for us to sympathize with her dressed like that. The costume was accurate, but it was still wrong. High schools often wander into this kind of mistake in costumes because they tend to use whatever they can find in the second-hand stores without thinking about what signals the clothes may give to the audience. But every costume gives a message to the audience, even if the audience doesn't know anything about period. My point is not that the costume itself must be absolutely accurate; it is that the *signal* you send with the costume must be accurate. Emily could have been dressed in the forties in such a way that she still seemed simple and pure and old-fashioned; she just couldn't tell us that when dressed like Joan Crawford.

Design Must Serve the Show, Not Impress the Audience

Remember that the purpose of the design is to make a context for the show, not to impress the yokels. Some shows — many musicals come to mind — depend on the beauty or the gaudiness of their design for a major portion of their impact. But most shows do not. Good design is not always expensive design. It is especially hard for a school teacher to hold to this principle. Most of our audiences are relatively unsophisticated, and they are impressed by expensive scenery and costumes. Design impresses people, but it doesn't entertain them. Make your design serve the show at all times, and in the long run, it will pay off for all concerned.

Concept Staging Can Be Counterproductive

You hear the word "concept" a lot when you read about or listen to "big-time" professional and collegiate directors. What it means in practice is trying to direct the play through the scenery and costumes rather than through the actors and words. When it works, it's exciting. But most of the time it doesn't work, usually because they get so wrapped up in their concept that they forget to include the information the design is supposed to give us. Thus, you will read of productions of Shakespearean plays set, for example, in bombed out subways to make them "relevant" to our concerns about nuclear destruction. The problem with this is that if the set makes sense, there's no reason to see the play: As soon as the lights come up, we know what it all "means." At the same time, it often gets in the way of the play, making Macbeth look pretty stupid there in his underground shelter worrying about those walking trees when he doesn't even have a window to look out of. Whatever you do, never, ever allow the design to actively con-tradict what the actors will be saying and doing.

Always remember that the show controls the design and never vice versa. Far too many productions in the modern world are designed to make a striking visual statement rather than to serve the script. Make all your design decisions only in terms of what you need to make the show play well and clearly.

CHAPTER FOUR

BLOCKING

The director's most basic job is to make the action of the play clear to the audience. All dramatic action is both defined and revealed by a process of change — change in emotion, change in relationships, change in situation, etc. The director shows these changes to the audience by constantly adjusting how the actors are arranged on the stage.

Blocking is a term we normally use for this process of arranging the bodies on-stage. To far too many people, this is a casual process, little more than "traffic direction," and many people think the director just makes it up as he or she goes along. Good blocking is never just traffic direction. And it is never casual. It is the way you visualize your analysis of the script. If you do sloppy or unfocused blocking, the show will be sloppy and unfocused, no matter how brilliant the acting or how beautiful the scenery and costumes.

I'd like to be able to wave a magic wand and say: "This is the way you should block a show." That's not how blocking works. There is no one perfect way to arrange the characters on the stage. This does not mean that we cannot or should not discuss blocking. Nor does it mean that it doesn't matter how you arrange the actors on the stage. It matters a great deal. There are a number of fundamental principles of blocking that you should always consider, and which you should continue to use throughout your rehearsal period. As we discuss these below, remember that they are principles, not rules. They are important because they work — most of the time. Sometimes you will have to do something else, simply because you have to. But most of the time, you will make any play better, just by applying these basic principles.

Blocking serves two important and overlapping functions:

(1) It translates your verbal analysis into a physical world the audience can see and hear.

(2) It provides the practical foundation on which the actors build their performances.

If you do a good job of blocking, the audience will get the maximum understanding, and your cast will give better performances than anyone expected. If you do a poor job of blocking, the audience will misunderstand or be bored by much of what they see, and the actors will look worse than they really are. Blocking is an absolutely critical part of the director's work.

All Good Blocking Begins From a Simple Premise

- For the action of the play to be clear, the changes in the course of that action must be clear.

- For the changes to be clear, they must be made visible.

- Hence, *any change in the course of the action should be accompanied by an equivalent change in the visible activity on-stage.*

If all the information of the show could be conveyed by words alone, there would be no reason to stage the play. The audience could just sit there and let someone read the script aloud, or stay home and read the script on their sofa. An audience comes to both watch and listen to a play, and you must provide information in both modes, both visual and verbal. The visual information must support the verbal information. The visual staging reveals what the words say. It is not undertaken at random, or for variety, or even for the sake of artistic principles (although these may affect the way in which you choose the specific piece of blocking). It is undertaken to express the changes in relationships that occur during the course of the action.

If you have carefully analyzed the script, you already know *when* significant alterations in your stage blocking should be made. At any time some change in situation occurs, you also change the blocking. The question now is merely: Which blocking best expresses that change?

Obviously, no specific piece of blocking will serve only one single purpose. All the various changes must also fit together. This demands a certain amount of "traffic direction." Without some help, actors will eventually start running into each other. Someone has to keep them from doing this, and the director is obviously the person. Some directors ridicule traffic direction, but no good production can function without it, for it makes all the "important" staging moments possible. Blocking is done in two stages. The first is preparatory blocking, done in the planning stage. You can do this on paper after you have a ground plan and before you start rehearsals. Then you can do it over again with live bodies in rehearsal. In the course of any rehearsal period, you will probably change at least a third of your original blocking. Much of what you plan on paper simply will not work when there are real people wandering around on the stage. And you will never want to turn the performers into puppets who spend all their time worrying about how many steps to take and when. It is far easier to go in with a plan and then modify it than it is to make it all up in rehearsals. Take the time, even after you become very experienced, to block the show on paper before you get to rehearsal. It will clarify your analysis and save you time and agony later in the rehearsals themselves. It will improve both the look and the emotional impact of the show.

VOCABULARY

Before we look at the ways you use blocking for dramatic effect, we need to establish a basic vocabulary.

The primary function of this vocabulary is to give you a standardized way to write it down. You can talk to the actors in any number of ways, depending on the kind of help they need at any given moment. When you write it down in the production book, you have to write it in a form that everyone understands.

Proscenium Vocabulary

Most blocking is done with vocabulary developed for the proscenium stage. Thrust stages are supposed to have audiences on three sides, but in practice eighty to ninety percent of the audience sits on one side of the stage, which means that most such stages are really proscenium stages with wide aprons. Thus, most thrust stages can use the same basic terminology as that used on the proscenium.

Generally, a proscenium stage consists of several large spaces (Fig. 4.1). The part of the stage that is visible to the audience is called "on-stage." The part of the stage that is out of audience view is "off-stage." Off-stage areas may be called "backstage," which applies to all such areas, and the "wings," which are technically only the spaces immediately off-stage to the right or left. Any part of the space on-stage that would still be visible to the audience if the main curtain were closed is called the "apron."

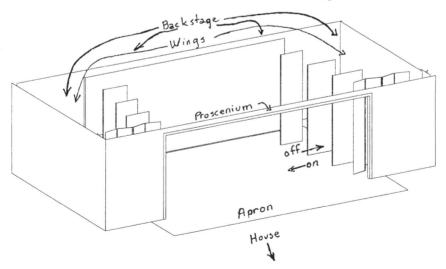

Fig. 4.1: Basic Spaces on a Proscenium Stage

57

On this stage, it is a convention that right is to your right when you face out toward the audience, and left is to your left in the same circumstance. This holds true no matter how you may be facing: Right is always the same direction. If you happen to be looking away from the audience, the right would be on your personal left. This is easy to remember on stage, but it is often difficult for directors, who always talk about directions in the actor's terminology while standing in the audience area. One of the little tricks of the trade is learning to point with your left hand when you want the actor to move right.

A Stage Has Fifteen Imaginary Areas

For reference purposes, the on-stage area of a standard proscenium stage is divided into fifteen imaginary areas (Fig. 4.2). The part of the stage closest to the audience is called *down*, from a time when all stages were raked and that was in fact the lowest part of the stage. Conversely, the part of the stage farthest from the audience is *up*. The lane crossing the stage between these two is the *center*. Similarly, an imaginary lane runs from upstage to downstage at the right and left sides of the stage and down the center of the stage. However, since most stages are wider than they are deep, additional lanes are drawn between each of these extremes, the right-center and left-center lanes. These lanes overlap to produce the fifteen areas, called as shown.

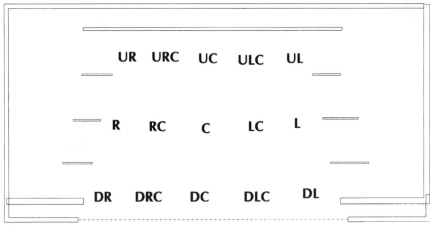

Fig. 4.2
Basic Acting Areas of a Proscenium Stage

These areas are not precise. No one draws little rectangles on the real stage. The terminology is used to give the actors a general idea of where they are placed and to enable you to make a record of that placement. The size and shape of each area will vary depending on how much of the stage space you are actually using. For example, in Fig. 4.3, we have drawn an imaginary set piece and modified our areas to fit the stage space that is actually used.

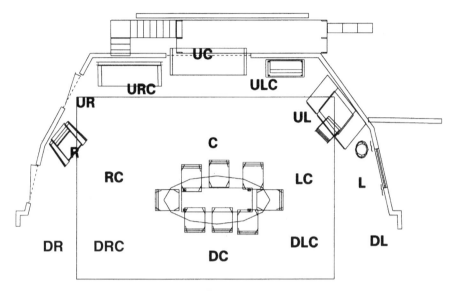

Fig. 4.3
Basic Acting Areas Adapted to a Stage With Scenery

Vocabulary for Stage Direction

In order to dictate direction of movement, another set of terms are used. Unfortunately, these are built off the same words, which occasionally leads to some confusion (Fig. 4.4 on page 60). As might be expected, movement toward the audience is called *down,* movement away from the audience is called *up. Right* is toward stage right, *left* toward stage left. The diagonals are indicated by combining the two directions concerned: diagonally to the right and toward the audience is *down right,* to the left and away from the audience is *up left,* and so on. There is no "center" direction, because center is only a place, not a direction.

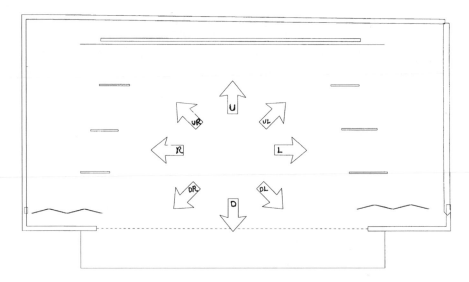

Fig. 4.4
Basic Directions for Movement on a Proscenium Stage

The confusion comes when people confuse the names of the directions with the names of the spaces. You may move down-right without going anywhere near down right on the stage. It all depends on where you start the move from. If the actor is standing at center and moves down right, he will end up eventually at down right. But if he begins at left, when he moves down right, he will end up at down center or possibly even down left center.

Thus, directions must be given, and recorded, very carefully. Technically, each direction should indicate both the direction moved and the place stopped, but sometimes one or the other will be sufficient. The word *cross* means to move across the stage, and directors tend to prefer that, in order to be distinct from *move,* which means a gesture or a change in posture. Cross is abbreviated by an X. Thus, if you want an actor to move to a chair in the DRC area, you can record this in one of four ways:

(a) Cross down right to down right center [XDR—DRC],

(b) Cross to down right center [X—DRC],

(c) Cross down right to the chair [XDR—chair], or

(d) Cross to chair at down right center [X—DRC chair].

Any of these will do. However, it is essential that in your book you not confuse the way you record the directions. Always write the direction directly after the X, and always separate the place stopped by some means — the word "to," an arrow, a line, etc. If you do not maintain consistency, when you refer to the book next week you won't be able to tell what you meant at all.

Arena Vocabulary

Since the 1960s, many groups have begun performing in spaces where the audience may be seated on several sides of the stage at once. This is usually called an *arena* stage or *in-the-round* (even though the stages are still rectangular). Arena staging is very attractive to many contemporary schools, for several reasons. First, it eliminates most of the elements of scenery, or at least those elements that seem to eat up time and money. Since the audience is on all sides, you don't have to build, paint, and decorate any walls. Secondly, it puts more audience closer to the stage. One hundred people, for example, can easily be arranged in an arena with no person farther away than the second row. This means that young actors can speak naturally; they won't need special training to project their voice to the back of the auditorium. It also avoids the problems of playing in a large auditorium to a small audience, as so many drama programs must do in schools with old auditoriums that were designed to hold all of the school at once. A crowd of 200 in an auditorium designed for 1,000 makes the play feel like a disaster; in an arena, those same 200 people feel like a sold-out crowd. Many teacher/directors convert a room to an arena for an even more practical reason: It can belong exclusively to the theater program. With a separate, small theater space, you will not have to fight with the choir and band and assemblies for time on the big stage. There are lots of new technical problems to balance the attractions of such a space, not the least of which are the problems of lighting, of defining entrances and exits, and of compensating imaginatively for the loss of scenic elements. Even so, it is now common for a school director to have to work on an arena stage at least part of the time.

Establish an imaginary compass or clock for defining stage space.

Because the audience is arranged on most sides of the stage space, there is no "up" or "down." Thus, you need a different blocking terminology (although the blocking principles are not so different as one might originally think). The most rational way to determine direction is to use an imaginary compass. Standing at the center of your performing space, arbitrarily assign one direction as "north," then work around the four points of "east, south," and "west." It does not matter if that matches up with reality, since most of your cast won't notice the difference. Just be consistent.

Then divide the stage into areas, as we did with the imaginary lanes on the proscenium. Draw an imaginary circle around the center, which will be called "center." Draw a similar circle around the outer edge of the space, split it into eight imaginary areas identified from the points of the compass (north, north-east, east, etc.). If the space is large enough, put an imaginary circle between these two. Each space in it would then be identified as the combination between the two extremes. As the area between DR and DC on the proscenium is called DRC, so in the arena, the area between C and N would be NC, between C and NE would be NEC, and so on. (Fig. 4.5)

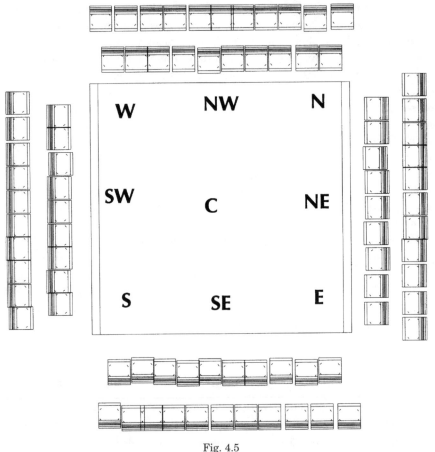

Fig. 4.5
Compass-Based Acting Areas on an Arena Stage

Directions given to the actors and recorded in your book would then be done in the same way as with the directions on a proscenium: (a) XNE—NEC, (b) XNE—chair, (c) X—NEC, or (d) X—chair NEC.

Alternatively, some directors prefer to think of the arena as a clock, with the outer edge broken into twelve imaginary areas. Thus, in this method, an actor could be directed to cross to two o'clock rather than to NE (Fig. 4.6).

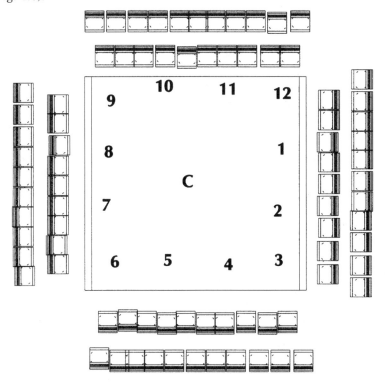

Fig. 4.6
Clock-Based Acting Areas on an Arena Stage

***

Once we have the vocabulary, we can begin to plan our blocking. As indicated earlier, what follows are fundamental principles, not rules. However, they are principles derived from dealing with audience responses, not from artistic theory. Since blocking exists to clarify information for an audience, then the only valid test of that blocking is: Does most of your audience respond as you wish when they observe any particular moment? If the blocking doesn't "work," then change it, no matter how well it may fit some theory or rule or tradition or experimental process.

MAKING RELATIONSHIPS VISIBLE

One critical function of blocking is to make the changes in situation and relationship visible and clear to the audience. This is expressed through four different types of changes: personal, interpersonal, group, and temporal changes.

Personal Change

At the personal level of activity, a character moves to express a change in emotion or attitude. This may be small (a twitch of the mouth, for example) or large (the character jumps up and throws a book across the room). It may involve the face, the hands, or the whole body. It essentially expresses how the particular individual character feels about a situation, another character, or a situation in general.

This is the level at which the individual actor can and must contribute the most, for this is in essence the very definition of acting. Yet, the director still has important functions at this level. The director can edit and select the best and most effective expressions given by the actor. The director can also suggest and encourage alternative ways of expression for the actor to try. The younger or more inexperienced your actors, the more suggestions you will make.

The important thing to remember here is that the actor is *always* expressing a change in relationships, not "interpreting" a line. The tendency for almost all student (and many experienced) actors, is to think in terms of gesture: What do I do with my hands? Rather, both actor and director should be thinking: What change has occurred or is in process of occurring, and what is the best way to express that change?

Interpersonal Change

As soon as a character begins to express something on-stage, that automatically begins to have an effect on the other characters in the play. This effect is a change in interpersonal relationships. For the director, these emotional changes are visibly expressed by changes in the physical relationships of the people on-stage.

When working with more than one person, several important factors must be considered.

Distance

As relationships develop, characters move closer together or farther apart in a psychological or emotional sense. This can and should be expressed physically. In simple terms, this is done by moving the characters together as they establish closer ties and moving them apart as those ties are interrupted or broken. The traditional love scene, for example, ends when the characters both accept that they are in love. This is visibly expressed by their close physical contact, usually a hug and a kiss. In a well-blocked love scene, this should happen only at the end of the scene. The balcony scene in *Romeo and Juliet* is the classic illustration. Shakespeare starts the scene with the characters as far apart as possible — Juliet on a balcony, Romeo on the ground. Simply by following Shakespeare's indications we find them drawn closer visibly as their love becomes more open, until at last Romeo climbs the balcony and they embrace. Not all relationships will be laid out so obviously in the script, but every pair of characters on the stage have some emotional connection, which can be visualized by the physical distance between the characters.

Attention

Characters may express changes in their relationships by changing their direction of movement or attention, even while they stay the same distance apart. In simple terms:

• People tend to look toward each other when they agree and to look away when they disagree.

• People tend to turn toward the other when they accept an idea or a person and look away when they don't.

• People tend to attend closely when they like what they hear and to ignore or try to ignore what they dislike.

• People tend to attend closely when they are personally involved in something (even when they dislike it) and ignore something which has no importance to them.

Authority

Physical relationships between characters should also reflect the nature of the relationship itself. That is, it can express who is dominant at any given moment and who is subservient. It can also indicate those moments when the characters share a moment of equality. Blocking reflects this relationship by showing the relative power of a character on-stage.

In general, authority is established in two ways: (1) placement on the stage itself and (2) placement in relation to the other characters.

There are "strong" and "weak" positions on any stage, which are described in our discussion of *focus* below. Characters who are placed in those "strong" positions tend to dominate any relationship with other characters on-stage who are placed in "weaker" positions. Thus, it is important that in your blocking you use this to reflect properly the actual relationship depicted at any given moment.

Similarly, characters may reveal authority through their physical relationship to the other characters on-stage. The most common expression of this authority is height, as when a king stands and a court kneels before him. However, there are no fixed rules in this particular area, because context is extremely important. A person towering over someone else sitting on the sofa may convey great power and authority at one moment. Yet at another time, the person sitting calmly on the sofa while others are standing around may clearly be in control of a situation. This is one area of blocking that requires careful attention and sophistication.

If there is a general principle which holds in almost all situations, the person with authority at any given moment will be the person most easily and completely visible to the audience.

Conflict

Characters change their physical relationships when they come in conflict with each other. This conflict may express itself in two apparently contradictory manners.

Obviously, characters tend to move together as they think or feel together and move apart as they come to think or feel differently. Characters who are angry with others often express that anger by jumping up and going to the other side of the room.

But, characters may also express conflict by an urge to engage in conflict. They may just as often close with their opponent; in fact, it is far more common for people to move toward each other when in conflict. When we get really angry with someone else, we get "in their face." Just as lovers must eventually touch to express their agreement, so fighters must eventually touch to express their disagreement. The critical factor to remember is to save the physically closest moment for the most intense moment of the conflict.

Intensity

The nature of the relationship between two characters can also be illustrated by the extremity of the physical relationships in the blocking. That is, as changes in a relationship grow more intense, the distances over which the blocking expresses these changes become more extreme. When a character disagrees, for example, he may turn away, but if he disagrees violently, he does not just turn but also stalks across the entire room. Similarly, if he disagrees, he may step toward his opponent to emphasize the disagreement, but if he violently disagrees, then he may charge directly up to the other person where he can shake a finger directly in the other person's face. Extreme intensity of feeling is expressed through extreme changes in blocking. Conversely, extreme changes of blocking will be interpreted as extreme intensity among the characters, so be sure that you use these big moves only when you really mean them.

Expectation

The joker in the pack here is the question of expectation. The basic principles above are obvious, because they are based on the normal actions of everyday life. But there is a tremendous dramatic power to be gained when you don't do what is "normal." Any child soon learns that when the parent stops yelling and gets very quiet and still, then the parent is really angry. The quiet moment draws its power as an emotional expression from the fact that it is abnormal, unexpected. When someone does the unexpected, it is more powerful precisely because it is unexpected. When everyone in the building expects a character to move, it may be more expressive to have the character stand still. When everyone expects a character to take charge of a scene by standing, she may more effectively take charge by remaining seated. When everyone expects the characters to kiss, they may better express their relationship by walking away from each other. This is, of course, one of the most common ways we make a scene funny. But it is a blocking principle that can be just as effectively used in "serious" or "dramatic" moments.

It is important to remember that the unexpected has dramatic power only at moments of greatest intensity. Its expressiveness is directly proportional to the amount of audience involvement in the proceedings on-stage. If no powerful expectations exist, doing the unexpected will have no impact.

Similarly, the unexpected is expressive in direct ratio to its rarity. You can only do something unexpected a handful of times during any show. If characters always express their anger calmly, then that soon comes to be the accepted expression of anger, and it has little dramatic power.

Group Change

Just as each character's relationship with another is expressed by the blocking used for the two of them, so also the blocking can be used to illustrate each individual character's relationship with larger groups.

At any given moment, each character is emotionally more or less integrated into the group of characters on-stage. This integration or isolation is expressed by the way the character is physically integrated with, or isolated from, the other characters. A character may be blocked to move comfortably among those with whom the character is in agreement. Similarly, the character should be separated from those with whom he or she is uninvolved or over whom he or she is in authority.

There is one major exception to what we have discussed: The character who is in conflict with a group of others almost never closes with the group at the moment of extreme conflict. When that character is in conflict with the group, you must block the actors to show this. It is extremely difficult to visualize such conflict if the character is placed within the group. He or she should always be outside the group so that we can see the character as a distinct figure.

This practicality is underlined by some basic psychology. Although we usually try to get close to individuals when the conflict is most intense, if we are in conflict with a large group, we try to keep all the group in view, if only to prevent any sneak attacks from someone we can't see. If the dramatic conflict of a scene is supposed to be one against several, as in any scene with a teenager arguing with her parents, the individual should be blocked away from the group so that she physically shows her emotional opposition to the group as a whole.

Temporal Change

All plays happen through time. From moment to moment, the situations change, the emotions change, and the relationships change. You must also consider that the audience has been watching the show for some time.

This means that you can't have the actors move around in the same way all the time. Things repeated lose their effectiveness. If everyone moves to DC when they have an important speech, it won't take very long before the audience is bored, because each moment will look like every other moment.

Good blocking considers the following points:

Repetition — Within any script, some things occur repeatedly. The writer does that for a purpose. For example, in *You Can't Take It With You*, the first and last acts end with the family at the dinner table. This is the one moment of each day in this chaotic household when the family expresses its unity. When Mr. Kirby and Tony join the dinner in Act III, it visualizes that they have now joined the Vanderhof family. Good blocking would arrange this last scene so that it looks as much like the first scene as possible, with only two additional bodies added. And it would keep Tony and Mr. Kirby away from the table until you are ready to make the point that they have been accepted. Ideas that the playwright repeats for dramatic purpose should be underlined by the repetition of blocking.

Theme and Variation — More often, however, the playwright will choose not to repeat a moment exactly. The play will introduce an idea and then develop a series of variations for dramatic effect. For example, in the Hanukkah scene in *The Diary of Anne Frank*, the scene begins and ends with the Hanukkah celebration and song. The first time, the song is celebratory; the second time, after they have heard the intruder, it is a way of restoring terrified spirits. The dramatic importance of the second version is how the song puts the group back together, the same but different. Good blocking for that scene would find a way to bring everyone back to the table as they were at the beginning of the scene, yet somehow slightly altered in arrangement so that the difference in the two situations was also clear.

Development — As the play progresses, relationships develop, and the blocking should illustrate this. We have already discussed most of the common means for this in passing. As people grow together, for example, they tend to move closer to each other. With *Anne Frank*, for example, Peter and Anne tend to keep their distance emotionally in early scenes until they become close friends and chaste lovers in Act II. Thus, although they move together and apart in the course of each individual scene, there is a kind of "average distance" they maintain in each scene. This average distance decreases as they grow to like and understand each other.

The scale of activity, the distances moved, the spaces between persons involved, should all intensify as the dramatic conflicts intensify and relax as those conflicts momentarily relax. You should always adjust the scale and tempo as needed.

Also, one of the most significant things to keep in mind is that you can use the blocking to set up audience expectations. As we have discussed earlier, sometimes the most effective moments occur when you do something unexpected. The effectiveness of such moments is increased if you have encouraged such expectations in prior scenes. For example, to set up a character, you could have him turn away from people before he expresses any anger. Then, at the moment of greatest anger, he could attack without first turning away. The audience will immediately understand that this is the most important and most deeply felt crisis in the play for him. Such a device only works if you have set it up with other blocking throughout the show — if he did something different at each moment of conflict, doing yet something else different now will not express the seriousness of this moment.

MAKING CHOICES VISIBLE

One essential function of the blocking is to exteriorize all choices made by the characters. As we saw in our analysis of the script, each change in relationships among the characters is caused by a choice made by one of those characters. Thus, if the play is to be clear to the audience, then each choice made by the characters must be made clear. Some of those choices, of course, were made in the past or off-stage and are explained in the verbal exposition. Any choices made on stage during the course of the action, no matter how well or completely discussed in the dialog, must be visualized in the blocking.

To make choices clear, keep three principles in mind while blocking:

• The audience must be able to see the nature of the choice;

• The audience must see the character deal with the choice; and

• The audience must see and understand the choice when it has at last been made.

The "Casket Scene" Example

In *The Merchant of Venice*, Bassanio must choose the proper casket to win the hand of Portia. A well-blocked production must make all aspects of that choice clear to the audience.

First, all three caskets must be visible to the audience. How could we understand the nature of the choice if we can't see what he must choose? Similarly, the three caskets must not only be visible but must also be distinct — that is, we must see three separate items for him to choose from, not three piled up on each other in a single place.

There is more. Bassanio is not just choosing a casket; he is choosing something that will demonstrate he is worthy of Portia. In other words, the casket is merely a step on the way to her. Thus, we should not only see the caskets but also see a visual relationship between the caskets and Portia.

In addition, we must see Bassanio's face. It is not enough to see Bassanio. We must see him consider and decide, and we can only do that if we can see his face.

At the same time, since it is his choice, we must also place Portia so that she cannot give him clues. (Unless, of course, you have interpreted the scene, as is sometimes done, to indicate that she cheats and gives him a clue because she loves him. If she cheats, it must be visible to the audience, because that is part of the choice.)

When he has chosen a casket, he must indicate it in a manner so clear no one is in doubt as to his decision. That is, he must touch it or pick it up or point it out in an unequivocal manner.

Finally, since the correct choice also delivers Portia, she must move toward him to indicate that he has made the proper choice.

Good blocking of this scene makes all of these points visible. And the same kind of analysis and planning must be given to every other choice made by every other character in the course of the play.

Visualize a Character's Choice

Most choices in most plays are "either-or" situations. The easiest way to block such choices is the most obvious way. That is, the chooser should be placed between the choices. When the wife says, "Decide now, her or me," the husband should be between the two women. If the "other woman" is not present, the husband should be between the wife and the door. The audience sees a visualization of the choice, sees the chooser decide, and then understands the decision made, because he either moves back toward his wife or he goes out the door. If at all possible, at least one and generally both of the choices should be downstage of the chooser, so that we can see the chooser's face as he considers the options or turns back and forth between them.

The more important a choice is, the more clear and exaggerated the visual clarification should be. And nowhere is this more important than at the climax, which is always a moment of final choice made by one of the principal characters.

This seems so obvious that it should be hardly worth mention. But many productions, amateur and professional, break down at this point more than at any other.

MOVEMENT

One of the difficulties of discussing or illustrating blocking is that we have no way to put on paper the most important parts of the process. We can discuss and record only where characters stand at a specific time, but they, in fact, spend far more time in motion to and from such positions. Many of your decisions about blocking must deal with the nature of movement on-stage. Movement, as well as activity and position, contributes to the complete visualization of any given situation.

Generally, the following aspects of any movement must be considered:

Appropriateness — Is a movement appropriate to the emotional state or dramatic situation being depicted? Would the character do this? Could the character do this?

Scale — Each movement operates within some scale. As intensity increases, the physical relationships among the characters become more extreme. Similarly, the scale of movement alters with intensity. Casual moments require casual, short movements. As emotions and changes grow more extreme, movement covers greater distances.

Tempo — As the intensity of a scene alters, the tempo of movement should also alter. Generally, this means that at the most intense moments, the movement is done more quickly than at casual or relaxed moments. But sometimes for dramatic effect you may go against expectations and do something very slowly to express intensity.

BUSINESS

Sometimes, directors must provide other movement that is not really concerned with the play's action. People light cigarettes, serve tea, shuffle through papers, examine the paintings on the wall, dial the phone, and so on. This is the kind of thing that is usually called *business*. For the most part, this tells us nothing about the plot, but it does tell us a lot about the characters and the background. Actors can and should develop most of this themselves, but the director must edit and shape this business. With amateurs and students, the director often has to invent the bulk of the business as well.

The problem with most business is that it is ultimately controlled by its own rules rather than by the play's needs. For example, you may express everything you need to express about a relationship by the way you offer a cup of tea. Even so, you must still pour the tea into each and every cup, put down the teapot, pass out the cups, provide sugar, pass out spoons, stir each individual cup, and so on. That demands its own time scale. Conversation has to be matched to that time scale. The classic problem is the actor who suddenly has to talk while his mouth is still full of food. Some playwrights plan scripts this way — the dialog of *The Odd Couple* is paced to match a poker game, for example. But many times directors try to insert such business into scripts that did not originally use it, and it doesn't always fit. If the characters have tea, you can't have one person pour one cup and then hand out four, just because there aren't enough lines to go around. The audience would then reject the tea process itself, start to laugh at the wrong things, and the show as a whole would be ruined. So you have to put the play on hold while you finish the business.

Remember that business is different from action. First make the action clear, then worry about the business.

Similarly, much of your "traffic direction" will actually be business. Sometimes, you may send a character over to the window just so that the person about to come through the door won't run into her. If that happens, you should always add some business at the window so that the move contributes to the overall environment. The last thing you want is people moving around just because you told them to move around. For example, you may tell her to look out the window to see if someone is coming, or merely to establish for the audience that there is a world outside that window that may come into play in a later scene. You may also use this same piece of business to increase the dramatic value of a later moment. The character at the window may turn to meet the person who is coming through the door, which will be more effective than if she waited on the sofa until the door opened.

You may invent business to make the actor feel more secure or to increase the sophistication of the individual characterization. This is especially important with inexperienced actors. As a group, they tend to want something to do with their hands. In order to calm them down or to stop them from trying to gesture on every word, the director may need to give them additional props to use or to suggest specific pieces of business. Such selections and suggestions must still fit within the context of all the other blocking and help to visualize individual characterizations, even though they were initially included for the actor's benefit. We'll discuss this kind of business again in several later chapters.

FOCUS

In blocking any scene, the director must also direct the audience's attention to the activity or character that is most important at any given moment. That is, the blocking should focus the audience's attention. This is done by placing the most important element of any given moment in the strongest position *vis-a-vis* the other characters on-stage.

Attention can be focused using a combination of several basic principles.

Keeping the Individual Visible

Before examining particular ways in which the director focuses attention in a group, we should consider some ways in which you keep the individual actor visible. Many directors insist that such traditional devices be ignored, with the result that what was once not discussed because everyone knew it is now not discussed because no one seems to remember it.

First and foremost, remember always that the purpose of being seen on-stage is to be SEEN on-stage. Second, the purpose of expressing anything on-stage is to have that expression SEEN AND HEARD by as much of the audience as humanly possible. On the proscenium stage, this means that an actor who is doing anything significant or important MUST face toward the audience at such times. When more of the front of the body is visible than is hidden, the actor is said to be *open*.

There are exceptions, of course. Just as there are times when it is more dramatic and interesting to have the character do the unexpected, so there are times when he may have a potent effect with only his back visible to the audience. But this works only when it is unusual and when the emotion concerned is more easily expressed by body posture than by facial expression. Most of the time, the audience wants to see faces.

Similarly, audiences want to hear what actors are saying. Even with the best speakers, this is easier when we can see their lips. Some actors can be heard clearly while facing away from the audience, but most can't. Students in particular can't. A proscenium stage is arranged that way precisely so the actors have to talk in only one direction. To arrange your staging so that the bulk of your sound is aimed at the wings is to lose clarity and frustrate the audience.

Obviously, you can't make a pretense of drama and at the same time have everyone face directly forward to the audience all the time. Characters must, most of the time, talk "to" the other characters on-stage. This means that they must deal with people who are upstage or in some way on the side. The actor and the director have to "cheat" so that their physical position will allow the actor to make contact with other actors and at the same time still be visible to the audience.

These are the traditional methods for cheating. You'll need to teach them to your cast:

• Unless facing directly forward to the audience, always stand with the upstage foot forward (Fig. 4.7 on page 75). By sliding the upstage foot forward, the actor can still look toward actors at his side. At the same time this keeps slightly more than half of the body and face visible to the audience. By contrast, when the downstage foot is forward, the body turns diagonally upstage. Even if the face maintains the exact same position, the downstage shoulder blocks off part of the face for part of the audience. The actor loses visibility and with it loses interest and strength.

• When an actor makes a cross, always begin and end that cross with the upstage foot (Fig. 4.8 on page 76). This turns the body open at the beginning of the cross, when the reason for moving is being expressed. Then it turns the body open again at the end, when the reason for stopping is being expressed. With some practice, an actor can also learn to step so that the downstage foot always takes a slightly smaller step, which keeps the body slightly diagonal throughout the cross. Even if the young actor can't master this, leading and stopping with the upstage foot will cheat the body open at the most critical moments.

• Always reach forward with the upstage arm, reach back with the downstage (Fig. 4.9 on page 77). Actors find this awkward at first, because right-handed people want to do business with their right hand, and left-handed people with their left. To reach forward with the downstage hand closes the body off from view, and in many cases will even hide the gesture itself from view. To reach back with the upstage hand invariably turns the actor's back to the audience. It can be done, of course — no one will fire you or shoot you if actors temporarily turn their backs to the audience — but why should they if they don't have to?

74

Fig. 4.7: Standing Open

The person on the right is much more visible by simply sliding the upstage foot forward.

Fig. 4.8: Walking Open

The person on the left is leading with the downstage leg; notice how it turns the head away from the audience unintentionally.

Fig. 4.9: Gesturing Open

In the left group, the girl has hidden herself from the audience simply by gesturing
with the downstage hand. Notice how much more visible and interesting she is
in the group on the right by simply changing the hand used to gesture with.

- Never hold anything in front of the face while talking. It blocks the sound
  and it blocks the view. Telephones are the greatest problem here — always
  hold the phone on the upstage side of the face (Fig. 4.10 on page 78).

- Talk to the downstage earlobe rather than the eyes of other actors. This
  is a very small adjustment, but it keeps the faces of both participants
  open while still giving the appearance that the characters are looking at
  each other.

- Look at other actors at the beginning and end of a speech, but talk out
  toward the audience in middle. When making a long speech or when
  talking to characters who are predominantly upstage, the actor cannot
  afford to lock in on other actors for fearing of losing part or all of the
  audience. However, she can give the impression of looking at those other
  characters without actually doing so. As the speech begins, an actor
  should look at the other actors, and then look away toward the audience
  as the speech continues. Then, just as the last word is said, focus should
  go back to the characters addressed. If the speech is very long, she may
  briefly look back to the persons addressed at occasional, dramatically
  effective moments, but keep the bulk of the speech aimed outward.

Fig. 4.10: Telephones
Changing the phone to the upstage hand makes the entire face visible.

- Cheat all diagonal crosses into slight curves. When moving diagonally upstage, start the move more up than to the side and then finish with more horizontal movement that allows the actor to cheat open at the end. When moving diagonally downstage, start slightly more horizontally so that the move then ends with a more nearly vertical move in which the actor is more visible than he would be on the pure diagonal.

The Arena Stage Techniques

An arena stage changes things. These little cheating devices are not quite as important. Since there is audience on all sides, there is no way to avoid blocking the view of at least part of the audience at any given moment. The director's job is simply to make a decision which side will be blocked from a view of which actor at any given moment and to minimize this whenever possible. However, the arena does demand one artificial convention not used on the proscenium:

- Characters in arena staging must turn regularly so that each side of the audience sees them approximately the same amount of time as any other side. This is particularly complex when there are scenes in which characters sit. In the arena, they simply must stand and move around more often than on the proscenium, purely for the sake of variety and audience comfort.

There is a tendency in contemporary theater to ignore or to belittle these traditional stage practices. They have disappeared from many acting and directing textbooks. Perhaps they have fallen into disrepute because they were once taught as rules, and we live in an era that has rejected old rules. These kinds of things are not really rules so much as practices developed from hundreds of years of painful experience on the proscenium stage. As such, no one must follow them slavishly. But if you do not require your actors to use them most of the time, most of the time the audience will not be able to see and understand what is happening on stage. These practices have been used for hundreds of years because they work.

Using Stage Space

Any stage has some parts of it that are stronger than others. When we discuss blocking, *strong* means simply "more likely to attract audience attention." A stage may all look the same when it is empty, but as soon as you put actors on it, they attract more attention in some parts of the stage than in others, no matter what they might be doing or saying.

In general, the following principles apply on all proscenium-style stages:

- **Closeness** — Downstage areas are stronger than upstage areas (Fig. 4.11 on page 80). The downstage actor tends to attract more interest and attention because she is closer to the audience.

- **Centrality** — Center is stronger than either left or right (Fig. 4.12 on page 80).When the character moves to the right, for example, he may become stronger to those sitting at the right, but for those on the left he gets further away and loses interest. The center area is a compromise that balances out the interest level for those on all sides of the audience. One of the fundamental reasons why we have directors is to keep actors from fighting over who gets to stand DC when they speak. Only some outside authority can force them to give up that dominating position.

- **Visibility** — Brightest is strongest. All other factors being equal, we tend to watch that which is easiest to see. Bright light focuses attention. This is, after all, the reason for the spotlight, on-stage as in the art gallery

Fig. 4.11: Downstage/Upstage
The closer figure automatically draws more attention.

Fig. 4.12: Centrality
Although all are about the same distance away, we
automatically focus on the one in the center.

or department store. In the early days of proscenium stages, this encouraged actors to rush downstage, because all the light came from the footlights. Since we have invented electric spotlights, we have much more flexibility. In fact, most school stages are so poorly designed that there is almost no light on the downstage areas and you can rarely get actors down to the front of the stage, even when you need to do so.

Using Scenic Focus

Fortunately, there are some ways available by which you can both counter the power of the traditional strong points of the proscenium stage itself and vary the ways in which you focus attention. The scenery can be arranged so as to encourage additional positions of strength. These include such devices as:

• **Elevation** — Generally, an actor on a platform will be stronger than actors on the floor, even (or especially) if that platform is upstage (Figs. 4.13-14 on page 81). While a platform actually increases the actor's distance from the audience, it does compensate by giving the actor additional height.

This is a fundamental way to establish authority. One who is taller is almost always the more authoritative figure, and thus authority figures tend to end up on platforms. The platform does not give strength in all situations, however (Figs. 4.15 below). Characters on platforms are stronger than those on the floor only if the audience can see them both at the same time. If the platform is too high, as in a balcony or a second floor, audience members may be unable to watch the people on the balcony and on the floor simultaneously. When that happens, other factors will come into play and the audience will watch the person who is easiest to watch, usually the person on the floor who is closer. Thus, crowds are often draped around balconies to keep them from distracting attention from the principal performers on the floor.

Fig. 4.13: Focus by Height (a)
The highest figure draws the most focus.

Fig. 4.14: Focus by Height (b)
Highest is still the center of attention, even if off to the side.

Fig. 4.15: Focus by Height (c)
The figure on the floor now controls focus, because the two high points cancel each other out.

- **Frame** — Characters within an artificial frame tend to be stronger than those characters outside it (Fig. 4.16 below). Thus, you can focus attention on actors by placing them in an open doorway, in front of a window, beneath an archway, etc. Most good sets for proscenium productions must keep this in mind, so that possibilities for framing are available. At the same time, be careful not to make the framing elements of the set so obvious that they dominate the stage and destroy all other staging options. A second way to frame a character is with the lighting. By changing the intensity of the lighting, you can make weak areas stronger and strong areas weaker. Thus, you may play an entire scene in only a small portion of the stage — on one platform or off to one side, for example — and still hold audience focus as long as you dim the lights on all other areas down or even completely out.

Fig. 4.16: Focus by Framing

Compare to Fig. 4.12. The people stand in the exact same positions, but with the addition of the arch, we tend to focus on the figure in the archway rather than the one at center.

Focusing Groups

Not only are there strong and weak areas on the stage, but there are also strong and weak ways to arrange characters so that they draw or lose the audience's focus. This is influenced by four basic factors:

(1) All other factors being equal, an audience will watch motion.

One way to draw attention to a particular character is to put the character in motion.

Motion also distracts, so in most cases, a character will move just before saying an important line, for example, and then stop while actually saying the line. This draws attention to her and then, once that attention is drawn, ceases not to distract from other more important elements of the situation.

This is not a rule. Obviously, there are times when a character continues to move while talking — this is called gesture, for example — and other characters move in reaction. Sometimes, the character may move and talk at the same time for dramatic effect or when the movement underlines some attitude between the characters. It can easily be overused and become boring. It is merely one way to attract audience attention when you may need it.

There are also some ways of moving that are stronger than others. Some patterns of movement draw more attention from the audience than other patterns of movement covering the same distances. In general, the relative strength of such moves is also related to changes in height or visibility.

- Vertical movement, from upstage to downstage, is usually very strong. The actor changes height quickly and keeps his face visible to the audience for the entire time he is in motion. However, remember this is always relative to the audience's perception. For audiences that are far from the stage, the change in height may be minimal and thus the power of the cross itself will not be so great as on a stage where most of the audience is very close and feels a sudden surge of authority from such a cross.

- Vertical movement from downstage to up, is usually very weak. The actor both loses size and moves with her back to the audience. This is why it is almost always better to break an actor's upstage exit into several distinct parts. First, have him cross to the doorway and pause; then, have him turn back into the room for his last line, using the doorway as a frame to increase focus. Then, after the line is done, he can turn his back and exit. To say the last line in the middle of stage and then turn to exit through an upstage door without looking back is always weak and should only be used when you wish to underline the weakness of the character involved in relation to those left on-stage.

- Horizontal movement on the same plane of the stage is usually weak. Although such movement is immediately clear to anyone in the audience, the character stays approximately the same size relative to the audience and is only partially visible because his body is turned to the side. This is the kind of cross that is most useful when you are involved in traffic direction, because it shifts people around without significantly altering their relative authority. It is also a good movement to use simply to get attention before doing something else, such as saying a line, because such a change in position is obvious to everyone in the audience. (Remember this when planning your ground plan. If your principal entrances and exits are placed at the sides, characters must use horizontal crosses to use them; this will make entrances and exits weaker than if entrance ways are placed farther upstage.)

- Diagonal movement is usually strong. For example, a cross that moves from upstage to downstage on a diagonal provides the same amount of change in height as the vertical cross while maintaining full visibility of the actor's face in the process. At the same time, the horizontal portion of the diagonal cross makes it clear to everyone that some movement is taking place. Similarly, when a character crosses diagonally from downstage to upstage, she can mitigate the weakness of the vertical movement by keeping at least part of the body open to at least part of the audience.

(2) All other factors being equal, an audience will watch one person rather than a group.

One simple way to focus attention is to isolate one character from the rest of the group. This can be done in a number of ways:

• The group can be in a line, with the isolated person below the line (Fig. 4.17).

• The group may be in a semi-circle, with the isolated person at the focal point of that semicircle (Fig. 4.18).

• The isolated person may be to one side of the stage and the group at the other (Fig. 4.19 on page 85).

Fig. 4.17: Individual vs. Line

Fig. 4.18: Individual vs. Semicircle

Notice in both 4.17 and 4.18 how hard it is to separate the individual from the mass on the line or semicircle behind. Although this seems like the most obvious and simple way to focus attention, it often fails unless there are other factors, such as spotlights or different colors of costume.

- The isolated person may be on a different level, such as a platform, from the rest of the group (Fig. 4.20).

Fig. 4.19: Individual vs. Group

Fig. 4.20: Individual vs. Group
Notice how effective this is, even though the group includes a high figure
and is centered. The individual still stands out as the major focus point.

There are problems associated with each of these solutions, not the least of which is their inflexibility. You can easily isolate one person on one side of the stage, but what happens if you then want to shift focus to a different individual? In general, isolation is rarely used without being combined in some way with another method of focus. But isolation can be judiciously used to focus attention on an individual.

(3) All other factors being equal, an audience will watch whatever is different.

When you can't isolate a particular individual from a group, you can still focus attention by the use of variation.

- Audiences will focus on the person who is different in height (Figs. 4.21, 4.22 on page 86). Although the tallest person is usually the strongest person, if all are standing and one is sitting, the audience will focus on the one sitting.

- Audiences will focus on the person who is doing something different. If all are drinking tea and one puts down her cup, we will watch the one putting down the cup. Similarly, if everyone is active, we watch the one who is still.

Fig. 4.21: Focus on the Different (a)
With most standing, the single seated figure takes the focus.

Fig. 4.22: Focus on the Different (b)
With most sitting, the standing figure draws most of the attention,
even if in an otherwise weak position, off to one side.

- If all are moving, audiences will focus on the one moving in a different direction. If all move right and one moves left, we will watch the one moving left.

- Audiences will focus on the person with the most distinctive or unusual appearance. A costume can often be used to help a character take and hold focus. This is the reason stars traditionally insist on the most attractive or most distinctive costumes. Sometimes this involves color — lighter colors tend to attract more attention than dark, brighter colors attract more attention than those tending toward brown or gray, etc. Sometimes this involves decoration — the more spectacular the costume, the more likely it is to hold focus. However, it always involves difference. That is, if the entire group is in spectacular clothes, the woman wearing the simple black gown will draw focus from more spectacular clothes. The difficulty, of course, is that a costume is on-stage as long as the actor is, so this method must be used sparingly and with sophistication to keep focus changing.

(4) The audience will look at what the actors are looking at.

This is so simple that many directors forget how valuable it may be. It is human nature to look where others look. If we see people looking up at the sky, we automatically stop and look up ourselves. If we look at one actor and he is looking at another, we will shift our focus to that other one.

One of the fundamental ways in which you can focus audience attention on one person or thing is to have all the other actors on-stage look in the same direction.

Triangulation

Most of what we have been talking about is common sense. We know these tendencies from common, everyday experiences. For the most part, even beginning directors will use them without conscious thought in short scenes or plays with small groups. The difficulty arises when you try to block and focus scenes with many different groups of people over a period of two hours.

In groups of three, of course, the actors fall into a natural triangle. This is in many ways the perfect visual arrangement, because it is infinitely variable. Characters can stand perfectly still, and yet you can change focus from one to another effortlessly. (Figs. 4.23-27). Any character at any point of the triangle may take focus at any time. All that is really needed is for the characters at the other two points to look at him. This makes it an ideal arrangement for scenes in which several persons participate approximately equally. As long as the characters look at the person talking, then focus can shift back and forth without having to move the bodies around in exaggerated or unnatural ways.

Fig. 4.23: Basic Triangular Blocking (a)

Fig. 4.24: Basic Triangular Blocking (b)

There is now a clear delineation of group vs. individual,
but it is still very clearly three individuals as well.

Fig. 4.25: Basic Triangular Blocking (c)

Note how the girl has shifted focus to the adults without anyone moving, just by changing the direction of her gesture.

Fig. 4.26: Basic Triangular Blocking (d)

All focus is on the character at DC.

Fig. 4.27: Basic Triangular Blocking (e)

Same positions as in 4.26, but now all focus is on the character UL.

Any time anyone moves, the triangle stays in effect. You may arrange different kinds and sizes of triangles. You may even arrange vertical triangles using platforms or steps, with one point higher or lower than the other two points. You may mix vertical and horizontal triangles. You can vary the arrangement of bodies (called the "stage picture") almost infinitely, without losing control of focus.

Larger Groups

It is when we move into larger groups that things start getting complicated. There are only a handful of basic ways in which those people can be arranged.

Unfortunately, many people resort to the weakest arrangement, simply scattering bodies around wherever they end up. Scattering is actually quite useful in moments of transition, and it is of course the way to go for moments of chaos. But it must be used very rarely, precisely because it has no focus. Since it is arrangement at random, then any focusing effects are produced at random as well. The audience may and will look anywhere at all. If that's what you want at that moment, then do it, but such moments are usually pretty rare.

Circles

Circles are another common "real-life" solution. On-stage, they are disastrous, for an obvious reason — half of the circle hides the other half from view (Fig. 4.28 on page 90). The audience can see only the backs of those on the downstage side, and can see nothing at all of those on the upstage side. The cast might as well be off-stage. It can be used, and used effectively, if you find some reason for the people on the downstage side of the circle to sit down on the floor (Fig. 4.29 on page 90). This makes it useful for scenes with long speeches. But there are practical problems. It takes a long time to get everybody seated, and even longer for them to stand again after the long speech.

Semicircle

The semicircle does have the advantage that you can see the people in it. Most of the people are visible to the audience, although in varying degrees. There is a natural tendency to focus on the person in the center of the group (Fig. 4.30 on page 90). If you want to focus on any other individual in the group, she must step out into the center area (Fig. 4.18 on page 84). This makes it a common and useful pattern of focus in scenes with a single soloist against a crowd, as with a musical number with chorus. It is also useful if you want the principal person to stand at DC or UC. That makes it the traditional pattern for crowd scenes, such as the crowd in a neat semicircle listening to Marc Antony's oration or watching Hamlet's sword fight. But it has little or no flexibility — if you want to change focus from one person to another, then the first person must step back into the semicircle while the second steps out. That is your only option.

Line

The line is similarly limited. It arranges a group so that focus is essentially balanced. No one in the group stands out (Fig. 4.31 on page 90). That's why chorus lines are in lines: You are not supposed to watch one Rockette, but rather to watch all the Rockettes equally. Its disadvantages are that you

Fig. 4.28: Circular Grouping On-Stage

Fig. 4.29: Circular Grouping With Downstage Characters Seated

Fig. 4.30: Semicircular Grouping
Note how the eye is drawn to the actor at UC.

Fig. 4.31: The Line

see them all equally. An individual can become the focal figure only by stepping out of the line. This has somewhat more variety than the semicircle, in that two or three can step out of the line and still be separate. It has less dramatic impact because the people who have stepped out of the line can no longer have any plausible contact with the group still in the line. In a semicircle, the "soloist" could look to either side and see part of the group, and the audience would accept that he was speaking to the group. With the line, everyone else is behind the "soloist," which means she essentially is talking to the audience rather than to the group. There are times when this works effectively — the entire show *A Chorus Line* is built on this principle, for example, and many musical comedy production numbers fall into it naturally — but it lacks the flexibility and the plausibility to be useful in most shows.

The Triangle

When dealing with larger groups, the most valuable arrangement is the triangle, which is just as flexible for crowds as for groups of three. (See Figs. 4.32-36). In some ways, it is even more flexible, because you can vary the group to be either at the points of the triangle, or along the "sides." If a group is arranged along the sides of a triangle, a single person can be isolated at one of the points. Similarly, you can focus on small groups within larger groups. Simply arrange the small group at the strongest point of your triangle, and then the larger group will almost automatically fall into the "background" for the scene.

In practice, the triangle will be the single most useful device the director can use for applying all the focusing principles.

Fig. 4.32: Triangular Groups (a)

One person on a point, the group along a line running between the other two points.

91

Fig. 4.33: Triangular Groups (b)
Two individuals at two points, a group at the third.

Fig. 4.34: Triangular Groups (c)
Grouping treated as if along the sides of the triangle rather than at the points; the two lines form two sides of the triangle, the individual stands in the middle of the third side and takes focus.

Fig. 4.35: Triangular Groups (d)
Large groups clumped at points of the triangle.

Fig. 4.36: Triangular Groups (e)
Major group within a larger group; the large triangle focuses attention on the group at DR, while within that they form their own triangle.

VARIETY AND STYLE

When you are blocking and rehearsing your production, you will never confine yourself to only one method of focusing the audience's attention. You will combine two or three of the different principles we have discussed. You will mix semicircles and triangles, make triangles that include platforms, focus on downstage at some critical moments and upstage at others. That is why I prefer to talk about blocking as a matter of basic principles rather than basic rules. Some things work for certain situations, others don't.

In general, we try to mix up the various methods of blocking simply for the sake of variety. You should never want all the scenes to look alike. This can happen easily in almost all types of plays. Most "classic" plays, for example, were written for theater companies that had no stage furniture, no directors, and almost no rehearsal time. Playwrights soon learned that they had to write a lot of scenes for only two or three people who simply came downstage and talked with only such movement as the actors themselves felt necessary. Shakespeare and the other Elizabethans at least interspersed occasional crowd scenes, but you can go for pages and pages in Molière without ever getting four people on-stage at the same time. The same problem often appears in musicals, which move back and forth between "crowd" scenes in which the chorus stands around behind the soloist, and scenes with only two people that always end in a song, usually a solo. In 1981, John Ford Noonan jokingly called his new play "A Coupla White Chicks Sitting Around Talking," but it was a telling joke. Most plays of the last thirty years are little more than a couple of characters sitting and talking. Sometimes you have to force some variety, just for variety. Even so, there are certain limits to the amount of variety you want to include in any staging.

Style or Tone

Every production will have a style whether you intend one or not. One of the keys to good directing is learning to recognize this and to adapt it to good effect in each individual production.

The question of staging style is inextricably intertwined with the question of characterization. Essentially, we tend to talk about style in terms that run along a continuum from "artificial" to "natural." Thus, actors tend to talk about stylized performance as opposed to naturalistic performance, and stylized characters as opposed to realistic ones. This is perfectly valid, up to a point — there is no doubt that there is an eloquence of language, an "artificiality," in *Romeo and Juliet* that is not present in *Blue Denim*. Similarly, there is a formality of social custom, an "artificiality," in *The School for Scandal* that is not present in *The Odd Couple*. At the same time, we must not be blind to the fact that this is often a difference in social

93

custom as much as difference in theatrical "reality." All the fans and hand-kerchiefs and wigs in *The School for Scandal* are the norm for the persons depicted in their time. They are perhaps exaggerated for comic effect, but no more exaggerated than the perversities of Felix and Oscar (*The Odd Couple*). It is not that the characters are artificial, but merely that their customs are different from our own.

The director determines the style for the performance. You decide to accept certain kinds of business while rejecting other kinds. Each character has his or her own style, in the sense that people in real life have a style — there is a way they hold themselves, a way they carry themselves, a way they express themselves that expresses their personal image of themselves or the image they wish to project to the world. This is built up in perfor-mance by types of business. Stanley Kowalski has a different style from that of Professor Harold Hill, although both are in fact traveling salesmen. A Harold Hill who scratched his armpits, mumbled, and fumbled for the right word simply would not work. Hence, as part of the style of Harold Hill, any decent director would reject scratching his armpits, no matter how "natural" such business might be.

Similarly, each individual actor must fit into the group while still being a unique individual. Once Stanley starts scratching, then the rest of the cast must do similar business. If he scratches his armpits while everyone else folds their napkin and dabs their lips after every sip of beer, it will be funny. The entire milieu must make Stanley's activity believable and acceptable, which will automatically establish a style for the perfor-mance as a whole. This may be just as "artificial" as Restoration Comedy. The point is that it must be consistent throughout the production and then treated by all the performers as if it were natural.

Formal Staging

Formal staging is staging in which the number of arrangements and movement patterns are extremely limited. Shows done on bare stages, for example, tend toward the formal, simply because they offer the director fewer options about ways to vary the staging. A director with ingenuity can stage a show with very informal style within the context of the nearly bare stage, so one does not automatically mean the other. But in general, for-mality is forced on you by scenic limitations.

Casual Staging

Similarly, the casual production generally tends toward a crowded or complicated stage. The more furniture you put into the stage space, the less formal the blocking patterns and the more options for the director to vary blocking patterns. The relationship is not automatic. Sometimes you can produce a very formal show within the context of a casual stage. But, in general, the relationship holds.

What difference does this make? At one level, none at all. There are no plays that *must* be given formal or casual stagings. On the other hand, the formality or casualness has an enormous impact on how the audience responds. Try to establish some consistency.

Important Reminder

This has not been a discussion of rules. Rules are a matter of fashion, and they change from time to time and place to place. These are basic principles only, from which you can select practices most useful to the given moment in the given play on your specific stage.

There is only one actual rule for blocking:

You have eyes and ears, and imagination: Use them.

Always remember when planning blocking and then later when testing it in rehearsal that ultimately all blocking must clarify the moment to the audience. Try to watch as an audience member rather than as an examiner. Once you have given the actors the blocking, try to ask "Is this working?" rather than "Are they doing what I told them to do?" If it doesn't work, then change it. Try some other solution suggested in these principles, or try something that completely violates whatever we have been discussing. The only valid test is the result.

SPECIAL PROBLEMS

Arena Staging

Most of the principles we have discussed in this chapter hold true on the arena stage, even though they were originally developed for proscenium staging. But the arena stage offers some unique problems of its own. The most important point is: *remember at all times that you will be working in an arena.*

If you are not extremely careful, your mind will select one side of the arena as the most important side and start to stage a proscenium show without intending to do so. You write blocking on paper, and paper always has the same top and bottom, so you start to think the stage faces only one way. You work in a rehearsal room and sit or stand in one place, and soon you forget that you are seeing only one side of the show. The best way to deal with this while planning the show is simply to turn your blocking charts around now and then, just to shake up your own mind. Similarly, in rehearsals, *always* move around the room so you get used to watching the actors from all the sides the audience will see them.

Another significant problem is that positions of strength on an arena stage are different from those on a proscenium stage. An actor who comes close to the edge of the arena stage generally is in a very weak position (Fig. 4.37). When you are close to only one side, your face is invisible to the other three. Staying center helps some, but even there, the actor's face is visible to only half the audience (Fig. 4.38). There is only one spot on an arena stage where no people are sitting directly behind the performer — the space in front of an aisle. When you stand there, with your back to the aisle, your face is visible (at least in part) to more than three-quarters of your audience.

Fig. 4.37: "Downstage" on an Arena Stage
Although close to the audience on one side, the actor shows mostly back to all the other sides.

Fig. 4.38: Maximum Visibility on an Arena Stage.
In front of the aisles, no one has their back to anyone in the audience, and at least some part of the face is visible to roughly ninety percent of the audience.

One of the most attractive aspects of the arena is its intimacy. Even this sometimes leads to blocking problems. Because characters are close to each other, and because the audience is so close that actors may speak in normal tones of voice, it is tempting to allow "normal" groupings of the actors to develop as they would in real life. Unfortunately, the more actors talk to each other, the less the audience can see them (Fig. 4.39 on page 97). The closer together they stand, the more they hide each other from the view of the audience.

Fig. 4.39: Conversation Grouping on an Arena Stage

Not only does each person show back to some part of the audience, but the closer they come to each other on-stage, the more they block the view of the front of other actors. The most natural arrangement is thus the least valuable.

Similarly, although actors are usually stronger the closer they come to the audience, they can come too close. Most audience members like to keep some distance between themselves and the performance. When the actors invade that distance, people tend to grow uncomfortable and nervous. This in turn means they start worrying about the actor rather than thinking about the play. There is a point at which the actors see audience members as individuals rather than as a generalized audience. When they do so, they tend to lose their own concentration and mental focus. Thus, although in theory you can move actors right up to the people in the first row, it is usually better to establish some dead space between the stage and the audience (Fig. 4.40-41 on page 98). (This will also help to keep the stage lighting out of the eyes of the audience.)

One insurmountable problem of the arena comes from furniture. When the actors are standing, you can move them around. Although not all the audience can see them all the time, everyone can see them at least part of the time. But when actors are sitting on a sofa, they always have their backs to part of the audience (Fig. 4.42 on page 98). They can't turn around on the furniture the way they can turn when they are standing.

This problem can be minimized but never solved completely. One possibility is to keep the actors moving around more than you would on the proscenium. However, this negates much of the intimacy of an arena stage, which is one of the reasons you do shows in an arena to begin with. Actors can sit and talk more naturally and intimately in an arena than on a proscenium, and to keep them walking around tends to break that intimacy. A second method is to arrange the furniture so that the back of each piece is against an aisle (Fig. 4.43 on page 98). This minimizes the number of audience members sitting directly behind the seated actor and maximizes the number of people who can see at least part of the face.

Fig. 4.40: Actors Near the Audience (a)

Fig. 4.41: Actors Near the Audience (b)

Fig. 4.40 is what it looks like in the rehearsal room, where you are usually
standing, and where you can go to the back of the room; 4.41 is what it looks like
to the person in the front row. This is not only distracting, but it is often very unnerving.

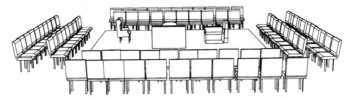

Fig. 4.42: Arena Furniture (a)

"Obvious" furniture placement. Notice how anyone seated will be
completely hidden from view of a large part of the audience.

Fig. 4.43: Arena Furniture (b)

The "four corners" approach. It's a cliché because it works; anyone seated anywhere
will be at least partially visible everywhere. However, the aisles are the only
way the actors can get on-stage, so remember that you have to leave room
behind the furniture for actors to make entrances and exits.

Two-Character Scenes

The most difficult blocking problem is not the crowd, but rather the smallest group: two persons. Crowds take a long time in rehearsal, but in planning, they are easy to work with because they provide a lot of options. Two-person scenes eliminate almost all your options. The fundamental problem is that a pair is always in balance. With only two points, you can't triangulate, nor can you do many of the other things you do with larger groups.

The most effective general principle I have found in such scenes is to use the distance between the characters as the visualization of their relationship. Changes in that relationship are visualized by changes in the distance between them.

Each scene works in a sort of push-pull relationship: characters are pulled toward each other, or pushed apart, as the dramatic relationship develops. In most cases, this push-pull process will climax with the characters in their closest relationship at the most intense emotional moment of the scene. However, it may often work for the climax to come when the characters are farthest apart, on the principle of unexpectedness discussed above. In either case, the point to remember is that, even with only two persons on-stage, the blocking still visualizes the emotional relationship between the two.

On the proscenium stage, it is often difficult to find a way for the faces of both characters to be seen by the audience, especially in those close, climactic moments. One common solution for this is to have both face the audience and one stand upstage of the other's shoulder, talking in effect to the back of the other person's head. This is "artificial," of course, and as such should be used sparingly, but there are times when the audience must be able to see and comprehend the faces of both actors at the same time. In such cases, this staging is not merely a useful solution but also the best.

Tables

Many plays include scenes in which people sit at a table. Unfortunately, when people sit at a table, some of them have to turn their backs to the audience. In arena staging, there is no solution to this problem: No matter what you do, someone will always have his or her back turned to some part of the audience. The damage is lessened because most of the audience is so much closer to the scene than on a proscenium stage.

On a proscenium stage, the table can pose serious blocking difficulties. If people sit all around the table, half of them have their backs to the audience. At the same time, since the stage is usually raised, the people whose backs are to the audience also block off the audience's view of the people whose faces should be open. The result is, no one can see anyone at the table (Fig. 4.44).

Fig. 4.44: Table Treated Normally
The drawing is done to show the table seen as the audience sees it, with their eyes above the stage but still slightly below the top of the table. In this "real life" arrangement, four of the six persons sitting in these chairs will be invisible to the audience.

If the scene is brief, this is not a serious problem. For example, *You Can't Take It With You* ends Act I and Act III with the family at the table while Grandpa says grace. If Grandpa stands to say grace, which is not uncommon in old patriarchal families, he can be visible to the audience no matter where his chair may be.

But in many plays, characters sit around the table for a long time. *The Odd Couple* is built around recurrent poker games, *Ah, Wilderness* requires a very long and sensitive dinner scene, the Hanukkah celebration in *Anne Frank* is long and critical, Banquo's ghost appears in *Macbeth* at a banquet table, and so on. These scenes cannot be played with people simply seated all around the table.

The "Last Supper" Method

The traditional solution to this problem is the "Last Supper" method: People sit at the two ends and on only the upstage side (Fig. 4.45 on page 101). It's unnatural, but it works. More importantly, it is essential when, as in Leonardo's painting, you want the audience to be able to see and to focus on each of the participants at some point in the scene. This method is limited by the number of bodies on-stage. An arrangement that seems logical with four or five characters looks absurd with eight or nine — not to mention the problem of finding tables long enough to seat the entire cast on one side. Even so, this remains the favored method of blocking tables on stage. Figs. 4.46-47 (on page 101) show some variations that allow you to expand the number of people without making the table itself look absurd.

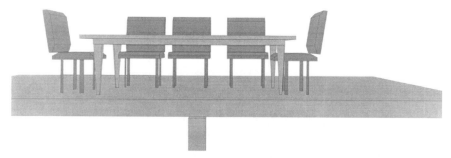

Fig. 4.45. The "Last Supper" Table

All chairs are open to the audience. Unfortunately, if the table has to hold more than the number shown, it starts to look very phony. It also starts to be such a big table that there is no room left on the stage for the rest of the scene.

Fig. 4.46: Angled Table

While not perfect, this does allow you to gain some visibility for all the persons seated; if you leave the chair on the DL corner empty, you can seat five with good visibility.

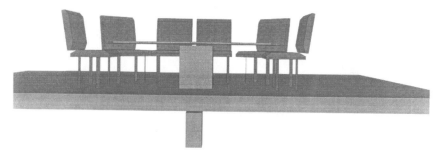

Fig. 4.47: Oval Table

When the table top is oval, you can squeeze more chairs into the "Last Supper" arrangement without looking unnatural.

Remember also that there are some cases in which it is not necessary to see everyone at the table equally well. In Harold Prince's staging of *A Little Night Music,* he completely reversed the Last Supper arrangement, putting all the couples on the downstage side of the table with their backs to the audience. As a result, we could see character's faces only when they were flirting behind their spouses' backs, which emphasized the intrigue of the various characters. Similarly, if only one person is important in the scene, you might turn the table vertically, so only the person at the head of the table is clearly visible to the audience (Fig. 4.48).

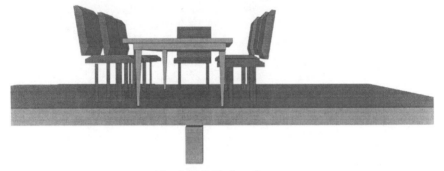

Fig. 4.48: Table for a Purpose

The characters seated to either side become weak and all attention focuses on the one person at the head of the table. This is also good for table scenes dominated by two persons — the dominant figure sits at the head of the table, and the second most important figure sits on one of the downstage corners, near to the audience; everyone else at the table disappears from consideration.

The critical question is: Who do you want the audience to focus on during the scene at the table? The answer, and that answer alone, should determine the way you place the table in your ground plan and the way you block your actors around the table.

CHAPTER FIVE
CASTING

Before rehearsals can begin, you must select a cast. The only way anyone knows to do this is to hold auditions. On the surface, these look like the same kinds of auditions professionals hold, but in practice, they should be quite different.

There are at least four unique reasons why you need to think differently about the audition process in schools, churches, and similar situations:

- **You are a teacher as well as a director.** Directors and producers at any level naturally want the best available actors. Ideally, they look for performers who already know how to build a character, control their nerves, speak clearly, and so on, because such actors minimize risk and simplify the rehearsal process. Professional directors cast actors who have already demonstrated a certain skill level by acting in other shows. In fact, they usually cast actors who have demonstrated their ability to play a particular role by playing a role very much like it somewhere else.

  You are a professional director and at the same time you are a professional teacher. You are being paid precisely to show your students how to do that which they do not yet know how to do. This holds true even if you are not in a formal school — church groups and youth theaters of other kinds all have a mission to help the young people do something new, to learn to be more than they thought they were. This means you should not exclude any students simply because they are inexperienced. Part of your purpose is to give them the experience.

- **All your actors are teenagers.** Their egos are very fragile. All actors face rejection all the time, and all feel it. Nothing you can do as a director can eliminate that, because it is part of the process of selecting a cast. But some casting procedures can do more damage than others. Your situation, dealing with the most fragile of all actors' egos, demands a casting process that does the least amount of damage to both the "winners" and "losers" in your audition.

- **Your program must have a constant supply of new blood.** Professionals can choose from far more actors than they can ever find parts for — more than ninety percent of union actors are out of work at any given time — so they use auditions primarily to eliminate actors from consideration. You have to use auditions to both eliminate and to include.

Even if your program is successful, every three or four years all your actors will grow up, graduate, or leave. If you expect to sustain, much less expand, the program, you have to find a casting procedure that welcomes, or at least does not frighten off, "new" students.

- **Everyone has some talent; you just don't know about it yet.** Every human being, at some time during almost every single day, pretends. We pretend that things are better (or worse) than they are. We pretend that we like something we don't like. We pretend that we feel something we don't feel, and so on. What is that, if not acting? This is different from acting on the stage only in that it is unscripted and often very brief. The actor on-stage must pretend something that someone else has thought up in advance (the script). Then, that pretense must be sustained convincingly for a relatively long period of time (the performance). But it is only an extension and development of real-life skills.

Every year you lose your most experienced performers and get a bunch of new people who have never acted on-stage before. No matter what you do, sooner or later you are going to have to give someone their first chance. You might as well make it part of your planning.

AUDITION METHODS

Everyone in the theater hates auditions. Actors (even the most experienced) hate them because they are a lot of work and pain and yet the end result is almost always rejection. Directors hate them because they never really tell you what you need to know before you cast someone. Anyone with a grain of compassion hates them because you know that you are going to hurt someone's feelings, no matter what you do. Unfortunately, no one has ever found a better way to cast a play. You have to audition.

This is never easy, but in a school production it is even more difficult than usual. There are five basic audition methods used in the modern theater, each built around finding the answer to a particular question. None of these works in all situations, which is why there are so many different methods. I think there is a "best" way for schools and similar groups, but it is possible you could use other methods.

Resumé Casting: What Have You Played Before?

This method is the most common professional approach. Producers and directors (and casting agents) see actors in shows. When casting a new show, they sort through the faces and names that seem familiar, then try to remember what they were like in the previous show. If that seems like what is needed, then they call up the actor's agent and try to negotiate.

Professionals like this method because it means they don't have to take chances. No one is cast for a role without having demonstrated the ability to play a very similar role in the past. Unfortunately, it is also the dominant casting mode in most colleges, where only graduate students get roles in "mainstage" productions after years of lab and class performances.

Many school directors are tempted to use this approach because it eliminates worry. You know the people whom you cast can play their part because they have already played a similar part. So you can go worry about scenery or publicity or whatever. But after a couple of years, the actors you already know will graduate, and who will replace them? This method also shuts out people who might be as good or better but who have not yet played such roles. At the same time, actors who do get cast never get the opportunity to grow, since they always play a variation of the same role.

Interview Casting: What Kind of Person Are You?

This is generally used when professionals have not been able to find all the actors they need through memories of previous performances. When this happens, they will hold an interview. This means that they call in people who have good credits but with whom they are personally unfamiliar and just talk to them. If they like what they see and hear in the interview, the actor will be invited to read or perhaps even be offered a role without reading.

School or church theaters rarely if ever hold formal interviews, but that doesn't mean directors in such groups don't use this method. We just don't formalize it. We know many students from classes, sports, field trips, and so on. So it's very easy to put them into compartments and type-cast them based on how we think of their personalities. In theory, this is reprehensible, but in practice, there are times when it is not only defensible but valuable. If the practice is used to exclude potential actors, it really doesn't belong in the school theater situation. But sometimes you may feel that so-and-so would be wonderful for this part, and use that feeling to encourage a kid who has not acted before to take part in a play. It's hard to object to the method in such a situation, as long as you can disguise it in such a way that it does not discourage other potential actors.

Monolog Casting: What Can You Show Me?

This is the most common audition method in professional "open" calls. The auditioners present a memorized monolog as if it were a real performance, in character and with full emotion. This demonstrates how well they can play a role, at least a role that is no longer than about two minutes and doesn't have to interact with any other actors on-stage.

This is in many ways ideal. It gives new people a chance, because directors who didn't see a performance can now see at least a part of that performance. It also encourages a judgment based on performance rather than appearance or personality.

But, among students (and amateurs in general), it has one potent disadvantage. It frightens people away from auditions. Professionals automatically learn four or five monologs; that's their form of resumé. They have them in mind all the time. When they go to an audition, they basically pull out the one they think will work best in a particular situation. But amateurs don't have a stock of ready-made material. They have to find a monolog, study it, practice it, and memorize it. People who aren't actors often believe that memorizing is the hardest part of acting. A significant number of talented people simply will not do that much work, since the chances are that they still won't get a part anyway. Most of those who do memorize an audition piece will do it at the very last minute. In the audition, they don't act — they just try to remember what comes next.

There is one more subtle problem in amateur situations: The actor has to memorize and prepare something in particular, but what is it to be? Students don't know many plays, if any, so you are more likely to see imitations of movie or TV actors than you are to see prepared scenes. Students don't know their own personality, so how are they to select "good" audition material? If they select poor material, you have no way to find out if they could do something else better, because they know nothing else. In practice, prepared auditions are far less helpful than theory says they should be.

Cold Readings: How Well Can You Read?

In this approach, the actor walks in and is handed a script. Then he tries to act it out without memorizing, while holding the script in hand.

This tells something about acting skill, but not as much as prepared monologs. That's why professionals resort to it as a last possible choice. But it does offer a number of positive values, even for professionals. It gives you a glimpse of acting potential without the distraction caused by poor memorization. If you wish, you can give the auditioner some directions, and this will give you some idea how the actor might respond to directions in rehearsals. The scripts give the very nervous something to hold onto, which sounds silly but is often very important to amateurs. By reading a scene, you can see two or three people at the same time, which both lets you see more people more quickly and allows you to take time to see individuals more than once. Perhaps most importantly, since the script you read from is the show you are casting, it tells you how people might look and sound in the parts you want, rather than in the parts from some other play.

In schools or churches, it has one tremendous public relations advantage: It looks fair. Everyone starts from the same point, no one can prepare ahead of time, and no one is automatically on the fast track just because they've done other plays. Anyone who walks in the door gets the same chance as anyone else.

There is one obvious disadvantage. Readings tell you only how well the actors read. Many very fine actors do not read well at all. In the contemporary high school, most students do not read very well. It is very easy to be deceived by the simple fact that the auditioner can actually say all the words. However, remember that a good reader probably will understand the role sooner, memorize the role sooner, and start to act the role sooner than will a poor reader of equivalent acting experience.

In most cases, you can modify the reading by sending groups off into the hallway or a corner to practice together for a few minutes. That way, all but the worst readers get over the hump. Everyone gets a chance to at least try to do more than just read out the words.

Improvisation: How Well Can You Make Up Your Own Play?

One or two persons are given a situation, and they simultaneously make up and act out that situation. The advantages, of course, are that no one has to prepare and no one is hampered by faulty memorization, faulty selection of material, or poor reading ability. Unfortunately, there are disadvantages, not the least of which is that the actors tend to do what they've always done, to play the same kinds of characters as they've always done. Thus, in practice, you get merely a disguised form of interview and typecasting.

More importantly, however, is that improvisation tells you only about improvisation skills. In the play you are about to do, the actor must read, understand, interpret, and play someone else's material, after doing it over and over to make it come out as nearly the same as possible every time. The skills of improvisation and of acting are only tenuously related, and many of the greatest actors of the modern world have been terrible at improvisation.

***

Given all the factors involved, I recommend the "reading" audition. It intimidates the fewest young actors and tells you more *useful* information about the actors you don't already know than any of the other methods. You may of course use whatever method seems best in your situation, but think about it carefully before you select your audition approach.

Basic Framework

Whatever audition method you select, the following framework is essential in all of them.

- **Access to the script must be absolutely fair.** If one person gets to look at the script before auditions, then *anyone* gets to look at the script before auditions. Since you have a limited number of scripts, this often means that no one gets to look at the script. But that's all right. You may see poorer readings, but you will see more students. They want the auditions to be "fair." It's more important in the long run that everyone is treated equally than that some people get a little extra help, even if they are people who need help.

- **All auditions should be open.** That is, anyone in the school or church group who is willing to do what is done in the audition should be eligible to audition. No "seniors only" productions; no auditions for "only people who have taken drama class," etc. If students have learned something in your drama classes, for example, they will do better auditions and get cast anyway. If they haven't, there's no justification for guaranteeing them parts. This is a particular problem in church and youth groups. When I was very young, I did a musical at a church where, after I cast the show, the minister overruled me and literally threw several of the kids out of the cast. He claimed that he didn't know them, that they weren't really members, and that anyway, we should favor the kids who were regulars. It was embarrassing to me, and I never worked for the group again. I didn't object to the criteria, just that they had not been clear before we started. Now I would also argue that it was wrong because one of the reasons for doing such projects is to attract young people who have not been regular. However you deal with this issue, the most important thing is to be clear and consistent. If the auditions are open to "anyone" in the group, then they must in fact be open to anyone who fits the definition of the group.

- **All auditions should be public.** Any potential auditioner should be able to observe the auditions, as long as they remain quiet. There are a lot of experienced people who disagree with this idea, because they find that some students work better without an audience of their peers. It is true that having an audience makes some nervous auditioners more nervous, but it is not a bad thing for you to find out who has the worst nerves. Professional auditions are almost always private.

In schools and similar groups, however, this sense of fairness and openness is of primary importance. If the theater group is a small, inbred group, it will always be an outcast activity among the rest of the students of the school. I've never seen a school in which most of the students wouldn't love to be in a play. But when it comes time to audition, practically no one actually shows up. There are a lot of possible reasons, but the single most common is that they don't believe they have a fair chance anyway. No matter what you do, some, perhaps most, students will believe that you play favorites and don't want any new people. You will probably choose the same people in a closed audition as in an open one, but most students won't believe that. They will think that auditions held "in secret" will mean they don't have a chance for a part. Somehow, when they can see the auditions of other students, they tend to believe that the program has more room for newcomers.

Even more importantly, many students come to auditions looking for a reason not to audition. They think they "might" try out for the play, but they want someone else to go first. If they sit and watch for a while, they relax. They see that it's not so terrible and that everyone else is doing it. Their friends encourage them, you encourage them, and finally they get up and audition. I've found a lot of terrific performers from people who came to auditions "just to see what it's like" — closed auditions would have kept them away and made all of us poorer.

PREPARATION

- **Before you hold auditions, be sure that you have scripts on hand.** Even if you don't use the scripts in the auditions, you can't start rehearsals without them.

- **Schedule enough auditions.** You must have enough time to see the people you expect to appear. Remember, however, that you have to concentrate for the entire period, so don't schedule sessions longer than two or three hours. It's better to have several sessions in which you are alert than one long one in which you are exhausted. In addition, students often have previous commitments. A single audition time might eliminate a number of people who simply can't come at that particular time. I usually have auditions at least two different days. I also try to have at least one afternoon audition for those who want to stay after school and one evening audition for those who work or play sports in the afternoon.

- **Announce everywhere.** No one in the school should be able to say they didn't know about auditions.

```
┌─────────────────────────────────────────────────────────────────────┐
│                                                                       │
│  Audition Information Form                                            │
│                                                                       │
│  Play: _____ │
│  Name _____ Date _____ │
│  Sex _____ Yr. in school _____ Ht. _____ Wt. _____ Hair _____ Home phone _____ │
│  Home address _____ │
│  Parents'/Guardians' names _____ │
│  Class schedule:                                                      │
│  Period    Class                   Room        Teacher               │
│  1. _____ │
│  2. _____ │
│  3. _____ │
│  4. _____ │
│  5. _____ │
│  6. _____ │
│  7. _____ │
│  8. _____ │
│  List recent roles you have acted and groups you have performed with: │
│  _____ │
│  _____ │
│  _____ │
│  List other public performance experience (e.g., choir, band, dance recital): │
│  _____ │
│  _____ │
│  In general, rehearsals for this play will be held _____ from _____ P.M. │
│  beginning on _____. Performances will run from _____ to │
│  _____. If you know of any conflicts for any of these times (e.g., job, family │
│  commitments), please list them below:                               │
│  _____ │
│  _____ │
│  If not cast, would you like to work on (check as many as you like): │
│  Stage manager ____ Props ____ Costumes ____ Scenery ____ Lighting ____ Sound ____ │
│  Publicity ____ House manager ____ Usher ____ Other (specify): _____ │
│  Director's comments:                                                │
│                                                                       │
└─────────────────────────────────────────────────────────────────────┘
```

Fig. 5.1: Sample Audition Form

- **Prepare audition information forms.** (See Fig. 5.1. above.)

  Most of the points on the example are self-explanatory. However, a couple of lines may need comment. You need to ask for a parent or guardian's name because a large proportion of your students will be living with guardians or stepparents with different names, or with only one parent. You need a class schedule so you can contact those students who are not in your classes. (I also use class schedules to tell me about students I don't know — their list of classes tells me a great deal about their general intelligence and attitude toward school. My last school required that students maintain a certain grade-point average to participate in extracurricular activities. Most schools have similar requirements, and if yours does, add a question about grade-point average to your form. I often ask people to describe their clothes down in the "comments" area, because it helps me to remember them — students can't provide you with photos, so anything that helps distinguish students you don't already know is a big help. (If you can afford it, take Polaroids of the unfamiliar auditioners.)

- Prepare yourself. Look at your analytical notes about each character, and then plan auditions that will tell you what you need to know. If you are auditioning for *Our Town,* for example, don't ask people to improvise scenes between a policewoman and a teenager with drugs in his pocket, or a burglar and a pregnant lady trapped in an elevator. Ask people to do what will show you what you need to know in order to cast intelligently.

AUDITION PROCEDURES

At the auditions themselves, the following procedures will make things go more smoothly.

Always be early, and come with everything you need. Bring scripts, of course, if you are using scripts for the audition. Since all auditioners must fill out your audition form, be sure you not only have the forms themselves but also plenty of pencils. Make sure you have chairs or props if you want to use them.

If you will use scripts, it will save time if you print out an information sheet that lists all the scenes that will be read. With this in hand, students need not interrupt continually to ask what page the scenes are on. It also helps to write a brief description of each of the characters on this sheet, so the auditioners know what you are looking for in the auditions.

Even if you give the auditioners an information sheet, begin with a brief speech in which you say again what is on the information sheet. Some people don't read, some won't read, and some don't believe what they read unless the teacher repeats it. During this speech, be sure to give a brief summary of the plot, since most will know little or nothing about the play. Answer questions. Then, begin the auditions by whatever method you have selected.

One additional advantage of the information sheets is that students who arrive late (as many will) need not interrupt everything to find out what's going on.

When you do auditions, remember to audition everyone trying for the same role in the same way. Don't change your reading scene or your improvisation idea just because you've seen it several times. You can't compare people for roles unless they have done comparable things.

It's okay to ask auditioners to do something else or something different after they have done their first audition. People often try for a role that they may not be suited for. Others do something during their audition for one role that suggests they could possibly play an entirely different part. If so, ask them to read a different scene later in the auditions or to play a different improv, or even to do the same thing again in a different way. The purpose of the audition is to allow you to get some idea of what they might be capable of doing — you can't get this if you aren't flexible. Time is the only limiting factor here. If you have a lot of people to see, you should see everybody once before you see anyone a second or third time. Again, fairness.

Similarly, if time permits, always allow students to audition a second time. This gives them a chance to read for a different role, after they have heard more about the play, or to do the same role again, but (one hopes) better. This, too, encourages the impression of fairness. More importantly, it gives you a chance to find out if people do get better. Many people are terrified the first time, even very experienced people. The second reading gives them a chance to try again when their nerves are a bit more relaxed. If a student really does read better during the second chance, then you will be able to select a better cast and make a better production. There are limits, of course. Some people just like to monopolize attention. Others will want a third or a fourth try. If time allows, let them try again. You want to find out the best they can do, and not everyone does their best first try.

Make notes on what you see. I write at the bottom or on the back of the audition information forms. You may think you will remember someone, but after twenty-five or fifty auditions you will only remember a few outstanding moments, which is not the same thing as remembering the best readings for a full cast.

Finally, don't make any decisions during the auditions. It's very tempting to say "Aha, that's it!" and then sleep through the rest of the auditions, only to discover that you don't remember enough to decide on the rest of the cast.

Callbacks

Callbacks are additional auditions at which the director asks some people to come back for a second look. Most people use them on a regular basis. You need a callback when there were so many people at auditions that you can't keep them all straight. You need a callback when you can't make up your mind from the first auditions. You may also need a callback to test potential groupings. For example, when your auditions are on several different days, you may see your best Helen Kellers on Tuesday and your best Annies on Wednesday; you need a day when they are all in one place at the same time so you can test how each combination might work. Similarly, when you read scenes or do improvisations, the quality of work done by any individual is limited by the skill of their partner. There may be some people who did not do well but who looked promising, so that you want to pair them up with a more skilled partner who was not available at the original audition. Finally, people who use prepared monologs or improvisations need to test the best people with actual scenes from the script. They can do this in a callback.

If you decide you need a callback, remember that you don't need to call back everyone. Call only those people you need to see again, and don't waste time calling back everyone you might cast.

And don't announce any part of the cast until you have finished the callbacks: what you see there may change all your casting plans.

MAKING A DECISION

After auditions are completed, you must come to a decision. This is, of course, a whole series of decisions. People often think that you just put the best person in the biggest part and try to hide those less talented in the smaller roles. This is not how it's done. Good casting is making the best possible use of the actors you have.

This does not mean you ignore such factors as experience or talent. Some of your students will have more of these than others, and you should use them to best advantage in the most demanding roles.

But the most demanding roles are not always the biggest roles. In practice, the only consistent difficulty about long roles is that they have more lines to memorize. If you have made a careful study of the script, you will have a good understanding of the requirements for each role. Thus, you should understand the roles that need your best performers.

To make the best arrangement of actors, start by making a list of all of the characters in the play.

Then, beside each character's name, list everyone you saw in auditions who might be able to play the role acceptably. Don't rate them yet, just list them. If someone's name shows up for several different characters, that's no problem. You will find that it is in fact quite common, for good young actors are often capable of playing several different roles in a particular show.

Next, make sure there is at least one name listed for each role. If not, go back over your audition sheets and notes until you think of someone who could take the role. Don't limit yourself only to those people who read for that particular role; someone may have done something applicable while auditioning for a different role. Don't ignore someone just because you have already listed them beside another character. This is all just preliminary.

Now, you're ready to start making decisions.

Start with the role you see as the most difficult or demanding. This is not automatically the "lead," although it will usually be a large role. Among the names listed, who was best suited to the role? Very often, if you have thought carefully about this role, you will have only one or two possible choices to consider for this part. Once you have made the choice, mark that actor off your list for any other roles he or she might be listed for.

Then go on to the next most difficult part and repeat the process. As soon as a person is selected for a role, he or she is crossed out of the list for any remaining roles. Gradually work down to the easiest role.

It will sometimes happen that the person best suited to a particular role is not cast there, because you need them more in a different role. For example, if you are doing *The Miracle Worker,* the best Annie may also be the best Helen. But Annie is a much more difficult role, and you will have many more choices for Helen, so you cast her for Annie anyway, even if she was the best Helen.

You may also have to revise your opinion if someone seems best for one role but is also the only person suitable for another one. Your best Annie, for example, may be your only Mrs. Keller. In such a case, you have to cast her in the part where you have no options. To do otherwise means casting someone who is unsuitable in a role, which can only hurt the show as a whole.

It would be nice if this solved all your problems, but there are still other factors to consider.

How will the various people fit together? For example, will the children look like children when they stand next to the people cast as their parents? Will the romantic couple fit together — in particular, will they be close enough in height and size that they will be taken seriously by the audience?

Can the cast be scheduled? Some of the people in the cast will have schedule conflicts, which is not usually a problem since everyone need not be at every rehearsal. However, everyone in the same scenes must be at the same rehearsals. If Mr. Keller wrestles on Tuesday and Friday evenings and Mrs. Keller sings in a church choir on Thursday, the only time they can rehearse their scenes together would be Monday and Wednesday. Can you do a practical rehearsal schedule under those constraints? Eight of the cast members in *The Diary of Anne Frank* are trapped in a room together, all on stage in all the scenes; you have to be able to get them all at rehearsals at the same time. If not, then you must cast someone else in the roles who can get to the rehearsals.

Never cast someone who did not audition. No matter how great you think that person will be, and no matter how poor your choices, resist the temptation. Confine your casting to the people who came to the auditions at the scheduled times. On occasion, there may be someone who wants to audition and who can't make it to one of the announced sessions. In that case, you may see them audition by appointment at some other time. But they must audition. Even more important, this special session must be witnessed by some other students. The problem again is that all-important appearance of fairness. Everyone must jump through exactly the same hoops, with no playing favorites. Casting people who didn't audition negates the whole purpose of the auditions.

(In general, students don't seem to mind if you replace someone who drops out of the cast later in rehearsals with someone who didn't audition — that's an emergency. Sometimes they don't mind if you go after other students when you literally didn't have enough bodies show up at the auditions — if you need seven girls and only six showed up, then you can usually safely bring in someone you think will be good. But only if you cast all six who struggled through the audition first. And even then, it's risky. You may improve the cast for this particular show, but you will weaken the next one and the next by implying that you have teacher's pets who always get a part, no matter what.)

Personality and Popularity

Finally, you must make some consideration of individual personality. It is a common misapprehension that the larger roles are "starring" roles. This has some validity in professional theater and films, where a star serves a purpose. This concept has no place in amateur theater, especially in theater with teenagers.

Real stars are people audiences will pay to see, no matter what they are playing. In that sense, everyone in a school or church play is a star. Most of your audience comes because they know someone in the cast. The person with the smallest walk-on role has just as many friends and relatives as the person with the "lead." Each will contribute equally well to the audience.

Teachers are often tempted to increase their audiences by recruiting or casting "popular" students, such as a cheerleader or the star athlete.

These students rarely contribute more than any other student would contribute to the box office. In some cases, they may have a negative impact. One of the oddities of student life is that, as soon as someone becomes popular, he or she is hated by other students precisely for that popularity. If popular students give you the best auditions, then cast them. But little if anything is to be gained by casting them in hopes that their popularity will rub off on the theater program. If they're the best available people, use them, but don't give them parts for any other reason.

The same holds true for truly unpopular kids. Every show you will be tempted to cast someone simply because "it would be good for them" or "it might turn them around." Resist that impulse. This is very hard to resist, because your program exists to provide opportunities for young people to find success and self-esteem. That's one of the main reasons you get a salary. But there is a difference between giving an opportunity to a kid who hasn't yet had a chance and trying to save a kid who has already blown several chances.

The thing to stress in casting decisions is that you should consider only what the particular play needs. The play production fits within a context, but you should have dealt with that when you selected the play. Once you have a suitable play for your group, then cast to make a good production. Do not cast for any other reason.

Having said that, there is, of course, one exception. Never cast people whom you have used before and who were irresponsibly disruptive. Again, one of your reasons for existence is to teach kids how to be responsible. That's one of the major "real-life" skills to be learned from rehearsing and performing a play. Everyone in theory should get a chance. But some people do not learn, and you can not afford to keep trying to teach them. If you know that a particular student has a long tradition of cutting rehearsals, of persistently bad-mouthing other actors, of refusing to learn lines or blocking, or disrupting rehearsals when they do come, do not cast them again. This sounds obvious, but very often these disruptive students are among your most talented people, or at least think that they are talented. They see TV and movies; they think that's the way "stars" are supposed to act. Let them go be stars somewhere else. You can live without them, no matter how much talent they might have.

Gender and Race

It is an inescapable fact of life that most plays that exist were written for casts that were originally "white" and that most of the roles in those plays are for males. It is just as inescapable that in an American high school, your students will represent dozens of different racial and ethnic backgrounds and that females will outnumber males at auditions by a ratio of 3:1 or more.

This can be a problem, but it does not need to be. In the schools, you are already exempt from the supposed rules of reality. All your actors are the wrong age anyway, so they will never be absolutely realistic. So there is no reason why you need worry about some mythical racial or ethnic reality in representing the characters.

Casting for Race

If the basic action of the play requires a single character to be a member of a specific racial or ethnic group, then you must find some way to represent that. There is no way to make any sense of *Othello*, for example, unless Othello himself is some kind of African; in the old days, we solved that problem with makeup, but now the social climate says that solution is unacceptable. In most plays, however, racial or ethnic associations are purely a matter of tradition rather than necessity. Dickens, for example, said Fagin was a Jew, but there is nothing in the plot of *Oliver* that would require you to cast only a Jew, or to make someone else "look Jewish." Situations that require ethnic casting are very rare. For the most part, if one arises, you should ask yourself why you are doing such a show in a modern American high school to begin with.

Ethnic Casting

Much more common is the kind of play in which everyone is theoretically a member of some specific ethnic group. Hamlet, for example, is ostensibly about Danes, or *The Diary of Anne Frank* is definitely about Jews. This does not mean you can cast only Danes or only Jews. The traditional method of all theatrical casting is to cast from the local talent pool and let makeup and/or costume deal with the cultural or ethnic questions. Thus, there are Japanese productions of *My Fair Lady* with all-Japanese casts who speak not a word of English, no matter what their accent. *Hamlet* is done all over the world without a Dane in sight, and there have been, at last, German productions of *The Diary of Anne Frank* without a Jew in the cast. And none of their audiences noticed.

In school or similar groups, you can cast anyone from any race or ethnic background in any role. Your students do not look right for most parts anyway, due to their age. There's no reason why you should expect them to look right in a racial or ethnic sense, either.

In fact, this should simply be a matter of policy. All casting is color-blind. Period.

This is not as easy as it sounds. Most minority students believe that drama is only for the "white" kids. You will have to work very hard just to get students from various minority groups to even try for a role. There is no doubt that, in the current climate in many schools, some minority groups ostracize any one of their members who tries to excel in school, which includes acting in school plays. It is not enough to just say, "Auditions are open to any student." You will have to scout the school constantly, trying to find minority students who will come to auditions.

Casting Must Be Colorblind

One of the problems that will arise in practice is *really* being color-blind. Twenty or thirty years ago, this meant looking past skin color to give minority students a chance. Now, more often than not, it means holding the minority students to the same standards as you do students from the majority.

There is no easy, hard and fast rule. If you cast minorities purely to have minorities visible, you are just as racist as if you excluded them purely for their visible racial characteristics. On the other hand, if you don't get some minority students in your shows, you will soon have no shows. You have to deal with every situation as it arises. The most important thing is to remember, always, that the only visual "reality" you have to work with is the visual reality of your school's population. It is hard to be color-blind. Maybe it's impossible. But you can try. And you must try.

Gender Casting

The question of gender is even more complex. Most roles in most plays were written for men, because that reflected the world in which the plays were originally performed. Not too long ago, doctors, lawyers, business-people, soldiers, politicians, and practically any other profession you can think of were all male. So when they appeared in plays, they were played by male actors.

In the world in which your students now live, this is no longer true. There are no more male-only professions. So there need not necessarily be any male-only roles in plays.

As always, there are exceptions. When gender is a part of the plot, gender must be accepted. Fathers and husbands, for example, should be male; mothers and wives female. Even this is flexible in some cases — I have seen *The Fantasticks* done with two feuding mothers rather than two feuding fathers. It worked well enough. (It would not have worked if one was a mother and one a father, because the audience would have expected a parental romance as well). The play will make no sense if you violate reality too much. Even so, a large number of roles in most plays can in fact be played by either gender. When you are making your casting decisions, always keep that in mind.

If you do decide to cast a female in a role that was originally intended to be played by a male, it is always best for her to remain female in appearance. That is, the male doctor simply now becomes a female doctor, even in a period play where female doctors would not have been normal. I have never seen any group dress up a girl in boy's clothing and successfully pretend she was a boy. It distracts the audience too much, and most of the time, a large portion of the audience will spend the entire show giggling whenever the girl opens her mouth. All-female schools, of course, have done this, just as all-male schools have often had boys play girls' roles. Once you have both boys and girls on-stage together, it is better to change an ostensibly male role to a female role than to have the female pretend she is male.

Just as in the area of race, there will be some people who complain. There will always be people who see racism and sexism where it does not exist. If you cast in a truly colorblind way, there will still be some who complain that you are demeaning minority students by expecting them to "act white." There will be people who complain because you do not do plays that require racial casting, because you don't have any specifically African-American or Latino plays. If you cast females in traditionally male roles, there will be some who complain because you also cast females in traditionally female roles as well. There will be others who complain that you seem to be trying to be "politically correct." You can only try to minimize the complaints.

You should not approach this issue purely in terms of potential complaints or pressure groups. Your shows are intended to both entertain and to educate your *entire* school community. Anything you can do that includes members of all parts of that community is a plus for your program, your show, and for you personally. The more people you reach as a teacher and as a director, the greater will be your own sense of personal accomplishment.

Double Casts

Sometimes, when there are few roles or few large roles, or when directors simply can't make up their mind, they will be tempted to double cast some roles. Two different people will play the same role, and alternate in performances.

This does increase your audiences a bit, and it does give more students an opportunity. It saves you from making hard choices. It also doubles your rehearsal time. Everything double cast has to be rehearsed twice. Since most groups don't have enough time to do one good rehearsal period, there is no way they can do one twice as long. For those people who are not double cast, that means rehearsing their scenes until they are bored with them. Most groups with double casts end up doing two poor productions instead of one good one. For me, that trade-off does not justify the increased opportunity — if the cast is not to be given the opportunity to do well, why bother with doing the show at all?

Understudies

In general, I have found that understudies never work out satisfactorily in high school. If they are to be prepared to take over a role, they must have some rehearsal. As with double casts, where is that rehearsal time to be found? If they do rehearse, then how can you not let them perform (in which case they are double casts, not understudies)? If they are not to rehearse, what good will it do to have them?

In addition, there is a practical problem. If you understudy Helen Keller, ninety-nine times out of one hundred the girl playing Annie will be the one to get sick. If you understudy Helen and Annie, Mr. Keller will be the one to leave town. You will have to replace someone in almost every cast, but there is no way to predict which one that will be. So, if you need to understudy one, you need to understudy them all, and you are back with double casting.

This does not mean you should not be prepared for cast replacements. If you need to replace someone in the first week or two of rehearsals, simply refer to your casting list and take your second choice for the role. In most cases, they will be more than thrilled to take over the role. If you need to make a replacement later, there are ways to do this without formal understudies.

Casting Everyone

Some schools try to remove the traumas from auditions by adopting a policy that everyone who auditions will get a part. This is done by expanding the crowds, or by writing in crowds, to use everyone.

In theory, this makes the program open to everyone and removes the more vicious, competitive aspects of the dramatic process. In practice, it makes the program seem of no value to most students. If anyone can get in without any effort, students will not value the program at all. Students are young, not stupid — they know when they are being patronized. They know, or quickly learn, that they are only being paraded on-stage in hopes of getting their parents to buy a few tickets. As a result, they will cause distractions and problems during rehearsals.

Cast everyone you need. Cast as many as you can, given the context of the show. But always remember, the purpose of the production is a good show. The only thing students learn from doing a show poorly is how to do something poorly. If you want to do a good show, you must approach it with some standards from the very beginning.

***

Kill the "Star" Syndrome

Once you have chosen a cast, make a neat list and post it in the designated place for any and all to see. Kill the star syndrome early — make your list in order of appearance, not by size of role. Be sure the notice includes directions for attending the first cast meeting. Make sure that everyone who is cast initials the cast list so you know everyone has seen it.

As soon as everyone has seen and initialed the list, send a letter to the parent or guardian of each actor announcing their selection for the cast. In this letter, explain what the play is about and what demands you expect to make on all the students. In particular, explain exactly when and where rehearsals will be held, and invite them to attend at any time they wish. The best way to gain and to keep parental approval is to keep them informed.

Dealing With Unhappy Actors

Sometimes students will be unhappy with the role they have been cast in and decide to drop out. Try to talk them out of it, because you obviously want them in the play or you wouldn't have cast them. Be as honest as you can here, but don't let yourself start discussing the other students. It may help to explain how you reached your decision. If you reached it the way I described above, you can turn this into a positive by stressing that, although this is not the role the student originally wanted, it is a harder or more significant role. Always point out that you cast them because you thought they were the best person for this role, not because you thought they weren't the best one for some other role.

In most cases, this talk will solve the problem, but in a few, the student will still quit. If that happens, look at your casting notes and get hold of the next person on your chart immediately. They will be disappointed that they were second choice but will usually be happy to get a part after all.

Some directors like to contact students individually before they post the cast list, precisely so that the people cast will never know that they were the "second choice." This rarely helps. Somehow, they always find out, if only because the person who turned down the part always tells everyone at the school. And any delay starts to look like favoritism again. To look fair, do everything you can in a very public manner. The appearance of fairness is always essential.

CHAPTER SIX
REHEARSAL

Rehearsal is a most peculiar institution. It can be an exciting and useful time. Simultaneously, it can be the most exasperating of all times in the theater. This is the period in which actors learn their lines, practice the blocking you have developed, and evolve the details of the coming performance.

The French call it répétition, which is accurate; you spend an enormous amount of time simply doing things over and over until everyone is secure. But that doesn't begin to suggest the life, energy, and stimulation of a good rehearsal period.

In Old French and Middle English, the root word is a farming term meaning to harrow again, to replow or recultivate a field that has already been cultivated. In a good rehearsal period, this is precisely what happens. The director lays out the basic shape of the show in the initial blocking. Then the director and the actors together go over and over the play, digging a little deeper each time, always asking questions about the script and about the performance, always looking for some better way to do things. In rehearsal, you are always changing, rearranging, reinforcing, adjusting, until the cultivation pays off and performances begin to grow. Then the play appears and is ready to be shared by the audience.

In the chapter that follows, I outline a typical rehearsal period for a typical play. This description is generalized, drawn from many rehearsals with many young actors. While it provides a guide to what should happen, and what common problems you can expect to meet along the way, each rehearsal period will be different in some ways, depending on the needs of your actors and the specific requirements of each unique script. This is a way of organizing and preparing for rehearsal that usually works, but you still must be willing to make individual modifications as circumstances arise.

SCHEDULING

For the director, rehearsal is life, since the director cannot perform and since this is, in fact, what you do for a living. In a very real sense, your work ends the moment an audience starts through the doors. Some directors deal with this by rehearsing forever — rehearsals go on and on for a full semester, even when nothing productive is occurring. Others deal with it by rehearsing hardly at all — unable to deal with the slow progress of most performers, young or old, they avoid anything that might not be perfect by simply pretending there is no point in further rehearsal once lines and blocking are memorized.

A good rehearsal period, however, falls between those two extremes. It must be long enough to deal with the play in detail, to find what the play has to offer and to develop performances to the best of the actors' capabilities. At the same time, it must not go on so long that the actors become bored with their material.

No matter how good we are, there is always room for improvement, and there is always something about a production that could be "fixed" with just a little more rehearsal. But there is a law of diminishing returns in rehearsal as in any other part of life. There comes a point when more rehearsal is simply spinning your wheels. This is especially common among student actors. Student actors are still students, and most of them do not work seriously without a deadline they can see. When rehearsals take too long, they don't work in more detail. They just put off the work until the performance gets close enough to scare them. It is better to do intense rehearsal over a relatively brief period than to spread rehearsals out over several months, much less a full semester.

Ratio of Rehearsal Time and Performance Time

In my experience, you need roughly an hour of rehearsal time for each actual minute of performance. This does not include your dress rehearsals, which we will discuss later. This is brief by professional standards, where almost two hours rehearsal per minute of performance is common for Broadway-type productions. Nevertheless, if the director prepares carefully, it can be very productive. I have rehearsed less, but it only worked well when it was a show with a small cast of experienced students. I have rehearsed longer, especially with large casts. Crowd scenes always require enormous amounts of extra rehearsal, and special problems, such as singing and dancing in a musical, also demand a longer time frame. Even in those cases, don't stretch rehearsals too long.

This usually means six to eight weeks of rehearsal time for a "full-length" play, before dress rehearsal. If at all possible, it is better to rehearse five times a week for six weeks than to rehearse four times a week for eight. Students count days, not rehearsals. They work harder when the show is six weeks away than when it is eight.

In schools, this means rehearsals Monday through Friday. Students generally will complain about Friday rehearsals, because they like to think the weekend starts at noon on Friday. But for most of them, this is purely a front. Few of your students actually have dates at any time, Friday or not, and most are happy to have someplace to go on Fridays. When I had evening rehearsals, I always started Friday rehearsals an hour or so earlier than others, so those who had parties to go to could get to them easily. Few students ever complained, much less cut a rehearsal.

Church and community groups can, of course, also rehearse on Saturdays. Schools almost never can use Saturdays, and in many districts it is formally forbidden, for reasons I have never understood.

Frequency of Rehearsals

Schedule rehearsals as often as possible, for mental rather than practical reasons. No matter how diligently the cast works, there is a certain amount of forgetting between the time you work on a scene and the next time you come back to it. The longer the time between rehearsals, the more will be forgotten. This means more time spent repeating yourself and less time to work on something else that needs the work. The shorter you can make the weekend, the shorter you make the forgetting time. If at all possible, always go for the more concentrated schedule with five rehearsals per week. Holidays are a particular problem area. The longer the holiday, the more that will be forgotten. Thanksgiving and spring break both tend to just wipe out a show, so if you have to rehearse on both sides of those kinds of breaks, plan on needing an extra week of rehearsal just to get back to where you were before the holiday began.

Length of Rehearsals

Within the schedule above, I recommend three-hour rehearsals. In almost all cases, any rehearsals running less than two hours will be a waste of time — you always seem to be quitting just when something productive is about to happen. At the same time, anything beyond three hours begins to fall apart. Students generally are not able to sustain the concentration needed for a good rehearsal for more than three hours, even with breaks and variations of activities. I know of many church and community groups that do five or six hours on Saturday, but I have never found that to be productive. The longer the time slot, the more time young people feel they can waste. In practice, I found that most of my rehearsals had done what they could do after about two hours and forty minutes of work. That seemed to be the point at which attention began to flag. If you schedule rehearsals for three hours, then you can get the two hours and forty minutes you need and lift everyone's ego by letting them out early. You also still have fifteen to twenty minutes in reserve in case some particularly knotty problem needs extra attention or someone is significantly late to rehearsal.

125

Be very careful not to under-schedule your rehearsal times. It is always better to release the cast early than to hold them late. For one thing, most schools have a time at which all school activities are expected to end, and the school must close down at that time. Far more importantly, you have made an agreement with your actors and with their parents. If your rehearsals are in the afternoon, your actors will have jobs to go to or family duties to get home to. If you rehearse at night, parents expect their children home at the time you told them. If you run over even ten minutes on even one night, Junior has a ready-made excuse. He can run around for an hour or so every night thereafter and tell his parents that you kept him at rehearsals (even the best students will do this if you give them the chance). If you say a rehearsal will end at a certain time, it must end then, or earlier. This must be an ironclad rule, or you will spend half your life answering charges that you're destroying the students' grades and lives by making them rehearse until all hours of the night.

Evening Rehearsals

In my experience, evening rehearsals are more productive than afternoon rehearsals, even though they are less convenient for the director. Most students, and all teachers, are exhausted at the end of the class schedule; neither actors nor director have the energy and concentration to focus effectively on rehearsals in the afternoon right after the last class. Many students have problems getting in gear, because afternoon rehearsals feel just like another class. Also, afternoon rehearsals often eliminate large numbers of potential actors. All sports teams, for example, will practice in the afternoon. Most part-time jobs also occur then, so afternoon rehearsals automatically eliminate students with jobs or sports before you even hold auditions. Many high schools now have some form of staggered scheduling, so that a large proportion of the student body does not actually stay for the last class period. In such cases, it is always easier to get students to come back to the school for rehearsals after a four- to five-hour break than it is after a one-hour break. I don't know why; it just is.

At night, however, the attitude is quite different. Rehearsals are separated from "regular" school, so students tend to treat them differently from the way they treat classes. They are more attentive, more concentrated, and more eager to work. They even attend more regularly — students who have stayed home from school in the daytime will often show up for rehearsals at night, if only to avoid the boredom of staying at home. It's also easier to schedule space at night. Unless there's an actual game, few other activities will be on campus during evening hours, and those that are will only rarely want your stage.

Consider Everyone's Personal Life

However, individual circumstances may make evening rehearsals inconvenient or impossible. You have a personal life. People with families often cannot come back to school every night of the week. (Although in families with small children there are advantages: You can take the kids in the afternoon while your spouse is at a regular nine to five job, and then trade them off after dinner when you go to rehearsals.) In larger towns and cities, the teacher may commute an hour just to get to school; you couldn't possibly do it four times a day. Your school may be in a neighborhood where parents do not wish their children to go at night. In many districts, school policy may not allow any activities after a certain hour, due to questions of security or just a shortage of money for janitors. Evening rehearsals are always more productive, but they are not always the most practical.

In church and community groups, on the other hand, it is afternoon rehearsals that are often impractical. Your students come from several different schools with different schedules, bus service for the young people who do not drive usually is terrible, you may hold a day job elsewhere, and so on. Your problem will be that space is at a premium at night, because that's when church committees and outreach programs tend to be concentrated for exactly the same reasons as you need to schedule rehearsals there.

Availability of Space

As you plan more specific scheduling, you should also consider availability of space. As we have discussed, you will rarely have control of your stage space, for it will be shared with any number of other school groups. Except for the week of tech and dress rehearsals, this need not be a real problem. You may just as easily rehearse in a classroom. However, remember that the rehearsal room must be noticeably bigger than your stage area. You have to be able to mark out your floor plan for the actors, and you must have someplace to stand that's not on that stage space. However, you will soon find that it is very difficult to rehearse large groups in a regular classroom space, for two reasons. First, you can never get far enough away to see the whole group at once. Second, those who are "off-stage" have no place to go, which means they continually distract those students still "on-stage" in the rehearsal. If you can get the stage space itself only for limited times during your rehearsal period, be sure that you always schedule large-cast scenes on those days.

Finally, you must consider when the actors you want are available. As you begin to plan a schedule, be sure to re-examine all those conflicts and include them in your scheduling, even if it means taking scenes out of order.

No one should have to surrender their life just in the hope that they might get a part in the school play, and no one will. You always want students who do other things, for it is their participation in those other activities that will bring in new audiences and new performers on the next production. In addition, one of the things the rehearsal process is supposed to teach is the importance of honoring commitments. It is more than a little hypocritical of us to begin by telling everyone cast that they must first break all their previous commitments.

When I audition a show, students tell me about any known commitments. They promise that, if cast, the rehearsals for the play become a new commitment and that they will not take on any *new* commitments that might interfere with those rehearsals. In return, I agree that, if I cast them, I will allow them to honor those commitments made before they knew they would have a part in the play.

No play that you are likely to do in a school demands every actor at every rehearsal — even Hamlet is off-stage a third of the time. As long as you know about schedule conflicts in advance, you can almost always arrange your rehearsals so that students can be elsewhere on occasion.

Rehearsal Schedule

Once you have considered all of these factors, work out a tentative rehearsal schedule. Consider the advice in the following sections about what should happen at any given rehearsal, and turn part of that schedule into something firm you can give the actors at the first meeting. I normally give the cast a general schedule for the entire rehearsal period, showing such dates as the day lines must be memorized, dates of costume fittings, run-throughs, tech rehearsals, and so on. But I provide only a specific schedule showing what scenes will be worked on at each rehearsal for the first two weeks. This specific schedule is then revised and updated each week, so that students always have at least several days warning of any changes in schedule caused by last-minute emergencies or, most often, changes in the school calendar.

FIRST MEETING

At the first cast meeting, everyone who is going to be involved in the cast or in a position of responsibility should be present. At this meeting, you should do the following:

1. Introduce the actors to each other. If you have been successful in your auditions, they will come from different classes and lifestyles and may never have seen each other. Also introduce those students with backstage

responsibilities, such as the stage manager or crew heads, so the cast will understand their presence when they appear at rehearsals.

2. Pass out scripts. Number these, and have students sign for their scripts. This serves two functions. First, someone will leave a script behind at almost every rehearsal; the numbering allows you to know who the script belongs to. Second, this allows you to call the scripts back after the performances. Once all students have scripts, go over all cuts or changes you intend to make and be sure that all students mark all the cuts.

3. Explain again the plot of the play, indicating as you go which actors belong to which characters. Use costume sketches and scene models to show where the show is headed. (The set model is particularly valuable here, because most students don't visualize a scene sketch very well.)

4. Explain all your rehearsal rules and any expectations you have about the show or the cast. As far as rehearsal rules go, there are really very few you need. These include:

   • Be on time for everything.

   • Meet all deadlines to the best of your ability (learn lines when due, etc.).

   • Be quiet off-stage and concentrate on-stage.

   • Tell the director about surprise conflicts in the schedule early enough for something to be done about them.

   That's not very many, and there's not much reason for more. For those in their first play, you will need to stress that rehearsals are not parties; the pleasure comes from doing well, not from playing around. It's always good to remind young people of the standard organizational rules. In most schools and churches, this covers obvious points like smoking, drinking, academic eligibility, and so on. Some students tend to believe that, since the play is "special," all those rules are off. Remind them that all the normal rules stay in effect as well.

5. Go over the rehearsal schedule together, so that everyone understands the way the schedule works.

6. Take costume measurements for everyone. This is more than likely the only time you will have the entire cast in one place before your first run-through, so take advantage of that and get all the measurements you may need.

Send everyone home with orders to read the script and get ready for the first blocking rehearsal. Many directors like to read through the script at this rehearsal, but I have found this to be of little value. It does guarantee that everyone has gone through the script, but it does not guarantee that they paid any more attention than they would pay if you were reading aloud in English class. Having heard it read aloud, most of them will not read it again at home. Most importantly, most of your students do not read with much facility. If more than half read above the eighth grade level, you will be lucky, so most of the reading will consist only of people stumbling over words. Meanwhile, those who do read well will try to start acting, without having the least idea how the role should be played. You will be amazed at how hard it will be for you to change interpretations once students have said lines a particular way in this first reading. In balance, it is far better not to bother with a read-through at this time.

You must establish from the very beginning that not all work is done at rehearsal. Every actor is responsible for some study, analysis, thought, and preparation for the role, all of which must be done at home. If you send people away from the very first rehearsal with "homework," it underlines this point quite vividly. For this reason, I usually schedule the first cast meeting on a Thursday, with first blocking rehearsal to follow on the next Monday. This gives the slowest readers plenty of weekend time to read through the entire play and to start thinking about it.

Floor Plan Preparation

Sometime before the first rehearsal, go into your stage or your rehearsal room and mark the floor. It always takes two people to do this, so take your stage manager with you. Using your floor plan, mark on the floor *exactly* where all scenery pieces and furniture will be. Use one-inch masking tape, and mark exactly where each piece of scenery will be placed when the set is completed. (If you can find it, gaffer's tape is better. It looks like masking tape, but it is much easier to pull up when you're finished. It saves you scraping the floor with razor blades when you try to remove the masking tape after six weeks of rehearsal.) These marks will serve as a guide for both you and the actors while they learn the blocking.

If your show has different scenery for each scene, you will need to clearly distinguish your marks. In general, the most practical way to mark multiple sets is with colored plastic tape or colored gaffer's tape. Use a different color for each scene. (This will, of course, be more expensive than masking tape, but it's worth it.)

Rehearsal Furniture

In addition, be sure that you will have rehearsal furniture available. Folding chairs are the handy, all-purpose rehearsal furniture, since they can be easily shifted and stored and can be combined to make sofas or large chairs when needed. If you have furniture on hand that more closely

130

approximates what you will use in the final scenery, then you should use it as soon as possible. However, since many rehearsals take place in classrooms or on a stage that must be shared among many groups, it is often impossible to store such furniture, and folding chairs once again become the most useful item. If you have the real furniture available, try to use it early in the rehearsal process. The more actors work with the "real" thing, the more secure they will be in their performance. However, never bring real furniture or props into a space you do not control all the time. If you share the rehearsal space with other classes, or even with others of your own classes, do not put out anything you intend to use in the final show. You can guarantee that that is the one item that will be broken, stolen, or worn out before the show opens.

REHEARSAL PERIOD

Rehearsals themselves fall into six basic stages:

1. Blocking	4. Development
2. Understanding	5. Integration
3. Memorization	6. Dress Rehearsal

The amount of time devoted to each stage will vary, depending on the cast and the show, but you must always deal with all six stages in order to have a good production.

First Stage: Blocking the Show

The primary goals of the first week of rehearsals are:

- To give the actors the essential blocking

- To establish the broad action of the performance

- To clarify the meaning of the lines

During this period, it is best to work in sequence if it is possible to arrange your schedule to do so. Since the cast is unfamiliar with the play, they will be less confused if you begin with Act I, Scene 1 than if you take scenes out of order.

131

When the cast arrives, explain all your markings. A set model is particularly effective here. Also, clearly explain stage directions for those who may be unfamiliar with them, showing where each of the areas are on your stage and showing the directions of movement. It also helps to show the cast how to abbreviate typical stage directions when writing them in their scripts — it's surprising how many will spell out each term, with the result that they can't read the script through the handwriting. Another common confusion comes from using "C" to abbreviate "cross," which soon gets confused with the "C" for "center;" encourage them to use an "X" or an arrow. Be sure to repeat this each night, until all the people who were not scheduled for the first rehearsal have heard it as well.

Once you have finished your introductory remarks, send the actors on-stage with script in one hand and pencil in the other and begin blocking the first scene on your schedule. As the actors read their lines, dictate blocking when it is needed. Have them walk through each move, and see that they write it in their scripts. Then continue with the next few lines until you need to make another cross, and so on until you reach the end of the scene.

It is almost impossible to give any detailed dictation to a group of high school students and retain their attention. You must get them active as quickly as possible so as to focus them on the work at hand. Similarly, no matter how well you have planned your blocking, you will have to make adjustments and changes as soon as you see the bodies in space. You will be stopping to make changes anyway, so you might as well not waste an hour or so dictating directions you will have to change. Blocking will make no sense until they have physically gone through it. On-stage, DC may occupy twenty-five square feet of space; until the actors are actually standing where they need to be, they can't possibly know what that DC direction actually means.

Get Actors On-Stage Early

Students tend to assume that rehearsal hasn't really started until they are personally on-stage. If you begin the rehearsal period with a discussion, many students will assume that no rehearsal has begun. If this happens several times, they will assume that it will be okay to be a few minutes late, because the director "never starts on time anyway." The only way to beat this problem is to always start people on-stage at the moment rehearsals are scheduled to start. Then, if you need to discuss a point, stop after ten or fifteen minutes of work to have the discussion.

While you do the blocking, listen carefully to what the actors are reading. Correct any mispronunciations immediately. There will be many of them, even on the simplest script. Although it will be difficult, since you are

132

trying to watch the stage and read your blocking notes at the same time, make sure each person says all the words in the lines being read. It is almost guaranteed that any lines misread in these first rehearsals will be mis-memorized. Nothing is more difficult to correct than an actor who memorizes a line with one word left out or one word mispronounced. Don't worry about characterization or emotional expression at this point — what you want to hear is all the words pronounced properly. Once the blocking has been notated, you will have time to begin work on such things.

Repetition Is Important

Whenever you stop to correct a line reading or to dictate blocking, be sure everyone backs up and repeats the line before going on. This allows you to be sure the correction has been noted or the blocking written down. It also helps to make sure everyone on-stage is at the same place in the script. This is also a good habit to teach the actors to use at any time in rehearsals when you have paused for a direction of any kind: Always back up and repeat the line or business you stopped on before going ahead.

Everyone Must Make Blocking Notes

It is essential that you make sure the actors all write down the blocking that applies to them. Many will think that a particular move is so obvious that they will always remember it and have no need to write it in the script. They forget that it will be several days before they will see this scene again and that they will have dozens of bits of blocking to remember. Only by writing everything down can confusion be avoided. The time saved later makes it worthwhile to spend a little extra time now to see that everyone writes down blocking.

Be especially careful in large group scenes. Actors tend to believe that they can just follow someone else in crowd scenes. The end result is that no one actually knows what to do, because each person is waiting for someone else to lead the way.

In general, you should be able to do between a quarter and a third of the play in each of these blocking rehearsals. If you restrict yourself to that goal, then the dictation and walk-through of blocking should take no more than the first two hours of the period. During the remaining rehearsal time, go back to the beginning and run the scenes through without stopping. This allows you to actually look at what you have blocked. It also allows the actors to check their markings, to begin to get some sense of the scene as drama, and to feel like they have accomplished something after all. Make changes if you see something in the blocking that you think needs to be changed. Correct the cast immediately if someone misses a piece of blocking or misreads a line. Do not let anyone leave this rehearsal until you have made every effort possible to see that the blocking has been noted correctly.

If time remains after this run-through, then you can begin to develop characterization and business.

Repeat this procedure each night until the entire show has been blocked. A number of directors, particularly in the professional theater, do not do this. They prefer to work on a single scene until it looks pretty good and then go on to the next one. I have found this to be unproductive with amateurs in general and students in particular. If you work on Act I until it looks pretty good, you will not get to Act II until the fourth week, and Act III may not come up until the day before dress rehearsal. By that time the cast will have completely forgotten everything they knew about Act I. By working on every scene at least once before you come back and repeat any scene, you keep each scene fresh in memory, even though you may lose some sense of cumulative development in any single scene.

Every Actor Learns a Role Differently

This approach to scheduling keeps the whole show in the mind of both you and the cast. No one can say how any individual actor will learn a role. The critical points of a characterization are usually in the emotional climaxes at the end rather than in the exposition at the beginning. By rotating the rehearsal among scenes, you keep the whole play in view and allow the actors to grow in whichever direction they need to grow.

Normally, initial blocking should take no more than four rehearsals. It is important that, no matter how detailed your plans may have been, you do not burden the cast with details at this time. Give them all the blocking you have planned. Also, give them any significant pieces of business that will help them understand the blocking. But don't worry about detail. **Remember that rehearsal is re-cultivation and that you will come back to each scene in the future several times. Then you can add more detail to your directions as the actors themselves discover more about the roles they are playing.** There is a limit to what can be done in any one brief rehearsal, so do only what is most important.

Second Stage: Understanding the Show

The second stage of rehearsals begins as soon as you have concluded your initial blocking, in the fourth or fifth rehearsal, and continues until actors begin to work from memory. For most shows in a five-rehearsal week this period begins on Thursday the first week and ends after the second complete week of rehearsals; in a four-rehearsal week, it would begin on Monday of week two and end after week three.

134

The primary goals of this stage of rehearsal are:

- To clarify, modify, and reinforce the blocking and business initially given

- To develop each actor's understanding of the role

- To encourage the process of memorization

During this period, you should devote your attention to scenes in a much more concentrated manner than during the first stage. In essence, you want to work on shorter scenes for longer periods. Given the vagaries of most situations, this is a time when you can and should schedule scenes out of order. Students will have no particular difficulty adjusting to this. However, remember that you should deal with all of the scenes at least once before returning to any scene a second time. The maximum remembering time for most casts is five days; if scenes are scheduled with longer gaps between, student actors will forget much of what has been learned.

It is best to do several different scenes during one rehearsal period. Unless a scene is especially long or complicated, the maximum concentration time at this stage of rehearsals is about an hour. Schedule several different scenes at each rehearsal. Try to arrange them so that actors have to come only when actually needed. In *Our Town*, for example, you might schedule all the Gibbs family scenes on one night, and all the Webb family scenes on another. This is not only an efficient use of time and bodies, but it also significantly reduces rehearsal distractions. Even adults who sit around for hours backstage waiting to come on for one scene get bored and make noise. Teenagers will make far more noise far more often. Do yourself a favor and call people only when they are really needed.

At each rehearsal, get the actors on-stage and begin to work immediately. They can and should still have scripts in their hand, even if they have already started memorizing. For one thing, they need to refer to their blocking notes, and for another, they will be writing new notes. Do any discussion as needed. Don't be afraid to interrupt. There are times when actors need to go through the scene without stopping, but this is not one of them.

Lead the Actors Into a Detailed Analysis

The actor's analysis will only be as detailed as you demand. However, this analysis should always be done in the context of physical action.

Detail the Blocking Itself

When precisely is the best time of a particular line for the character to sit? Why does it say to sit at the beginning of a line rather than the end or in the middle? Which best fits the emotion the character is going through and the meaning of the line? Similarly, you can add business. Remember that the actors have scripts in hand and thus cannot do much business that requires them to handle props, but you should at the least indicate what you will eventually expect. Also, encourage the actors to add business that seems suitable. This not only encourages the actors to contribute to the process but is also a clear indicator of how well they understand what is happening.

Ask Questions

Do the actors read the lines so that they make sense? Do not expect performance levels, for you are still very early in the rehearsals, but do expect simple sense. Does the manner of speaking indicate some comprehension of what is meant? If not, stop and ask the actors what they mean. The teacher in me often demands that students go off to the dictionary, for they have to learn to do such work on their own eventually. Also remember that "What does the line mean?" also includes "What does the character intend by the line?" This is the point at which you apply your analysis of the script directly to the individual actor's work.

Many directors like to do this kind of work around a table in discussion, but I always do this work with the actors on their feet. It is important that the actors always think of the performance as one seamless whole. If you talk about "lines" separately from "business," students in particular have a distressing tendency to think that the two things are unrelated. The only way to avoid this problem is to always deal with "lines" and "business" simultaneously.

Speech Feeds Activity

Each feeds the other. It is a reciprocating process at the stage of line memorization. If students learn certain activities while they are learning their lines, the repetition of that activity will help them remember the lines.

Many directors believe that you should never interrupt the actors in a scene but should rather wait until the scene is finished and then give the actors notes to be changed the next time you go through the scene. At this stage, you will find that the actors interrupt themselves a great deal, losing their place in the script, missing a piece of blocking, stumbling over a line, trying to read their own handwriting, and so on. Your interruptions will not destroy any intense mood. If you wait until a scene has concluded to correct a piece of business or a line reading, most of them will be certain they had done it that way already, and the note will be wasted. And if you want to change something, don't let them continue in a way that isn't working.

Interrupt Only When a Change Is Necessary

It is essential that you interrupt to make changes only when there is a change to be made. Never stop the actor to criticize without a suggestion that will make things better. Don't say, "That's terrible, do it again." Nothing will come of that except nervous tension. It's all right to say "That's terrible" (if it is terrible), but only so long as you have a way to make it better. Say things like: "Do it again but this time look at the people you're talking to," or "Do it again and move at the beginning of the line." The critical point is that you must always offer *concrete* actions that can be taken by the actors to make the scene work better. If you don't have any ideas about ways to fix the scene, let it run the way it is. There is plenty of rehearsal time left in which to make modifications. Do what you can do at any given rehearsal, but never try to do everything.

If you reach the end of this period and all of the actors read the lines clearly, with some semblance of characterization, and do the essential blocking and business as you have laid it out, you are on schedule for a very good production. Rehearsal is a process, not a test.

Rough Run-Through

It is very helpful to end this period with a complete run-through of the play, scripts in hand. This allows both you and the actors to see how far you have come and how far you have to go. It refreshes the actors' memory of how all the small scenes they have been working on fit together. It stimulates their understanding of the continuity of the play and the characters they portray. Finally, it gives a clear ending to this period of rehearsal, reminding everyone that the next rehearsal, when lines are to be memorized, is going to be different.

In most plays, there will be one or two scenes that cannot be completely staged until books are out of hand. Such things as fights, kisses, dances, or complex crowd scenes must be choreographed because they are so complicated or potentially dangerous. In general, you will indicate those in only the most general terms at this time. Detailed work has to wait until lines are learned.

Third Stage: Memorization

After ten to twelve rehearsals, all the actors should begin to work without scripts with all lines from memory. It is difficult to do this sooner, because it takes even the best students a couple of weeks to memorize any

137

significant role. It is dangerous to do this any later, because most of the cast will put it off until the last minute, no matter when that last minute may be. If you have no deadline at all, some will wait until the night before opening to memorize the lines.

Unless lines are memorized relatively early in the rehearsal period, you will never get real performances from the actors. The longer you wait to work from memory, the more the actors will think that accurately repeating all the lines is the same as giving a good performance.

Schedule These Rehearsals in Sequence

As with blocking, expect to do no more than a quarter to a third of the show on any night.

Begin each rehearsal at the beginning of the scheduled scenes and send the actors on-stage without scripts. Do not let them take scripts on-stage at all — no scripts in pockets "just in case," or rolled up in the hand although they "promise not to look at it." Most of the cast will actually know most of the lines far better than they themselves believe. If you allow them to use crutches, they will rely on those crutches even if they don't need them. Shock therapy is the only thing that works. Get the pain over with in one difficult evening.

Do not interrupt for anything except when the lines make no sense at all or when the blocking has gotten so confused no one knows where they are in the scene. They have enough problems trying to remember what they know that they can't possibly retain anything new.

The Role of the Stage Manager

The stage manager should follow the book, leaving you free to watch and think (and sometimes cringe). The stage manager should not interrupt to correct a line unless the meaning has been lost. During the first trip through from memory, anything close should be accepted.

If the actor does not know the line, there is a simple and effective procedure: He or she should freeze and say, "Line." The stage manager then reads the first five or six words of the line — if the actor knows it, this will bring it back. If the actor still doesn't recognize it, the stage manager then reads the entire line. Then everyone backs up one line, does it again, and then goes on. If the actor never says "Line," assume it is merely a dramatic pause. Demand this procedure. People get embarrassed and try to make jokes or apologize. Those aren't necessary. Just say, "Line" and go on with things. Don't let students get in the habit of making a big comedy act out of a forgotten line, because that destroys all concentration in the scene.

Almost always, the first memory rehearsal will go well, almost perfectly. Each following night will get worse. There is a simple explanation of this phenomenon. If the cast had two weeks to memorize lines, they spent two weeks memorizing Act I. Then they tried to memorize Act II and III overnight. I don't know of any way to prevent this; it is simply the way the student mind works. If you had good rehearsals during the second stage of rehearsals, the memorization of later parts of the play will be better than if you had poorly organized rehearsals during that period, but that is about the best you can hope for.

Some people try to give some space between the Act I and Act II dead-lines, but that rarely works. Since you will be rehearsing Act I during that time, most of the actors' concentration will be on Act I, so they will still wait until the night before to learn Act II.

Wording of Lines Must Not Be Changed

Most of your actors will ask, "Do I have to learn these lines letter perfect?" In almost all cases, the answer should be "yes." There are very specific reasons the lines are written in the way they are written. Changing the wording may retain the general sense of the line, but it will usually destroy the playwright's characterization and emotional complexity. There is no sense in expecting letter-perfect work at these first memory rehearsals, but at the second ones you should insist on it. If you let the actors go much longer than that, they will begin to think they can freely make up lines of their own. As a result, they will never say the same thing two nights in a row. Not only does this violate the script you have selected, but it also destroys the performances of all the other actors on-stage who never can be sure what their cue lines will be.

At the end of this period in rehearsals, you are ready to begin *real* rehearsals. The actors may think they're almost ready for an audience — after all, they know their lines and what they're "supposed to do." But real rehearsal has yet to start. Up to this point you have simply been preparing the cast for rehearsal and testing your own plans for the production. In stage four you will get down to the work that will make your production a play rather than a talent show or assembly skit.

Dealing With Actors Who Will Not Learn Lines

You have an obligation to teach in rehearsals, which means working with students at different skill and intelligence levels. But you are under no obligation whatsoever to work with people who are not willing to make a minimal effort themselves. You have to live with enough of that in the regular classroom. There is no reason you should put up with it in an extra-curricular situation as well. The ultimate threat is simple: The actor who refuses to learn lines can be replaced. After all, if he doesn't know his lines, what have you lost by bringing in someone new? If the actors believe you will, in fact, replace them, they will suddenly discover they can find time to study their lines.

Much harder to deal with is the actor who is just not up to learning as many lines as the role demands. However, I must stress that this situation almost never occurs. Students who cannot memorize large chunks of material usually cannot read well either and will not do the kind of auditions that get them roles larger than they can handle. In rare cases when it does occur, I tend to believe that no one making a serious effort should be punished by dismissal from the cast. You selected the cast and thereby took the responsibility to get the students ready. As long as they make every effort in their power, you are under an obligation to stay with them and get them through somehow.

Fourth Stage: Development

This period begins as soon as you have been through all scenes from memory. Generally, this period should involve at least two full weeks of rehearsal, and for complex or particularly demanding productions, should contain even more.

Unfortunately, this is the period most groups tend to skimp. Do not let that happen. This is the heart of the rehearsal period, when you turn the mechanics of blocking and memorization into genuine performance. It is possible to rehearse too long, particularly with students. But there is more to a production than just remembering all the lines. You simply cannot get there if you don't learn to use the development period of your rehearsals.

Everything Must Be Fine Tuned

This is the period in which you dissect every detail of the performance, examine it, adjust it, and repeat it until the work of each individual performer begins to turn into a real characterization.

It is also an intense period. When problems continue, they will lead to greater frustration than in other periods, simply because it is the period in which so much progress is made in so many other areas. At the same time, the excitement that comes from the progress made will often be more satisfying than the actual performance itself.

As the director, you must be at your most concentrated and sensitive during this period. In earlier stages of rehearsal, you essentially had only one function: to explain to the actors what they needed to do. In this stage, however, you must expand that role and simultaneously serve as leader, taskmaster, analyst, advisor, supporter, critic, and surrogate audience.

Schedule Scenes in Small Units

These rehearsals should be scheduled in smaller units than those scheduled during the second stage of rehearsals. Sometimes in a single night's rehearsal you will schedule four or more separate scenes with as little as thirty minutes devoted to a particular scene. For the sake of retention, you should still try to see every scene in the play at least once in every five rehearsals. However, there is no reason to try to work with scenes in sequence. Scenes that are coming along well should be hit occasionally so they don't regress, but the scenes that are most difficult should get the most work. Actors cannot feel secure in even the easiest scenes if they are worried about the hard ones.

You will need a prompter throughout this period, so the stage manager or your assistant should follow the book at all times. Again, you yourself should never follow the script. If by this time you do not have a reasonably accurate memory of the way the blocking should look, something is seriously wrong with your own work.

Does Everything Make Sense?

Look, listen, then analyze to discover why whatever the actors are doing isn't working.

When a specific moment on-stage does not "work," ask these three questions:

1. Am I asking the actors to do the wrong thing?

For example, in Act III of *Our Town*, Emily has the very intense, emotional, and sad "Good-bye, world" speech which, when well done, should leave the audience in tears. However, when our Emily cried, it never felt right. Emily should cry in the kitchen when she realizes what she has missed, but by the time she has started back to the grave, a change has taken place. When we finally realized this, we also realized that Emily should stop crying, not start. I had asked the actress to do the wrong thing, and when we changed to something that fit the script more accurately, we produced a much more effective scene.

2. Have the actors assimilated the activity yet?

Is it the right thing, but they just haven't "got" it yet? If not, there are three possible explanations:

(a) the actor does not yet understand what should be done or why it should be done;

(b) the actor is resisting the activity, because he or she wants to do something else or doesn't want to understand; or

(c) the actor just needs more time.

The solution in the first two cases is explanation. Actors who understand what they are doing generally do it "better." However, you must be careful not to talk your show to death, particularly in terms of psychology. Always deal with these problems in terms of character objectives rather than character pasts. (See Chapter 7). Ask the actor what the character wants to accomplish by the activity, and then let that answer itself explain how it should be done.

Occasionally, an actor may continue to resist some direction, even after it has been explained. In such cases, it is tempting just to let the actor have his or her way. If left to do only what they feel comfortable doing, student actors will always do only what they have always done before. They will not try to do anything new, and thus will not learn anything from the role.

The solution is simple drill — going over and over a scene until the activity is securely learned. Nothing makes actors feel better than the security that comes from knowing that the body and voice can do something without thinking. There are limits, however, for there is only so much time in rehearsal for such drills.

3. Is there something mechanically wrong with the activity?

This is where as director you really earn your wings. The actors may be doing the "right" or the "best" thing and doing it well, and it still may not "work." Your job is to try to figure out why it still does not work and then modify or replace it as quickly and efficiently as possible.

For example, in the Hannukkah scene of *The Diary of Anne Frank,* Peter becomes so angry that he threatens his father with a chair. We worked and worked on that moment in the scene, but it just never seemed to look either threatening or honest. Nor did it feel right to the actor. Eventually, we realized that in our staging Peter had to take two short steps to reach the chair before he could grab it, and that this destroyed the spontaneity of the act itself. Thus, we solved the problem by going back and reblocking part of the scene so that Peter could be standing directly behind the empty chair and could grab it without moving. We had the right activity, but not the right timing.

More often, the actor may simply be having a mechanical problem with the activity. A very simple action can look very awkward, unnatural, or insincere simply because of the way it is done. Holding out a hand, for example, may look foolish for many purely mechanical reasons: the arm may be too stiff or not stiff enough, the fingers may be too close together, too far apart, too stiff, or too loose, the wrist may be too stiff or too loose, the arm may be too straight, too bent, too close to the body, or too far away, the shoulder may be hunched over too far or pulled up too stiffly, the body as a whole may lean in too far or lean away too far, the head may be off-balance. Any or all of these things may make a perfectly good and simple and potentially expressive activity look wrong.

Rehearse With Props, Set Pieces and Costumes Early

Finally, there may be times when a desired activity will be impossible to do, no matter how well motivated or how accurately performed. Unfortunately, this usually doesn't show up until you start working with props or scenery pieces. Thus, it is essential during this period, to insist on rehearsal props and rehearsal costumes that at least approximate the final requirements of the show. Remember, movement and expression are closely related to the clothes worn, because each type of clothing hampers certain kinds of movement while encouraging others. This is especially important for those parts of clothing that are different from the clothes your actors normally wear. Shoes are critical, particularly since most of your cast have lived in athletic shoes for most of their lives and have little or no idea how to walk in high heels or stiff leather dress shoes. For boys who live in T-shirts, jackets are very confining. Increasingly for girls, not just period skirts but skirts of any kind are exotic and uncomfortable. People who must wear skirts or dresses for costumes should always wear skirts for rehearsals. The sooner they begin this, the more help it will give their performances and the more problems you can solve before you get your real costumes.

Even in the best rehearsals, however, no matter how well you substituted rehearsal props and costumes, you will find that some parts of your rehearsed activity simply will not work with the finished props or scenery.

For example, I did *Peter Pan* for a community group. We worked for seven weeks of rehearsal on the assumption that Captain Hook would swing off the ship on a rigging rope into the wings, from which we would hear a splash. When we finally got on-stage, the set designer discovered that he could not safely place a landing place for Hook in the wings as he had been so certain he could do. And so, two days before opening, we had to come up with a way for him to "jump" into the "water" on a set that had been designed precisely to avoid that situation. We never did solve it satisfactorily.

This is why you *must* rehearse with props and set pieces as early as possible. You can use pantomime to prepare for props and tape marks to get through blocking, but real timing and really effective performance occurs only when the performers are comfortable with their surroundings. And even more important, you won't have time to correct mistakes if you "save" props and set pieces until the last possible moment. If you can't get the real thing, use sub-stitutes, but always try to get the real thing as early as possible.

Mental Fatigue

The other limits on rehearsal during this period are mental. The effort of building a real characterization and an honest performance demands an intense concentration that is sometimes more exhausting than intense physical labor. Don't be afraid to take a break now and then. If people are really tired or tense, it may sometimes be better to go to something else entirely. You can come back to the problem area at another time, either at the end of the rehearsal or on a different day. Be aware of mental strain as well as physical strain. Don't try to take more than the actors are able to give at any given moment.

Sometimes, however, things just don't work no matter what you try. No matter how many times the actors do it, and no matter how completely convinced you are that the business is the best possible business in a given situation, it just may not be working. When this happens, you may have to change what you want. Try a completely different activity, cut the problem-atic business if it can be spared, rearrange the blocking, and so on. The goal of rehearsal is a good show, not a perfect replication of your plans. It is always better to accept a second or third choice done well than to insist on your first idea done poorly by a frustrated and nervous actor.

By the end of the development stage of rehearsals, every actor should have acceptably performed each part of his or her role at least once. They may be erratic from night to night and unable to reproduce their best work at every rehearsal. But they should know not only what their "good" per-formance would look like but also how it feels to do each segment well.

Loss of Cast Members

During this period, you will probably lose at least one member of the cast. Most often, this is due to illness. You have to make a difficult decision about whether it would be better to wait out the disease or to make a cast change. In other cases, the actor(s) just disappear — the student decides that money is more important than the play and gets a job that conflicts; the family moves; a family crisis demands that the student stay home at nights; someone drops out of school — the possibilities are endless.

When you do decide to make a replacement, it is almost always better in such cases to "move up" someone from a shorter role. They have been at rehearsals and already know something about the role just by watching someone else rehearse it. Then someone from outside the cast (such as one of the alternates on your original casting lists) can be brought in to replace the smaller role, which will take less extra rehearsal than replacing the larger role with someone who hasn't seen any rehearsals.

Occasionally you will find that you want to "fire" an actor. This is very difficult to do. A decision to cast is a commitment to teach. If the student concerned is working and making every reasonable effort to play the role, then the lack of progress is not his or her fault but yours. You should not take your frustration out on them by publicly humiliating them. You have an obligation to live up to your casting decision and get them through the performance somehow.

There is one exception: the student who is not working. No matter how good performers may think they are, or even may be, they are worthless to you if they aren't at rehearsal and working. You are always better off with someone who will be present. If you have someone who comes to rehearsal but refuses to abide by standard rehearsal rules — who refuses to shut up when off-stage, or who continually ridicules the work of other students — then you will be better off without them, too.

Fifth Stage: Integration

During this next period of rehearsal, you put all the pieces together. Usually, this takes from one and a half to two weeks, depending on the complexity of the production.

There are two major goals of this period:

---

1. To establish sequence and concentration for the actors so that their individual activities begin to jell into complete roles
2. To solve any and all technical problems that surround the actors as quickly and easily as possible

---

You reach these goals in two stages: (1) putting the scenes back into sequence, then (2) integrating the finished sequences with the technical aspects of the production. In practice, the two stages overlap, but how much depends on individual circumstances.

The standard way to schedule rehearsals during this period is to start by running sections of acts in order, stopping to solve problems. This is especially helpful if the development period has been very fragmented. First the actors have to learn how the small pieces fit together. Then run the same sections again and again until you can do them without needing to stop. Gradually expand the sequences until you can run complete acts. Then finally you are ready to try a complete run-through of the show.

145

Before Beginning Tech Rehearsals

I schedule one or two "worst-scene" nights immediately after the full run-through. At those rehearsals we put extra work on whatever scenes still seem to need the most work. Then, depending on the show and the time left in the schedule, we have either run-throughs of each act or go directly to our last run-through before tech rehearsals begin.

It is essential with either method that this period end with at least one complete run-through *before* you begin your tech rehearsals. Tech rehearsals, no matter how well planned and prepared, will be demanding and distracting. Too many groups expect their actors to cope with these distractions and still improve their performances at the same time. It simply cannot be done. Always have an uninterrupted run-through before you start formal tech rehearsals, so that the cast knows they are ready for an audience. That way, they can relax while they deal with the tech integration problems, secure in the knowledge that they already know their roles.

After the last full run-through, no prompter should be used. The stage manager will have other things to worry about at this time, and the actors should learn to rely on themselves. You should not need a prompter after this point, even (or especially) in performance. Eliminating the prompter temporarily adds a new level of tension. But this is more than compensated by the new level of concentration and focus from people who know they are now on their own.

If you have done a good rehearsal period, and if the actors are able to concentrate on the Now of their performances, something very exciting will happen in these rehearsals. Someone will stop "acting" and come "alive." When it does occur, all it takes is one person. Once one actor has a single concentrated focused moment, it will spread in a chain reaction to those others on-stage. The actors will begin to notice things that they knew were there but that they never really noticed before, and their bodies will take over, leaving their minds completely free to *react*. You will see it first in their eyes. Such intensity can be stopped by any interruption, so it is very important that you let it go when it first appears, no matter what you might like to stop and adjust. Something eventually will go wrong on-stage and break the spell. But once the actors have been there, even for a brief moment, they know where they want to be and will go back there just as soon as the situation on-stage allows it to happen again. It does not always happen, of course, but if it does, it happens before, never during, the tech rehearsals.

Tech Rehearsals

In some organizations, tech rehearsals are the first time the cast sees the scenery, costumes, props, and lights. This is less than ideal, but it is often necessary. If you don't control your stage, you can't introduce scenery or costumes until the last minute. This kind of last-minute tech work can

146

destroy an otherwise well-prepared and capable cast's work. No matter when you add scenery, props, costumes, and so on, you will have to make changes. To add them all at once is like starting rehearsals over from scratch. To add them all at once only a couple of days before opening means that you have no time to help the actors make adjustments.

If you throw everything technical at the actors at once, and do this too close to the opening, the actors' characterizations may never recover. That is why, in Chapter 2, I stressed that you must have at least *two* uninterrupted weeks on-stage before you open. Then you can add in technical elements of the production as they are ready rather than waiting to throw them in all at once the Monday before opening.

First, Props

Anything the actors touch should be in their hands in time for them to grow comfortable with its use.

Second, Scenery

Even if it's not absolutely complete, set up the scenery. Most important are anything the actors touch, such as doors, and anything the actors walk on, such as platforms. The "real" furniture should go on-stage as soon as it's safe to put it out there.

Third, Costumes

You have been working already with rehearsal costumes. Even so there will be differences that will affect the way the actors think and move. The longer they work in the real costumes, the more those costumes will feel like clothes for the character rather than just a costume, and the better the overall performance will be.

There are practical limits here, of course. You will not want to add costumes until after all the scenery paint is completely dry and all the rough edges of platforms have been covered. Some costumes may be too fragile to be worn for extended periods. Similarly, particularly with musicals, you may find that it is more efficient to rent at least part of the costumes, in which case they cannot be added until they arrive. They will always arrive at the last possible moment in order to cut down your rental fee. Nonetheless, it is axiomatic that the longer actors work in and with their costumes before opening, the better their performances will be.

Fourth, Lighting

When scenery, costumes, and props are in place, you can add the lighting. But lighting should never be added to rehearsals with actors until the lighting is ready. *Do not ever set light cues during acting rehearsals.* Rehearsals are used to make the lights and the performers fit together. It may be necessary to make adjustments in the blocking to fit the precise focus of the lighting. It may be necessary to run some scenes several times in a rehearsal in order to time some light cues. But at no time should actors be standing around on-stage while the light crew tries to change the focus or the gel colors of instruments.

In many cases, of course, you will be the lighting designer and can deal with the lighting schedule yourself. In other cases, however, you may be working with a TD who supervises the auditorium. If this is so, then together you must have a separate rehearsal in which you tentatively set all the light and sound levels for each cue in the show before the actors go on-stage.

Lastly, Makeup

At the last tech rehearsal, you should add makeup. Some groups try to save money by not adding makeup until later, sometimes even opening night. This is a case of "penny wise, pound foolish." You always have to modify the makeup after you see it under the lights. If there are no succeeding nights, then obviously, no corrections can be made and the makeup will never be done well.

Separate Rehearsals for the Tech Crew

Remember, even in this period, you are on a tight schedule. You have that end of rehearsal, school/church curfew staring you in the face. Most organizations allow a certain amount of relaxation in this period, but there are still limits. You can't start keeping the kids till midnight just because you are having tech problems. So you have to deal with as many tech problems as possible before the actors get there.

For example, I always set the light cues on Saturday without the actors. You, the director, the stage manager, and the light crew come in during the morning and set the cues, focusing on one or two volunteers who stand on the stage to duplicate blocking positions. Before we leave, we run through all of the cues as if in performance. This guarantees that our cue sheets are properly copied and that the cues can, in fact, be run as planned. When we try the cues out in a tech rehearsal with the cast, we take notes about things we want to modify. Then, we make those modifications during the afternoon before the next evening's rehearsal begins. In the same way, all scenery changes should be rehearsed by the stage manager with the stage crew before the first rehearsal in which these changes are made. Sometimes the stage crew has to come in early. In most shows, however, they can practice on-stage while the actors are getting into makeup and costumes.

Even in the best situations, once you add the technical elements you are going to be in long rehearsals. Because you can't stay very late, you must add time on earlier in the evening. Sometimes you may start rehearsals with tech crews as early as 4:00 for a rehearsal scheduled to begin at 7:30. You will of course have to start makeup and such things at least an hour and a half before you want the cast on-stage.

Personal Stamina

It is at this point that your personal stamina becomes so important. No matter how much the school administration supports you, you must still continue to teach your regular load, which means you will have a workday of at least fifteen hours. You will not have time to do anything else this week but hold classes and rehearsals, so don't even pretend that you can have a personal life during this period. Many teachers give drama a bad name by essentially canceling their classes during this time. There is neither need nor excuse for this. This is a period in which you want your regular classes to be working on a long-term project or on assignments that can be graded in class time.

There is no magic way to insure success during this period. Organization and planning are the only things that will get you through. However, no matter how much you may be occupied with scenery and lighting and costumes and so on, you must always keep the actors thinking about character and emotion and objectives. If rehearsals have gone as they should before this, the actors know what to do. They know how to do it, and they have done it at least once before the tech rehearsals began. Your job is to see that they keep doing it, despite the technical distractions. The method you use will depend both on your personality and that of your cast members. But you have an advantage now — you have been working together for at least six weeks and you know something about each other.

Sixth Stage: Dress Rehearsals

The basic reason for a dress rehearsal is to give the cast and crew performance conditions without the threat of an audience. Thus, they learn that they can do the show well, gain the security that allows them to concentrate, and if all goes well, they make the breakthrough into a genuine performance.

A true dress rehearsal is not a tech rehearsal. Technical problems should have been solved before dress rehearsals begin. It is not a dress parade. It is not the time to reblock scenes. Nor is it the first run-through of the play. All of these things can and should be done in rehearsals prior to your dress rehearsals.

The dress rehearsal exists solely for the benefit of the cast. It should provide an intense, uninterrupted, concentrated repetition of the entire show. When it functions in this way, it can convince the actors to relax, to focus, and to let themselves become absorbed in the immediacy of the performance itself.

Since these rehearsals should be interruption-free, your own comments will have to be given in "notes" after the rehearsal is completed. This is merely a logical outgrowth of earlier procedures, for you have been interrupting less throughout the integration period.

Always have an assistant to whom you dictate your notes. If you try to write notes yourself in the dark of the auditorium, you will miss too much of the stage activity. However, be sure that you speak softly to your assistant — the actors are easily distracted when they hear a voice "criticizing" them from the darkness. Have your assistant write all your notes on small memo pads, one note per sheet of paper, rather than on long sheets such as legal pads.

With students, I give notes orally, and I give them to the entire cast and crew at the same time. If possible, I do this immediately after the dress rehearsal. Do notes this way for several reasons:

• It is educational — advice or support you give to one person may help someone else with a similar problem.

• It tells everyone concerned that something is being done about a problem area. It's not enough to tell the prop crew to move the telephone, for example. The actors concerned need to know both that the phone will be moved and where it will be moved to. Other actors need to know when you are making an adjustment in someone else's blocking or attitude.

• It allows you to give praise publicly, which with students is even more important than it is with older actors.

It's always good to follow up the oral comment with the written note. After you have made your comment, hand the note to the person concerned. That's why you wrote them on separate sheets.

There are sometimes difficulties with oral notes. Time is the critical factor — no note period should go on for more than thirty to forty minutes. Energy and concentration collapse after that time, and no one will remember any of your notes after that energy is gone.

It is best to have three dress rehearsals. If for some reason the first reveals a serious problem, you still have the second rehearsal to work on the problem. Then you can use your third to run through without interruption. If your tech schedule is seriously compressed, you may be forced to eliminate one of these, but you should *never* go into an opening night with only one dress rehearsal.

Since the purpose of the dress rehearsal is to provide performance conditions, you should schedule them like performances. If you will perform at 7:30, dress rehearsal should start on-stage at 7:30. In almost all cases, this means that students will be later getting out of rehearsal than at any other time. Parents should have been warned of this in the letter you sent home when each student was cast. However, this is not an open invitation to stay all night. If you have done your work in tech rehearsals, dress rehearsals will run within a minute or two of performance time. Notes will be brief, and the cast will be out of the building earlier than on performance nights.

Makeup

Actually putting on the makeup helps the actor focus on the coming performance. This is why each actor should do his or her own personal makeup. This will mean you may have to spend a few minutes extra teaching each person how to do it in tech rehearsals, but that time more than pays for itself in the long run. Not only does it help individual performances, but it also simplifies future shows, where you will have experienced people in the cast that you will not have to teach again. Boys resist this, in general, until you make it clear that there is no other option. I once thought that this was because they were afraid of being thought sissies if they put on makeup, but I eventually realized that what they really wanted was to have some cute little girl leaning over them and devoting careful attention to their needs. If there is a makeup crew, the cast will always spend more time socializing than thinking about their roles. It takes no longer to teach the actors how to do their makeup than it takes to teach a makeup crew. When each person does his or her own makeup, the socializing drops and the concentration increases.

Time for the Director to Bow Out

Since the goal of this period is performance conditions, you must act as if it were a performance. That means being available for emergencies before rehearsal but for the most part staying out of the way. The actors should do their own makeup and get into their own costumes with the help of whatever student crews you have assigned. The stage manager should be doing whatever it is that needs to be done. If you stand around "helping," they will never learn to do it. Always have a call before the rehearsal begins, just as you will before each performance. Once that call is finished, no one should see you again until the end of the performance (unless the stage manager calls you backstage for an emergency). Do not under any circumstances allow yourself to stage manage, to call light cues, or in any other way participate in the actual running of the show.

Once the lights go up, act like an audience. Watch the show, make notes, laugh where things are funny. Stay out front. Do not interrupt the performance for anything short of a disaster.

Curtain Calls

If at all possible, the curtain call should be blocked before the first dress rehearsal. It is part of the show and should be rehearsed just as any other part of the show should be rehearsed. An ideal curtain call reflects the spirit of the show as a whole. It can be very simple, complex, formal, or flamboyant, as long as it clearly tells the audience that the cast is pleased by the audience applause, not stunned or embarrassed by it.

Essentially, there are only two kinds of curtain calls, the subtractive and the additive. In the subtractive call, you begin with the entire company on-stage and then isolate portions of that group for attention and applause. This is especially useful in musical comedies and in shows with large crowds who are on-stage at the end of the show already. In the additive call, you start with an empty stage and gradually add people until the entire cast has been recognized. It is common in all groups to have the performers with smaller roles take the earliest bow and those with largest roles take the later ones. However, it is essential that the very last bow be a "company bow," in which the entire cast together as a group receives applause. There are no stars in school productions. The company is the star, always, and should always take the final bow together.

Whichever method you use, do it quickly; nothing is more embarrassing than having the bow last so long that applause stops between the appearance of performers. It is always better to end the bow with the audience still applauding than to string it out after the audience wants to stop.

PERFORMANCE

During a performance, you have only two duties:

> • Open and close the building
> • Establish an environment that will enable the actors to perform to the best of their capabilities

A cast call between fifteen and thirty minutes before the curtain rises will establish "the moment of truth." Open the house to let the audience take their seats thirty minutes before curtain. No one should be on-stage. Shortly after the stage has been checked by the stage manager, the cast and crew should all meet in the largest space you have backstage. All actors should have makeup finished and be in complete costume as well. This is done so that there are no avoidable distractions between the time the call ends and the beginning of the performance itself.

At this call, discuss the following:

• Any last-minute problems from individuals.

• A quick visual check of all costumes and makeup, to be sure they are complete and accurate. You need not do this personally — the costume crew head, for example, can check the costumes. The point is, someone besides the actors should. At this time they are too nervous and distracted to check themselves.

• Stage manager's reminders that are necessary to the smooth running of backstage areas during the performance. These should be brief. Examples: "Put the props back on the prop table when you exit"; "Keep the wings clear"; "Stay quiet backstage"; and so on.

• Last-minute reminders from the director. These should not be "notes" but simply reminders, encouragements, and suggestions to help the cast and company focus on what they will actually do in performance.

One of these, of course, must deal with stage fright. Stage fright is a universal phenomenon, and every performer who is serious about his or her performance gets it, no matter how experienced. It takes a million different forms and expresses itself in a million different ways. Your actors will have it. The goal is not to eliminate the stage fright — that can't be done — but to bring it down to a scale where it can be used to advantage.

One of the ways you can do this is through relaxation. Most acting textbooks give you some good relaxation exercises, and I always go through a couple of these with the entire company.

Then, when they are relaxed, I remind them that the audience wants them to be good, that they wouldn't have bothered to come unless they wanted everything to go well. (This is not always true with high school audiences, but you don't need to discuss the exceptions now.)

Most importantly, I try to focus their attention on a single thing. The theories of rehearsal and acting used in this book are all aimed at letting the actor's body take over all the mechanical tasks of performance so that the mind is free to focus on the *Now* of any on-stage situation. Thus, I try to isolate their minds from all distractions except the performance itself.

The method you use will depend on your own personality and experience. My method was an established ritual, something that we always did at every performance. This ritual became part of the tradition of the program, and we could no more have skipped any part of it than skip any part of the senior prom. It began with turning out the lights to eliminate visual distractions. Then we joined hands in a large circle and repeated together a concentration device that we had developed almost by accident. This served to separate the company from the rest of the world. From that moment, no one was allowed to think of anything "out of character" or to talk about anything not related to the moment on which we were concentrating.

What you say or do specifically is not important, as long as you say or do something together. It should not be active or loud, for you're not giving a locker-room pep talk. Instead, you are defining the focus of attention for the cast, removing distractions so that they may concentrate on what they have to do. You want to provide a cushion of support that says, "We're all in this together, we all know what to do, and we don't need to worry about anything else." This kind of hand-holding encouragement seems a bit gimmicky with adults, but it is often the little touch that makes a big difference in performance with students. If you have rehearsed properly and well, this will get the company over the hump of that stage fright. The show will start strong and stay that way throughout the evening.

When this call is finished, go out front and STAY THERE. There is nothing you can do backstage but destroy the concentration and routine. Some people pace, some hide in a closet, others sit and watch calmly. You will stay available for genuine emergencies, so be sure the stage manager and house manager know where you are. But in 99 out of 100 hundred performances, the stage manager will handle all problems without difficulty.

After the Show

Be sure to go backstage when the performance is over. The cast will be surrounded by friends and relatives congratulating them, whether they did well or not, and you will have some people who want to do the same for you. It is important that the cast see you backstage so they don't think you're trying to disown them. Don't make critical comments. It's wasted effort; the cast knows exactly what went "wrong." If anything, you want to encourage them to forget any such problems.

Many groups find, for security or space reasons, that it is better to have the cast meet their well-wishers in the lobby or even in the auditorium rather than backstage. If this seems better for your group, be sure everyone knows the routine beforehand. If the actors are coming out front to meet friends, make sure they come out front soon. I dislike seeing actors in costume mingling with the audience, but it is better to have the actors come out in costume than to make large groups stand around while they change.

Photographs

This is also a way for parents get to take pictures of their kids in costume without disturbing others. Never, under any circumstances, allow parents to take photos during a show. Be polite, but be firm. The flash disturbs everyone in the audience, distracts the actors, and tells everyone that the play is not really important. It is standard policy at all live performances, at any level, to allow no photos during the performance. To help solve this problem, I always took photos of the show in dress rehearsal — after all, I knew what the best moments would be — and did it without flash. Other organizations have a special "photo call" at the last dress rehearsal or after one of the performances in which scenes are restaged quickly, purely for the camera. Either option works. Be sure actors and their parents know that these "official" photos will be available as cheaply as possible for anyone who wants them, and it makes it easier to keep the cameras out of the performance itself. If parents still want their own informal shots of their budding stars, then they can take them after the show.

Accepting Praise

Sometimes it is wise to remind both the cast and yourself how to act when people congratulate them after the show. Since you are all intensely involved in the show, any "mistakes" will be magnified all out of proportion. Warn the cast that the audience hasn't been at seven weeks of rehearsal and so doesn't know when you made a mistake. It is not good for the actor or the progam to have someone say, "You were really good," only to hear the actor answer, "No, I wasn't, I was terrible." Someone will do exactly that unless you warn the cast to always smile and say, "Thank you."

On the last night of the performance, there will be a party somewhere. Remember that everyone has prior responsibilities. Make sure that *all* members of the cast help strike the set and props before you release any of them to go to a party. If you fail to do this, you will find that all the time you spent establishing a group identity for the show and for your program as a whole is gone. Those who stay to do their work get angry at those who sneaked out to get to the party early. Make EVERYONE stay for the strike.

CHAPTER SEVEN
ACTING AND STUDENT ACTORS

Most people assume that there is nothing to be done for student actors. It is just assumed that students will be bad actors. Some might be good some day, but right now they are "just" students. Directors who think like this actually encourage poor performances by their student actors.

Admittedly, most student actors are bad actors. But this is only because they are students — they have not yet learned a process that will take them successfully through analysis, rehearsal, and performance of a role.

The acting training that Americans use may eventually turn some of these students into good actors. If Louise is in your play now, you can't wait until Louise has been through four years (or six, or ten, or however long it takes) of acting classes to get a good performance from her. She goes in front of an audience along with the rest of your cast in six weeks. Training is a long-run activity; rehearsal is always done in the short run. You need a short cut of some kind.

So, you face a difficult problem shared by few others in the theater world. How do you make people who are untrained, or incompletely trained, look good in a very brief amount of time? My experience indicates that almost anyone can be a competent actor, *if the circumstances are right*. So the practical question is: How can the director/teacher improve the circumstances of rehearsal so as to get effective, genuine performances?

In addition, since you are also teaching some acting classes, you have to find a way to rehearse that does not contradict what you are teaching in your classes. That sounds obvious, but it is very hard to do. Almost no professional theatrical rehearsal is conducted along the principles of professional acting classes. The professionals just leave all that to the individual actors. You can't do that, for both practical and ethical reasons. At the most obvious level, if you don't use what you teach, why should students take your classes?

PROBLEMS WITH CURRENT ACTING THEORIES

The real problem is not that students aren't trained yet. The more significant problem is that what we usually teach student actors has little to do with what actors actually do.

Most acting classes in America are constructed on one basic assumption: In order to express a character, the actor must be able to express the actor's own self. That assumption underlies almost all commonly accepted approaches to acting in the country.

Much of this goes back to our perception of Stanislavski's teaching, called Method Acting. The Method is a complex approach to acting, with each Method teacher's method different from every other. All Method approaches eventually focus on a way to make a performance ring true by tying it to something within the actor's own experience. This is called by many names — affective memory, remembered emotion, emotional recall, sensory reactions, etc. — but all express the same fundamental essential concept. The actor is supposed to build a performance out of an understanding of personal experience. This is why most acting textbooks begin with units called "Understanding Yourself," or "The Actor and the Self," or "The Actor Explores the Self," and so on. The actor's own personality is expected to be the core of each performance.

Alternative Techniques

Over the past few decades, many people have grown frustrated by the difficulties of the traditional Method. As a result, teachers have produced a number of new approaches, all of which claim to be an alternative to the Method. These alternative systems grew out of the do-your-own-thing avant-garde of the sixties, and tend to follow two major branches. One focuses on improvisation and psychological role-playing. The other branch can be traced to Viola Spolin's theater games. In both these approaches, actors play games and do improvisations in order to prepare themselves for performance. Sometimes they use these to actually "develop" the play itself. The overwhelming bulk of both games and improvisations are focused on the actors' sensitivity and awareness of self. The aim of all such activities is to get the actor to make it "real," which in practice means "like the actor's personal experience outside the classroom." Unlike traditional Method exercises, games and improvisations are done in groups rather than in isolation. That is one of the major reasons we have embraced them in our classrooms. But that is the only genuine difference between the traditional Method and its supposed alternatives — the Method works on the individual as an individual, theater games and improv techniques work on the actor within a group. All are more concerned with the actor's personal experience than with analyzing or performing a script.

Problems With Acting From Personal Experience

While these approaches may have great success in classes, they don't consistently work in rehearsal, even with professionals. Some actors get so wrapped up in their own reality that the audience can't tell what's going on. This has always been the major complaint about Method actors — they mumble and forget that the audience needs to hear. Some actors so completely identify their role with their own selves that they rewrite the character to fit their own personality. Some get so involved in improvisation that they rewrite the script to include the improvised lines and scenes. Others become so attached to "process" that they avoid performance altogether.

Such problems are magnified with teenaged student actors, precisely because they are teenagers. That is, they are insecure, confused, immature, incompletely educated, awkward, alternately impassioned and lazy, and above all, self-conscious.

Any attempt to make student actors more aware of their true self usually leads to worse rather than better performances. They become even more self-conscious and awkward. Teenagers live in constant, daily terror that revolves around one single idea: No one must ever find out I'm different from everybody else. When they talk about "just being themselves," they never mean "being themselves." Almost always, they really mean "being accepted by others," which is not quite the same thing. They are terrified that if their "true self," whatever that might be, should be exposed to public view, it will automatically be exposed to public ridicule. For many people, of course, this feeling never goes away, which is why we have psychiatrists on the one hand and fashion victims on the other. The feeling and the terror is never more intense than among teenagers.

Even if we find a rare student who is willing to expose that true self, how are they to know what it is? Every time they think they have figured out who or what they really are, it changes. They get older, their chemistry changes, their voice changes, even the weather changes. They find a friend or lose one. They find a sexual partner or lose one. They discover religion, they find a new hobby, they get a job or lose one. Their parents get a divorce or remarry. They make good grades or bad, and on and on. It is the very definition of adolescence that the self is still unstable.

If we ask people in such a situation to build all their work on a foundation of self-awareness and self-expression, we are doomed to failure before we begin.

Most acting training of our time is not training, it is therapy. As such, it may be helpful eventually. It just doesn't turn bad actors into good actors, at least not quickly. Assuming the teacher has either the right or the training to do such amateur psychological therapy in class (which is a very large and undiscussed assumption in contemporary education), it still fails almost all the time in rehearsals.

It ignores why students want to be in a play to begin with.

STUDENT NEEDS

After I had been teaching for several years, I began to ask students why they were taking acting classes or why they were acting. I asked these questions in part for personal protection. I could see that I was doing something right, because the shows were good and the program was growing, but I had no idea what it was. I thought I'd better find out what it was, so I could keep doing it. As a result, I began a series of annual detailed discussions with my advanced actors.

We talked about a lot of different things — what they had learned, what they wanted to learn, and how particular exercises had worked. One of the specific things I asked was, "Why did you take your first class or try out for your first play?" In general, they told me what I had expected to hear — they wanted to be a star someday, they thought it might be fun, their friends or older siblings were already involved, they thought it might help them get over their fear of talking to people in public, even that they really wanted to take art but couldn't get into an art class in that period.

The real surprise came when I asked, "After your first experience, why did you do it a second time?" Almost never did they say they kept doing it because they liked the applause and attention. Nor did they say they did it because it helped them to understand their true feelings. The thing that kept popping back into conversation was that they liked having someplace to hide. Typical comments were: "It lets me drop all my problems and be another person." "I get tired of being me, and it's fun to be another person." "It lets me act things out without other people thinking I'm nuts." "It gives you something to say." Perhaps the best summary, however, came from the girl who told me, "You know why I like acting? Because it's the only place I always know what happens next."

This was not at all what I had expected to hear. I repeated these discussions for several years with my advanced students, and the results were always the same. They started for any number of predictable reasons. But, once they knew something about performing in plays, they kept coming back for one basic reason: When they were acting, they could hide themselves in plain sight. They weren't much interested in the idea of losing themselves, as in the Method cliché where the actor becomes so involved in the character that he plays it on-stage and off. But they loved the idea that, as long as they were saying and doing things someone else had written and which were supposed to be someone else not at all like them, they were off the hook. They felt secure and free in a way that could not be matched by any other part of their life.

Fear

The single most inhibiting problem for young actors is simple fear: fear of others, fear of failure, fear of self-exposure. Thus, when you work with them, you have to find ways to convince them that they will not fail. You have to make them believe that people will not hold them up to ridicule. Most of all, they must believe that people, and other students in particular, will not see "the real me."

The fundamental nature of all fear, for young and old alike, is that it is always a fear of the future. We can't fear the past, for it has already occurred. We can fear that something in the past will come back, or will be exposed, but even that can only happen in our future. The girl who liked acting because it guaranteed what would happen next was expressing a critically significant concept. If she already knew what would happen, then there was nothing to fear. Thus, she need not worry about it. Once we removed the fear, we also freed the part of the mind that was occupied by that fear. Then she was able to concentrate all her attention on something else, in this case, the immediate present of the performance. With those fears removed, the performance itself became such a pleasure that she wanted to repeat it.

Acting a role in a play offers a person an experience that is unique, something that cannot be found anywhere else in the world. That is: It is a chance to repeat a situation and to get it right. Getting it right can have many meanings, of course. Many casts "get it right" and do terrible shows, because their definition of right means only reciting the lines accurately and not knocking over the scenery.

The Director's Opportunity

If you're serious abut directing, then your definition of "right" will be more sophisticated than this. It is the director's job to make sure that a cast knows that getting it right means getting a good, complete, detailed, and alive performance. There is a way in which you can work with untrained students and still make good, even sometimes very good, performances.

No director can force good performances to happen, no matter how talented you may be. You can encourage and establish the conditions that make them possible. And without doubt you can prevent good performances from happening. Most of the time, that's what most directors do with students.

The most important thing you can do is establish a sense of security that will make good performances possible. Security is another dangerous term, so we need to be clear what we mean by it. When most people talk about providing a sense of security, they mean the kind of feeling good parents give to their children. This is the feeling that they will always be safe, that they will always be loved even when they fail, that there is always someone who will hug them, who will kiss it and make it better. Many drama teachers try to give their student actors this kind of feeling. They try to be everyone's surrogate parent, try to give everyone a warm, cuddly kind of environment where everyone is welcome, where everyone always gets a fifth chance, and where failure is not only accepted but encouraged. This is not the kind of security I mean. The sense of security you need to provide is much simpler. It is the security that the performer gets from knowing what happens next. When they know that, and know that they know how to deal with whatever happens next, then they will be secure enough to actually give a good acting performance.

This sense of security begins with a sequence of productive physical actions.

PRODUCTIVE PHYSICAL ACTION

Action Is the Fundamental of Dramatic Performance

Action is the foundation of the play. Characters do things to each other in a situation, thereby causing conflict which makes the plot of the play. Characters also do things on-stage, which it is the job of the actors to present. They do this through their own physical action — moving and talking and responding. That is the reason why they are called "actors."

For the actor, physical action has two simultaneous functions. The first is that the audience can understand the play only through the action they observe. What the character does and how he or she does it will express the emotion of any given moment. From this, as much as and perhaps even more than the words themselves, the audience understands what is happening on-stage.

More importantly, physical action encourages the duplication of an emotional state. This is opposite to the system usually taught in American acting classes. Almost all current American acting methods ask the actor to produce the proper emotional state, so that it can automatically lead to the proper, expressive physical action. But it can work the other way around by using the action to produce the emotion.

The James-Lange Theory

This approach was initially proposed by William James and Fritz Lange. As expressed by James in his *Psychology (Briefer Course)*, this was that: "...bodily changes follow directly the perception of the exciting fact and...our feeling of the same changes as they occur is the emotion."

To illustrate his point, he describes the common experience of seeing something in the darkness — the heart hesitates, then beats quickly before we are consciously aware of the idea of danger. The action happens first, and then the mind understands it as an emotion, in this case fear.

The James-Lange theory is currently out of fashion, but it has never been disproved. We have a large number of clear demonstrations of its plausibility in daily life. It is common knowledge that we can change our emotional state by changing our physical state. We tell ourselves to sit still when we want to calm down, we pace around in order to "work up" our anger or our courage, we count to ten to short-circuit our anger, we tell people to hold their head up when we want them to cheer up, and so on. Similarly, we know that if people pretend to believe something long enough, they will come to believe it without pretense.

Interestingly enough, Stanislavski moved toward this approach in the later years of his work. Most people have paid very little attention to this fundamental change in his approach, because that part of his writing was translated much later than his first book.

In *Creating a Role,* he describes what he calls the "line of physical being":

"Now that we have created the physical being of a part we must think about the more important task — creating the spiritual being in a role. Yet it would seem that it had begun to exist in me already, of its own accord...In every physical action, unless it is purely mechanical, there is concealed some inner action, some feelings."

The difficulty, of course, is to find the "right" physical action for each emotion desired.

Nineteenth-Century Elocution Instruction

People of this period learned certain stereotypical gestures for certain stereotypical emotions. This was a "method" drawn from the teachings associated with Delsarte and soon mismanaged and misinterpreted by countless elocution teachers. An actor was taught one pose for anger, another for joy, another for fear, and so on. The problem was not that these were wrong, but that these were generalized and predetermined. As such, they could not cope with the rise of theatrical "realism," when we began to expect our

163

actors to work in smaller theaters (or on camera), in more accurately produced surroundings, and playing less idealized or more complex characters
than before. As a result, acting came to look so stereotyped and artificial
that Stanislavski invented what became the Method. The true problem
was not that the nineteenth-century actors worked from physical actions;
it was that they came to adopt a set of artificial, stereotyped physical
actions. The process gradually became divorced from reality, and performances lost their subtlety and liveliness. But that is not inherent in the
idea of physical action.

The Right Physical Action

For our purposes, the right physical action is the one that to the audience looks like an expression of the desired emotion. In current acting
theories, this is supposed to be the ultimate end product of the actor's work.
With student actors, however, it should be the beginning.

The thousands of physical actions that compose a performance are
developed in a partnership between director and actor. When working with
experienced adults, professional or amateur, the actors will contribute far
more to this process, depending on their intelligence, maturity, and ego,
than students can be expected to contribute, with their comparative imma-
turity and inexperience.

Hence, the bulk of the work in this area, at least in the early stages of
rehearsal, falls to the director.

It begins with the blocking, which as we have already noted is the
director's primary means of expression. Blocking also establishes the fundamental physical actions for the characters: Where do they go when?
What do they do when they get there?

Then, as if in a spiral, the same ground is covered again and again in
succeeding rehearsals, each time modifying existing physical actions and
adding more detailed new ones. Some of these modifications come from the
director, and some come from the actors as they come to better understand
what they are doing and want to do. If these actions have been well-
planned, they will encourage the actor to understand and feel what the
character is feeling.

There are several advantages at any level to a rehearsal approach that
begins rather than ends with physical action. These advantages are more
pronounced when directing young actors who are dealing with the normal
personal difficulties of teenagers. Physical action leads to an emotion
without asking the actor to do any conscious self-analysis or self-exposure.
Then, when the emotion begins to grow, it seems spontaneous to the per-

former, which makes it even more valid and valuable. It also provides a method of reproducing the emotion, each time the action is repeated.

In addition, it provides a strong sense of security to the actor. Even if he or she never thinks of another thing to do, there is still no fear that something will go wrong. Rehearsals built around Method or improvisatory approaches ask the actor to try things and throw out the ones that don't work. This sometimes leads to marvelous results, as long as there is time to keep experimenting. If time runs out, however, the actor is left with nothing but terror. If you begin with the physical action, the actor can always fall back to what has already been established as the basic outline.

You can't establish everything in the very first rehearsal, and the director can't possibly dictate every motion. With young actors, repetition must begin early in the rehearsal process, precisely because they are more insecure and because they have less rehearsal time to deal with that insecurity.

Of course, none of this works if the actors are asked to repeat unproductive or unexpressive physical actions. We must remember that even the best action can seem mechanical when it is done mechanically.

The physical action that feeds an emotional state and that also expresses something to an audience is some action that relates the character to the other characters and to the surroundings. That is, it is dynamic. The actor puts the cup down, glares at someone else, grabs him by the arm, yells at her, flinches away from an expected blow, walks to the door, and so on. These are the kinds of things we are talking about under the name of physical action.

The Physical Action of Speech

It should be emphasized that physical action also includes the physical action of speech. Just as Stanislavski's idea of the physical being includes everything the character says and how it is said, so our physical action includes the way a line is said. It is easy to forget this when we use words such as "action" or "physical," because we tend in common usage to separate the physical world from the verbal world. For the actor, they are two sides of the same coin. The act of doing necessarily includes the act of speaking, because that speech is another form of doing to and with others. It also includes the words themselves.

Any given physical action can be done in a number of ways, depending on the situation. One can walk to the door expectantly, hesitantly, joyously, depressingly, tragically, and so on. One can say a line in an infinite number of ways.

Thus, if we are to avoid choreographing the show and reciting the lines

for the actors to mimic, we need a second controlling idea to use with physical action in order to guide the actor toward a valid and consistent
performance.

This is the concept of the *Other*.

FOCUS ON THE OTHER

The kind of physical action the director should concentrate on with the
young actor is something done to or with others. In the context of the play,
every action is done for a purpose — something is expected to happen as a
result. As a simple (and simultaneously complex) example, let's consider a
brief exchange between a boy and a girl, which she initiates by saying
"hello." She always says "hello" to him because she wants him to do something in response. What she wants will determine the way she says it. For
example, Anne will say "hello" in one way if she just wants him to say
"hello" and then go on about his business. She will say it differently if she
wants him to stop and talk. It will be different again if she wants to initiate
a seduction, different again if she wants him to go away and leave her alone,
different still if she wants to negotiate a contract. Similarly, she may say
"hello" rather than "hi" or "how are you?" or "hello, buddy" because she
hopes to get some reaction from him. Each of his reactions would be different depending on how she says this simple greeting.

Acting From Objectives

Everyone uses the term "objective" in acting and directing classes.
Unfortunately, most people then misuse the concept in rehearsal. Most of
the time, objectives are generally expressed as "I want..." As a result, they
tend to be no help. They simply repeat what the character actually says
without giving any clue to the way it is said ("I want to say hello"). They get
too generalized and internalized ("I want to be happy"). Or they just
encourage artificiality ("I want to say hello as if I were sincere"). None of
these forms are much practical help. If you want the objective to work, you
must always frame the question in terms of the other person.

Instead of asking the actor, "What do you want?", ask "What do you
want the other person to do?"

This works like magic.

First, it explains without requiring explanation. If the actor understands what the character wants to accomplish, the actor *automatically*
knows how to do the action. If an actor enters "because he is excited," then
he will spend all his time trying to figure out how to look excited and will
usually look phony. If he runs in "to make everyone else excited about the

fire he just saw," he will automatically look excited when he does so.

At the professional level, the director and actors spend a great deal of time in discussion. A lot of this is wasted time, in the sense that, no matter what words you use to express an analysis, you still don't have any idea about how best to show that to an audience. Nonetheless, it is still done because the mature, experienced, and established actors will have a great deal of perceptive (or intimidating) input to give. With young actors, that maturity and life experience is much more limited. At the same time, they have a very limited vocabulary with which to express themselves. Hence, discussion of the play will often provide no real help to the actors, not to mention that you have almost no time for such discussion in your very limited rehearsal schedule.

By aiming at physical actions done to the Other, you can stage and analyze simultaneously.

Analysis by means of this approach also works because we know we can always find an answer. Since someone else has written the script already, we know what happens next. We can know what a character wants others to do by what those others in fact do. To use a traditional acting problem, how do you interpret a scene in which one character says, "I'm leaving!," then stays on-stage for another two pages? Traditional discussion in terms of the character's internal life would give her objective as "I want to leave." In fact, she doesn't, for if she did, she would. There is some other, more important objective that she hasn't yet stated. If, after she threatens to leave, he asks her to stay and she does stay, then her objective in threatening to leave was in fact to get him to ask her to stay. Thus, the actor knows to say "I'm leaving" in a way that implies that she'd rather stay. (For example, she might use an implied "but," or she might not stand up, or she might walk more slowly than expected, or she might watch him carefully to judge his reaction. Although the objective is there to be found, without years of psychoanalysis, you still have many options about ways to express it effectively.)

A Way of Leading Into Character Analysis

You can say to a student actor, "See, you must have meant...because that's what the other characters saw." That may not be true in terms of the deepest goal, of course. It is very clear in terms of what can be seen at any given moment, which is, after all, the concern of rehearsals.

For young actors, this is critical. Most student actors hate "analysis," because it seems like the kind of open-ended, no-right-answer time wasting they do in English class. No matter how much you try to get them to analyze their role, they try to avoid it. If you ask them to use this approach, you get much better results. They know that, eventually, there is an answer that can be found, and so they are willing to look for that answer.

Your analysis is also testable in the sense that the actor has to "convince" the other actors involved. Conversations with actors go something like this:

ME: What does that mean?

ACTOR: It means such-and-such.

ME: Do you mean it?

ACTOR: Yes.

ME: Then why are you saying it to him?

ACTOR: Because I want to scare him away.

ME: *(To SECOND ACTOR)* Were you scared?

ACTOR 2: No.

ME: *(To FIRST ACTOR)* Let's try it again, look him in the eyes, and try to scare him. Convince him that you really mean what you're saying.

If it should happen that Actor 2 is convinced of Actor 1's sincerity at that particular moment, of course, you would have no reason to stop the scene to discuss it. The scene would be interesting and lively and dramatic and wouldn't need any particular improvement from you at that point.

This is, of course, a point that you will reach only after some time in rehearsal. In the spiral of rehearsal, you begin with the biggest, most significant actions and gradually narrow down to more detailed actions and more precision. Only at that time are you able to begin to ask the actor to think about such questions and to use them effectively. For only then is the actor sufficiently familiar with the script to consider them. A professional actor usually starts rehearsal with at least some version of the script already analyzed and often already memorized. Your actors don't see the script until the first rehearsal, or if they have seen it, don't know what role they will play until then. It takes some time for them to read and think about their roles, even if they are adept at it. So don't waste time in character discussions in the first week or two. That will only force the actors to make decisions before they have enough information to make them properly. In the meantime, by starting on-their-feet rehearsals immediately, you will provide a physical context in which the actor has the security to turn to real analysis.

This approach also works because answers to problems are to be found outside the individual actor's own personality. All the actor's concentration is turned away from self-analysis and self-exposure and turned toward other characters. The actor has to deal first with things that can be done, physical actions (including the words to be said, of course). Then he or she can "know" how to do those things by doing them to others. That shifts all attention toward a goal or objective and away from the actor's own feelings of inadequacy.

And the actor has a ready test of success that both reinforces good work and feeds the growth of the scene as a whole. The way that you tell if Actor 2 is convinced by Actor 1 is that he reacts as if he were. When that happens, you have stepped over into a whole new realm of performance.

Reaction

From an audience's point of view, a performed work becomes convincing not when individuals speak or move well but rather when reactions seem logical, believable, and/or proper. It is at this reaction level that performances most often seem false. One of the clearest signs of a typical "high school play" (or a TV sit-com, for that matter) is that the actors seem to be reciting their lines rather than talking to each other. A says something, then B says something, then A says something again. You can almost see each person counting the seconds until "It's my turn." Sometimes, one or more of the performers involved may be quite good; that is, they may say and do their lines quite naturally or dramatically. Still, they might as well all be in separate rooms, because there is no connection between them.

Reactions are the most difficult aspect of the acting performance. It's comparatively easy for an actor to "act," especially when acting is doing. It is much harder to "react," precisely because the reaction is sometimes, perhaps often, a feeling that becomes visible to the audience. It was to deal with just this problem that Stanislavski developed his original approach using the actor's inner life and experience. Those reactions can be produced more quickly and much more easily by the process we are discussing here, precisely because they are produced spontaneously. And they are produced from the things that are happening on-stage, not from some aspect of the actor's private life.

The actors gradually begin to "react" rather than to "act," precisely because they never think about making a reaction. All their attention is aimed outside themselves: What am I trying to do to and with them, and what are they doing to or with me?

This question only produces fully realized and genuine reactions when the actors also concentrate properly.

CONCENTRATION ON THE NOW

Most people, when they think of concentration, mean only to be quiet and pay attention, as in a class lecture. An actor requires concentration of a magnitude so much greater that we really need a different word. The best and most productive form of concentration is a mental focus that senses one thing and one thing only, that has no "distractions" because there is no room in the mind for a second thought of any kind. It is a form of focus on the *Now* so complete that the individuals concerned become oblivious to all else. Baseball player Yogi Berra, the subject of much humor for his quaint sayings, said, "I can't concentrate when I'm thinking." It sounds silly, but that is precisely the state you want your student actors to reach. Good performances come when the performers concentrate so hard that they stop thinking.

Fear Is the Major Destroyer of Concentration

Fear is why many people who claim to be concentrating in fact fail so miserably — they are concentrating on what they have to do next rather than what they are doing now. Thus, the speaker concentrating to make sure he doesn't forget his memorized speech stumbles over words and loses his place, because his attention on the present is distracted by his attention on the future. The only way to defeat that problem is to concentrate not on what the next words are but on convincing the listeners that these words now being spoken are important and meaningful. The only way you can make what you do now seem alive and genuine is to forget what you have to do next.

When people think of a typical high school play, they often have this problem in mind. They see awkward actors awkwardly going through the motions in an unconvincing manner. People generally call this a mechanical performance, although in fact it is a performance in which the mechanics have broken down.

If the actors don't believe the other actors will execute the blocking as learned, they will hesitate to make any cross until they are sure everyone else has made theirs as well. The result is that they look like people moving around from mark to mark. The cause of the problem is not that the director told them to move on a particular line to a particular place. The real problem is that the actors are distracted from doing it now by the fear that it might be wrong. The solution is not for the director not to block but for the actors to learn the blocking sooner so they can do it without conscious effort or fear.

The paradox is that you can only forget the future when you know what the future is. For your actors, this means that they only really know a role when they can forget the role. The next line will come out spontaneously only when they know so well what the next line is that they can allow themselves to forget it. They must pay attention only to what is happening Now. They can only do that if repetition has made them so secure about what must be done that they can cease to think about it.

Perhaps we can explain this paradox best with a metaphor. A musician does something similar to what is done by an actor. The pianist, for example, plays notes to make music. Playing the notes occurs on two different levels: one must make the notes in general — that is, know the instrument well enough to find all the notes required — and make the notes of a specific piece — that is, make this very specific set of notes in the specific order noted here. For the actor, the first level is the knowledge of the individual's body and voice — breath control, speech, movement, dance, etc. — that actors usually call "learning the instrument." The second is the specific role in the specific play under production. Even when the notes are made properly and well in both cases, music still may not result.

The music begins, as any serious musician will tell you, only when the pianist stops thinking about the notes. In effect, the music starts to "play itself." That is, the fingers know the notes so well that the pianist doesn't have to think about which finger to move next. The pianist lets the fingers make the notes while concentrating the mind on making the music.

Actors make the dramatic music, so to speak. They can't make the music until they know the notes, and know them so well that they don't have to think about them anymore. Your job is to see that the notes are in place so that the music has a chance to come out.

More often than not, the actors will not take that final step. But you will be surprised at how often they will. When they do, you will have performances as good as practically anyone in the country at any level can do. Perhaps even more important, even if they don't make that last step, the audience will still see a finished, "professional" looking performance, because all the notes are in place.

Repetition Is Fundamental

It is that repetition which metaphorically puts the notes under the fingers. Repetition makes the performer believe that things are going to happen as expected. Only when things have been repeated the same way several times will anyone believe they will continue to be repeated that way. This is far from being mechanical. Most amateur productions look terrible and mechanical not because the director blocked and controlled performances too much, but too little. When the cast thinks only about doing the blocking and getting the lines right, that means the director stopped too early. They are only going through the motions, because they don't yet understand those motions.

171

We really have no language to describe this, because the situation is so rare in real life. There is an immense amount of related psychobabble, but none of those terms is quite right. The best I can come up with at present is a concentration on the *Now* of performance. In one sense, this requires that the actor lose himself in the performance, but not in the way we normally use that phrase. When it really happens, the actor is so aware of himself and all the other things around that he feels like a different person. At the same time, the actor never confuses his or her personality with that of the character.

People in sports talk about this feeling a lot, usually in terms of a suspension of normal time. There is the sense that everything must have slowed down, otherwise you couldn't possibly have time to see and feel and understand so many things all at the same time. Movies express the feeling in the same way — in slow motion. And yet, paradoxically, time itself moves incredibly quickly, because you are completely unconcerned with it. When the "spell" is finally broken, you think, "How can it be over? I just got started." As the cliché says, time flies when you're having fun.

That happens only when you are completely concentrated on the immediate present, on the *Now* of a situation. Any awareness of anything else, past or future, will destroy that concentration, will "bring you back to Earth." When someone is really playing well, baseball players say, "He's playing unconscious." What you want your actors to do is to reach the level where they too can "play unconscious."

The limitations of rehearsal time can be overcome. When that happens, most people assume that you found some unusually talented cast members and let it go at that. But you can do it with only "typical" talent if you consistently lead your actors to a point at which they can focus completely on the *Now*.

Three basic things make the *Now* happen in rehearsal:

> • Physical action, properly chosen and then repeated until the actors are completely secure
>
> • Focus on the *Other*, which aims all these physical actions at other actors and characters in the play
>
> • Concentration on only one thing at a time

If you do the above, you can make the most inexperienced young performers look like experienced professionals. Equally, and perhaps more importantly, you can make a play that interests and moves its audience rather than a show that is "all right, considering..." That is, after all, why you're a director as well as a teacher.

A FEW HINTS

Whenever you have a problem with a scene, always talk to the actors in terms of the script and the character, never in terms of the actor and director. That is, always explain directions in terms of what the character is doing or saying, rather than as something that you have decided to do for no particular reason. In this way, directions are not automatically seen as personal criticism.

Whenever you have a problem with a scene, don't try to fix it unless you can think of something related to a physical action that might improve it. Don't tell the actor something is "wrong" unless you have an idea about what can be done right now to make it better. If you don't have an idea, let it alone.

Always Work as if in a Spiral

Fix the important things first. Don't worry about whether someone sits with legs crossed or not until after you know when and why the character sits and when and why she stands up again. In this way, the actors always have support. We often talk about building a performance. This is like building a house. You lay the foundation, build the shell, add the trim, and then decorate and furnish it. All too often, contemporary actors try to build the house of their performance by starting with the wallpaper, looking for tics, funny voices, or how the character felt about being potty trained. Build the foundation and shell first. Then if you get to the wallpaper, well and good. If you don't get that far, you still have a house.

Don't Ever Assume Something Will Fix Itself

Just because you and the actors have discussed something, doesn't mean the problem has been solved. Actors not only need to know what to do, but they also must know that they can actually do it. It is never a bad idea to do something one more time, "just so we feel comfortable with it."

CHAPTER EIGHT
RECURRENT PROBLEMS

In schools and in most churches and similar groups, you will be not only the director. You will also be responsible for all aspects of production, such as scenery, costume, lighting, or makeup. Because this is a book about directing, we have paid little attention to these technical areas. If you are seriously inexperienced, you can find lots of how-to information about these topics in dozens of other books.

However, there are some persistent technical problems that seriously affect your rehearsal and directing process. These require some comment, because they are not usually discussed in other sources. Some of these are common to any directing process in any group. Most of them, however, are problems unique to amateur groups or to teenaged actors.

BACKSTAGE ORGANIZATION

In general, the student production should be operated, as well as performed, by students. Play production in our situation is an educational as well as a theatrical process. One major part of the educational process is learning to take responsibility for a job. Students cannot learn how to deal with such responsibility unless you give them responsibility.

If a student can be taught how to do a job, then a student should do that job. This does not mean students should do every job, however. Students should never be asked to do jobs that they cannot be taught to do well in the circumstances available. For example, student directors and designers should be used only in the rarest of circumstances and with the most careful supervision. This is not because it means a loss of teacher control. Rather, these jobs demand skills and maturities that can only be developed by education, experience, and relatively adult sensibilities that are rare among high school drama students. However, with the exception of directing and design, you should start with the assumption that every normal production job will be done by a student, even if it would be more convenient or more comforting to find another adult or simpler to just do the job yourself.

Each production of a play needs people in the following positions of responsibility, all of which can be done more than adequately by students, with the following basic duties:

Assistant Director — assists the director in whatever way necessary. Usually, this means such things as note-taking, check-in of cast and crew during rehearsal, prompting, small-group rehearsal of scenes already blocked, and/or maintaining the production book.

Stage Manager — organizes and supervises all backstage operations, calls all cues for lights, sound, and special effects, prompts lines during rehearsals, and maintains the production book.

In practice, I tend to be very flexible about the duties of these two positions. The most important figure is the stage manager, who is, in fact, the student in charge of the actual operation of the show. This should be the most experienced and most dependable student available backstage.

Sometimes the assistant director is equally experienced and will share many of the stage manager's duties, particularly during rehearsal periods when the stage manager may have schedule conflicts that prevent constant attendance. At other times, the assistant may be a very promising, but very inexperienced, student to whom you want to give a quick but intensive introduction to all aspects of production. Sometimes the assistant will be just a note-taker, and at others he or she will be a student who will, next semester, be a student director. The assistant is essentially your assistant, the stage manager the student in charge. If there is any question in your mind about experience or responsibility, always put your best student in the stage manager's position. Good assistants are relatively easy to find, while good stage managers can be found only among your very best students.

Also, it helps to have a lot of people who are familiar with the show, just in case. As noted earlier, officially designated understudies are generally useless. But you still have to be ready for emergencies. Whenever possible, I appoint students of different genders to be stage manager and assistant director. Although I never assign them to be understudies, the fact that they are at rehearsals regularly and are familiar with the show means that they could take over most of the smaller roles in a given show at a moment's notice. For example, if a male actor got sick the day before we opened and I had a male stage manager, I could move the stage manager into the role, shift my female assistant over to be stage manager, and find a replacement to take notes for me among other people backstage. All in all, this works much better than having formal understudies.

Crew Heads

Prop crew head — organizes and supervises the prop crew in all functions. This includes finding, making, storing, and returning all properties used in the show, dressing the set for rehearsal and performance, and supplying the actors with necessary props during rehearsal and performance. This is a position of tremendous responsibility, but it is also completely within the range of most students. Since props are usually borrowed rather than made, or when made are constructed on a relatively simple scale, props require time and application more than artistic experience. Students can do this with minimal supervision.

Scenery crew head — organizes and supervises the scenery crew in operating any scene changes necessary during the run of the show. For reasons of both safety and legal responsibility, you cannot allow students to actually supervise the construction of scenery. Too many dangerous tools are involved. Hence, there has to be an adult supervisor during all construction and during the early stages of any scenery moving. You can depend on a student to organize and schedule the crews themselves. Once the scenery is built and painted, you can allow them to plan and supervise scene changes and other safe parts of the scenic processes.

Costume crew head — organizes and supervises the costume crew in measuring, making, and storing costumes and aiding the actors in using or changing costumes. In general, students should never be put in charge of designing costumes. They rarely have the personal experience necessary for such work. But they can organize almost every other aspect of costuming as it is done in most school situations. If you construct all your own costumes on site, then naturally you or another adult must supervise that construction, just as you must supervise the construction of scenery. If you send patterns and materials home, as many schools do, a student can maintain all the records, check up on progress, and so on. Once costumes are finished, a student should always be in charge of their storage and maintenance. A student can also keep the records for any rental items.

Light and sound crew head — organizes the light and sound crews and supervises their operation of the various boards during rehearsal and performance. As with other crews, you or another adult should actually design the lighting and supervise the hanging and focusing of instruments, for reasons of safety as well as experience. But students can learn to run the light and sound boards, teach others how to run them, and run them accurately during performance. They could do this long before computer boards, so they can certainly do it using the computers, with which they will usually be more comfortable than you.

Additional Positions of Responsibility

In one of my schools, backstage space was extremely small and the view of the stage itself very limited. Thus, I put the stage manager out front, in the spotlight booth at the back of the auditorium, which was a far more advantageous position from which to call light cues. However, that meant that he or she was not backstage at all once the show started. So we always had to have an assistant stage manager to take care of backstage duties. In some shows, this was the stage crew head, who was supervising scene changes anyway, and in others it was a separate person. Sometimes there is only one set, so the prop crew head can supervise all scene changes.

As for the backstage crews themselves, there are rarely any cases in which there can be too many volunteers. However, it is important that you remember that the volunteers are no help to you if they do not rehearse. Do not allow students to work backstage just to qualify for the party — make sure they can come to all of the necessary rehearsals. Once the show is in tech rehearsals, you must keep backstage staff at a minimum in order to prevent backstage distractions, but the problem is more often a shortage of people rather than too many.

DESIGN AND TECHNICAL QUESTIONS

Lighting

Without doubt, the single most important technical breakthrough for twentieth-century theater has been the electric light bulb. No theater in history could do the kind of things that even the most minimally equipped high school stage can do now through careful and imaginative use of lighting.

This is not the place to explain all the things light can do for you. There are numerous good textbooks in the field. However, there are a few fundamental points that affect the way you stage and direct a show and which even the best classes in college sometimes forget to mention.

The Function of Lighting Is Illumination

Sometimes academic and artistic lighting designers forget this basic function of lighting. Lighting can do many other things, but its first and most important function is to make what happens on the stage visible to the audience.

This does not mean that the stage has to be brightly or uniformly lit. It means that the point of the scene that you want the audience to focus on should be brightly lit, which is a different matter entirely.

The one thing that makes electric light different from all other forms of stage lighting in the past is that electric light can be focused. You can aim light at one portion of the stage and make that one portion bright while all other parts of the stage are darker or even completely dark. With even the simplest dimmer board, you can change which portion of the stage is bright from moment to moment and vary the brightness or color in an infinite number of ways.

Lighting Often Replaces Items of Scenery

If light doesn't fall on walls, there is no need to build the walls. It also means that the scenery built may be suggestive rather than realistic — the sunlight-colored light coming from a single direction will be understood as sunlight coming through a window, even if we don't see a solid wall with a window in it. Most importantly, good lighting can give to a performance a fluidity that is not possible in any other way.

Don't Be Intimidated by Lighting

School equipment is usually poor, lighting seems so "technical" and "scientific," and most drama teachers never took anything remotely electrical in school. This feeling has only been exaggerated since the introduction of computerized light boards. In recent years, the collegiate designers, given computerized boards to play with, have taken a few very simple principles and obscured them behind an incomprehensible jargon. That raises lighting designer salaries and allows them to intimidate practically everyone in their programs. Unfortunately, it also intimidates the students who could most use what they have to teach. Don't let the mumbo jumbo frighten you. The principles of lighting are very simple, and the rest is all learned by experimentation and practice.

Light is one of the most critical tools you have to work with. Use it. Get a couple of good lighting books. Then use your stage equipment. Experiment and take a few risks, for who is going to criticize you? You're the only person who is interested in your rehearsals. Make lighting work for you, not against you. It will make $500 shows look like $5,000 shows. At the same time, it can increase the dramatic impact of the actors' performances. Lighting is not an adjunct, it is a fundamental. Don't waste what it can do for you.

Sound

Not all that long ago, all sound effects were done live. That meant that, for the most part, playwrights chose not to demand much in the way of what we call sound effects. Like Shakespeare, they limited themselves to alarms, shouts, and the occasional cannon or clap of thunder. This began to change in the early twentieth century, as radio made audiences and writers alike more aware of the value of sound for setting time, place, and mood. Crickets began to chirp, traffic to pass outside windows, trains and sirens to wail in the distance, horses to gallop up to the doorway. Initially, these too were done live, but after the Second World War, recording and speaker techniques improved. Now almost all sound effects are done with recordings.

179

Sound is more complicated than one would assume. The fundamental problem of sound on-stage is that it must be audible to a large crowd and yet sound natural. This is where difficulty begins. It's not enough to put on a recording of the effect and play it through the auditorium speakers. You have to make the sound match the dramatic situation.

Avoid Auditorium Speakers if You Can

They are uniformly terrible. Speakers built into high school auditoriums were almost always installed when the building was opened, which means they are anywhere from twenty to sixty years out of date. If anyone thought about how they might sound — which is unlikely — they selected the speakers for their value as a public address system. That is, the speakers are designed to make the principal's voice cut through crowd noise at assemblies. This makes them practically worthless for music and for anything that sounds even vaguely natural. Even if they are good speakers, they will be in the wrong places. Most often, they are mounted on the sides of the proscenium, or perhaps directly over the center of the proscenium arch. Those are the two places sound effects will almost never need to be heard from. If you have crickets chirping, you want them to sound like they are chirping "outside" the house, not in the upstairs attic.

You Will Almost Always Need to Set Up Speakers of Your Own

This way, you can make the sounds come from the right place. It will also give you a bit more quality control. Fortunately, portable speakers are relatively cheap and can be found practically anywhere, since almost everyone has two or three stereos of some kind. However, remember that the speakers have a very specific function — they must sound natural on the stage. Avoid speakers and stereo systems with heavy basses; they sound great for rock and roll, but the crickets start sounding like stampeding elephants.

Always Retape Specific Effects for Instant Cueing

Under no circumstances should you try to play your sound effects directly from the original LP or CD. You can absolutely guarantee that the sound effects operator will miscount tracks and play the wrong sound, or that there will be a three-second delay as the CD player hunts for the right track. Always retape the specific effects you need onto your own tapes.

Unfortunately, technology has now left behind the finest way to actually record and use sound effects. Nothing has ever matched reel-to-reel tape. With that format, you could record each sound cue, overdub and mix several different sounds to get exactly what you want, splice them all into a single reel with all your music cues in the proper sequence, and put in leader tape so that every cue started exactly at the beginning of the sound.

Only computer "sampling" provides the same kind of control, but it is still a bit expensive and daunting for most school or community groups.

How to Work With Cassette Tapes

Most people now settle for cassette tapes. These are cheap and convenient, but they still have their problems. The greatest problem is that they are very hard to edit. You have to start the recording *exactly* at the end of the leader tape in order to cue the tape up properly for use. This is very difficult to do. But if you don't do it, there will be an unpredictable delay from the time you start the cue until you actually hear it.

The best way to use cassettes is to record each individual cue on a separate cassette. That way, there is no problem trying to find the start of the next cue "somewhere" on the tape.

Many Sounds Need to Be Done "Live"

Even with good speakers and original recordings, there are some sounds that just need to be done "live." Any sound that is short and sharp — like the gunshot off-stage at the end of *Hedda Gabler* or the door slam in *A Doll's House* — will be more recognizable and sound more natural if produced in the same acoustics as the rest of the play. (These short sounds are the hardest to do properly on tape as well. Since they're over in a fraction of a second, misaligning the leader tape by a quarter of an inch can mean that you punch the button and nothing is heard.) Crowd noises should be done live by all your off-stage actors and crew, especially if that crowd is also going to appear on-stage at some point. Use taped sound only if the crowd is so large or so unusual — like Times Square on New Year's Eve or the Super Bowl — that you can't get a close approximation to the sound using a handful of persons.

Plan and rehearse all your sound cues — music and effects both — exactly the same way as you do your lighting. Get them set up and try them out to set sound levels and specific cue points before you put the actors on-stage. You may have to change these once you hear the actors, of course. Sound effects never seem the right volume the first try. But there's no need to make the actors stand around doing nothing while you try three or four different ways of making the off-stage sound effect.

I say all this on the assumption that you can actually find recorded sound effects. It's not always as easy as it ought to be. Very few people put out tapes of pure sound, just to listen to, so your local record store may not have many to chose from. CDs are obviously better than LPs or tapes because there is no tape hiss or surface noise — assuming of course that the sound itself was digitally recorded and not just remastered from old LPs.

181

This is another of those things you need to buy when you see it, whether you have a current need or not. Someday, that sound effect will come in handy.

Microphones

Mention of sound naturally brings us to the question of microphones. Many people suggest that, since young actors have weak vocal training, they need some kind of sound reinforcement. The practical problem is that there is no way to do this properly. They've been doing it in Broadway musicals for decades, and they still haven't found a way to mike the singers and make it sound like they're really singing from the stage. All you accomplish with most miking is to make the audience hear sound coming from two different places — the stage and the speakers. This confuses more than it helps.

Even so, you will almost always have to mike a musical if you use anything more than a piano for the musical accompaniment. If you do, remember always that the microphones are in service to the show, not vice versa. Place microphones to cover the show as you've staged it, rather than restaging the show to fit the microphones. It sounds easy, but it is very hard, particularly since most schools own no decent microphones.

If you mike the actors, never mike the orchestra, too. They do this on Broadway, but it is just as absurd there as it is in the high school. No one is in an auditorium that big. If you think you need to mike both the singers and the band, then you really need to mike neither.

Remember as you plan that you are using microphones to make the sound of the actors clearer, not louder. Louder helps, but turning up the volume to maximum settings does nothing but give your audience earaches. Make what the actors say or sing as clear as you possibly can. This often means making all the volume settings as soft as you possibly can.

Remember, too, that no matter what you do, someone will always complain that they can't hear the actors. Resist the urge to solve all problems with the volume knob. The audience has to make some effort to listen. If you treat the stage like TV or stereos, your audience will treat it the same way. They will talk, read, wander around the room, and generally avoid paying attention, just like they do to all the electronic sound they hear throughout the rest of the day.

Music

Music is a fundamental aspect of sound that is often underused or misused. Even in nonmusical plays, there are numerous opportunities in which the right music, used imaginatively, can make a major difference in the effectiveness of the production.

Generally, music has two functions in live theatrical productions:

- It covers transitions.
- It underscores stage activity.

Underscoring means that the music plays underneath stage action, accompanying lines or business in much the same way as a film soundtrack score would operate. Some plays have such music indicated in the script and written into the scene — Eugene O'Neill, for example, specifies when the piano should play in the room off-stage during *Ah, Wilderness* and exactly what songs it should play, and Chekhov is very precise and detailed about using music. Most plays, however, give no such indication, because until recently all music had to be done live. No one since World War I has been willing to pay for the musicians. Since we are used to underscoring in movies and television now, we often think about trying to do it on-stage as well. This is difficult, because stage activity is never exactly the same from one night to the next, but it can be done.

Whichever role you choose for your music, it will only work productively if it is the right music. When selecting music, five basic factors should be considered:

1. **Mood** — Just playing music is not enough. Far too many groups just put on a tape and play whatever music comes next during the scene change, with often ludicrous results. All music is not created equal, and all music is not applicable to all situations. Pick the music to fit specific situations in specific individual productions. If you are not particularly sophisticated in this area, spend some time and study to become sensitized.

2. **Familiarity** — Remember, the music is supposed to encourage a feeling or attitude about the show, not be the show itself. If people begin to pay attention to the music, then they quit paying attention to the show. This does not mean that all music should be the equivalent of elevator music. Rather, it means that the music should be unfamiliar to the audience. Among students, where "old" music is anything recorded more than six months ago, this is not a difficult requirement. Practically any purely instrumental music will be unfamiliar to most of your audience. The reason familiar music becomes a problem is that it has its own associations. If you play "The William Tell Overture," for example, under the battle scenes in *Macbeth*, someone is going to think, and maybe even shout, "Hi-yo, Silver, away!" This will destroy their concentration on the play on-stage. If you play this week's latest hit song at intermission, part of your audience will start thinking about going dancing or what they

183

were doing when they last heard that song. Unless you can be absolutely sure the entire audience will share such a context, and you want that context to relate to what is happening in the play, such familiar pieces hurt far more than they help.

3. **Scale** — When directors select music to promote a mood, they tend to lean toward classical orchestral music, precisely because it has such a large emotional vocabulary. Unfortunately, most of us are tempted to use recordings from symphonies or from movie soundtracks. Few plays operate on the same kind of grand scale as such symphonic works. When the music comes on, the players seem to be overpowered by it. Avoid wide-screen music for shows that aren't wide-screen spectaculars. This means that you need to become familiar with chamber music, works for piano, small jazz combos, and such similar groups. This takes time, but it pays off in the long run.

4. **Unification** — Each show should have some unifying style or tone, some general feeling of scale, tone, place, or time that holds it together. Many groups destroy this unity by playing unrelated pieces of music at different times in the course of the production. Only rarely can you use the same piece more than once or twice in a show, for the moods will be different each time you need music. Even so, the various pieces you use should be similar in some way — all from the same period, all using the same instruments, all in the same style, or some similar manner of unification.

5. **Period** — This is a difficult point to discuss, but it should be considered. It usually helps to use music in period plays from the period depicted. People tend to think of harpsichords and flutes for Molière rather than rock bands. As a general rule, that makes perfectly good sense. People who know even a little bit about music associate certain times with certain kinds of music, and as soon as they hear the Glenn Miller band they think 1940s, for example. But the period music should still contribute to the mood. You wouldn't play "Chattanooga Choo-Choo" for *The Diary of Anne Frank*, even though it was a popular song at the time the play describes. The ideal situation is music from the period concerned that also has the mood concerned. If this is not possible, then mood always is more important than period accuracy.

Props and Furniture

Don't let yourself get overwhelmed or overloaded with scenery. Lots of people, even the most famous directors, let themselves get so wrapped up in scene design and scenic concepts that they forget they have to direct the play with actors. Scenery is the least of your problems. Sets are just walls. If you want to, you can skip them completely. Any number of successful and

intelligent productions have been done without walls. Arena staging is pred-
icated on being a theater without walls. Shakespeare had no scenery. Most
of the playwrights between Molière and O'Neill wrote for theaters that used
the same handful of sets for every show — every forest scene used the same
forest drop, every palace was the same palace, and so on. Walls and platforms are useful, but they are not essential. Furniture and props are.
Without a throne, no stage palace is a palace; with a good throne, no palace
needs walls.

Furniture

Unfortunately, props — especially furniture — cost money and time
most school groups think they do not have. Furniture in particular is a
problem. Sometimes you may find someone who will loan you furniture,
usually a parent of a cast member. But no one would loan you a piece of their
good new furniture for a contemporary play, and certainly they would not
loan you antiques for a period play. So you are pretty much stuck with what
is in your own home and what your group can afford to buy secondhand.

One secret here is upholstery. Most secondhand furniture, especially
around theater storage rooms, looks ratty simply because the upholstery is
worn out. If you re-upholster that furniture, it looks pretty good. That's not
as hard as it sounds, because you don't have to do a fully professional job. In
someone's home, new upholstery has to last years; on your stage, it has to last
about a week. And it only has to look good to the audience. Often, you only
have to recover half the furniture piece, the half the audience can see. You
can slip some extra foam or even a board into the cushions to square them
up, reshape arms and backs with temporary foam pieces, and hide it all with
new material. Because your repair only has to last for a short time, you can
often use material that is much cheaper than quality upholstery fabrics.

A second secret is wood. Stock up as many plain wooden chairs,
benches and tables as you can find. Plain is good. The more specific style the
chair or table might be, the less flexibility it gives you. Plain chairs can be
repainted. You can re-upholster them, or add phony backs or arms cut from
plywood or padded material. You can make them up with fancy painting or
tone them down — but only if you start with good sturdy wood. Tables can
be refinished, and for many styles you can put on new legs to change the look.
If the tops aren't what you really want, there're always tablecloths. Wood is
much sturdier than the various fake woods, fiber boards, and even plastics
that have become common in recent years. It will take more wear and tear
on-stage, and you can repair it more easily if something goes wrong.

You must have useful furniture. If you have nothing, get this first. Let
the walls come later.

When you do have furniture, use it thoughtfully and dramatically. Choose it or modify it to fit the place and period of your play. This is important with props as well. If you use plastic dishes be sure they don't actually look plastic. You can't always be perfectly accurate in period — you don't own an antique store. But most people don't actually live in their period. Compare the furniture in your own home with the layouts in home design magazines. Unless you're very unusual, most of your furniture is years older than current fashion, and most of it wasn't particularly fashionable when it was new. In most eras, most people have lived with a mish-mash of furniture, some new, some handed down from their parents, some even made by themselves. The secret is not to put something too "modern" into a scene. Don't put electric lamps into plays about the frontier, or a Danish modern sofa into *You Can't Take It With You*. If you can't use your props and furniture to define place and period exactly, then be careful not to allow what you have to distract.

Incidental Props

Little props in the arena or on any stage that is very close to the audience must be believable. If a character says he's reading Shakespeare, be sure that the book he's holding doesn't say in big bold letters *The Cat in the Hat*. It doesn't have to actually be Shakespeare, it just should not obviously be something else. If the family brags about its Ming vase, you won't have a Ming vase, of course; but it should at least look "Chinese" and not look like it's made of plastic. On a large proscenium stage, you don't necessarily have to pour actual tea into the cups, as long as the actors go through the motions as if there were tea. In an arena or any other close setting, however, you should pour tea and make the actors really drink it. This is not to say that you must always be realistic. You simply should not ever do anything that will distract the audience, that will take their mind away from the stage, or that will make them think you've made a "mistake."

Accurate Descriptions

Under no circumstances should you ever allow an actor to describe something differently from what the audience can see. If you can't find a red vase, then change the line so that the actor says the vase is blue, or whatever color you did find. This holds for anything, not just props. If the actress has brown eyes, don't let the actor compliment her on her lovely blue eyes. That sounds obvious, but I can't begin to count how many times I've heard this happen on-stage — I saw it happen at the Royal Shakespeare Company just last year. Actors will say what they've memorized, so make a point of telling them to change the line to fit what they actually see. Aside from the momentary confusion this causes for audiences, it is one of the first "mistakes" people point to when they make fun of "high school" and "amateur" theatrics.

Simplify Stage Props

One handy rule to keep in mind about props and furniture is: If no one uses it, you don't really need it. If no one is going to sit in the chair, why is it on-stage? Lamps are a particularly big offender here. Most modern rooms are lit by lamps, but on-stage, they just eat up stage space and the shades block the actors' faces. Unless you have a real dramatic need for a live lamp on the set, get rid of it. Audiences don't care and won't notice that it's missing. Set dressing is important, of course; all those pictures on the wall and doodads on the tables set up an ambience that completes the scenery. But if your time or budget is limited, simplify your over-all design to focus on the one or two pieces that will be most valuable and forget the rest.

What to Do With the TV Set

In contemporary plays, the TV set is a serious problem. Almost every room, if realistic, should have one, and many plays also require specific sounds to come from TVs (or radios). In general, you never want the audience to be able to see the actual screen, which means the set has its back to the audience. That means the TV should be downstage, where it blocks the sightlines for part of the audience and occupies space that ought to be available for the actors. One solution that is possible now in the age of remotes is to have the TV be "imaginary," on the fourth wall that faces the audience. People can turn it on and off with the remote and don't have to physically touch it. The other is to set it in one of the downstage corners. Furniture will look stupid because it doesn't face the TV, but then most interior designers do the same. If characters don't have to watch it for any extended period, this is usually an acceptable solution. In arenas, there is no easy solution. Wherever you put it, something or someone will be blocked from view. In addition, in arenas, someone can always see the screen, so if a specific program is supposed to be on, you will need to be able to play a tape of that program through the on-stage set.

COSTUMING

I would like to stress the importance of good costuming.

Recently, I attended a number of productions entered in the American College Theater Festival competitions while at the same time judging a similar contest for high school productions. This was an interesting and educational experience, because it allowed me to make very vivid and direct comparisons between theater production at the two levels.

The most striking fact was that there was no significant difference in the quality of directing seen — if anything, the high school directors did a slightly better job of making sense of their scripts and guiding their actors than did the college directors. After allowing for the physical maturity of the collegiate actors, there was very little difference between the quality of performance at either level. The high school kids acted at about the same quality level as the college students. With very few exceptions, however, the high school productions still looked "high school." It took me some time to figure out why, but the explanation was ultimately quite simple: The colleges were almost always well costumed and the high schools were almost always terribly costumed. This is the one significant difference between theater at the two levels.

Good Costumes Make the Actor Look Better

I discovered that those community theaters and professional companies most consistently greeted with audience admiration and good reviews, even (or especially) when the performances themselves were terrible, were the organizations that hired good costume designers. Good costumes make the actors look better, make the show look better, and do the bulk of the work for which directors usually take credit.

Good costume need not be expensive, but it must be good. To be "good," it must fit the following needs:

Characterization — A costume should be something that the character would wear in the situations of the play. It should tell people in the audience something about the character's personality and position in society.

Period — If the show is set in 1960, the clothes should resemble the clothes worn in 1960. Far too many people tend to lump anything more than five years in the past into some vague, all-purpose "olden days." Then they assume that, so long as the clothes were all found at Goodwill or the Salvation Army store, they will be "old-fashioned" and suit the play. "Old-fashioned" is not enough. Everybody should be in some specific period, and they should *all* be in the *same* specific period. If you look at photos or see actual productions of the most famous directors and designers, you will have noticed a spate of "eclectic" design during the past decade or so. This is design in which each actor seems to be from a different era or style. These people can get away with this, but you can't. Because they are directing at a major opera house or large rep company, audiences and reviewers assume there is some artistic principle at work which is too complex or subtle for most of the audience to figure out. The same thing at your high school would be interpreted as proof that the director knew nothing about historical period or artistic style.

Style — Colors, materials, patterns, or some similar factor somehow should suggest that you didn't just go down to Goodwill and buy the first six things you saw.

Completeness — Costumes should have accessories that finish the costume properly. Very often, the accessories are more important than the clothing — the right hat will change the same nondescript suit into a 1920s gangster outfit, a 1950s business suit, a 1980s sack suit, or a contemporary punk rocker's outfit. The wrong jewelry will ruin the most meticulously duplicated period dresses or destroy your illusion of contemporary wealth.

Fit — The costume simply must fit the actor. It sounds so obvious, and yet so few schools manage to do it.

Budget — Most high schools fail on all five of the above points, and blame it on budget. The sad part of all this is that good costuming need not take a lot of money. Many directors try to excuse their ignorance in this area by saying, "Well, we just can't afford to rent costumes." But rentals make no significant difference, except for very specialized, unusual, and gaudy costumes (*The King and I*). Many rental companies make costumes very cheaply, and their costumes often look it. Even if you rent from a quality supplier, the costumes that arrive in the box still may not fit, may have the wrong accessories, may even be the wrong period. Once an associate for a production of *Arms and the Man* decided to rent the military uniforms since men's coats are very difficult to make and uniforms of the period could not be easily faked from contemporary items. Imagine her surprise when she opened the box to find that Bluntschli's uniform was from the Revolutionary War, while all the rest were from the late 1890s. That's what the rental house sent, so that's what they had to use. The only guarantee that accompanies rentals is that they cost money. Unless you give them exactly the same attention as the costumes you make or buy for yourself, they will give you exactly the same problems as the costumes you make or buy.

Inexpensive Costuming

Small budgets necessarily force modifications and compromises. This should mean compromises only in detail. If you get silhouettes, fit, and accessories right, no one will miss that detail. Simplification and selection are fundamental stylistic design devices. There are ways to reduce expenses. For example, never throw anything out. Never build a costume without intending to use it again in a year or two — retrimmed, redyed, or taken apart and remade several years down the road. Never make costumes just to look pretty. But the point remains, for the same money your associates are spending to no avail, you can produce shows that will look as good as, or better than, they really are.

189

Learn something about costume theory, design practice, and construction. Then spend the bulk of your money where it will help you the most. Make your costumes support rather than interfere with the quality performances you are trying to train your actors to give.

Most importantly of all, make your costumes important. If you don't have enough budget to both build a good set and do proper costumes, *always do the costumes first*. The audience watches the actors. So put your first money on what the actors will look like. Then whatever's left can be put on what goes behind the actors. You can't send the actors out naked, but you can do a very effective and professional looking show on a naked stage. Costumes are far more important than sets to the effective staging of your show.

COMMON ACTORS' PROBLEMS
Makeup

The basic text in the field is Richard Corson's *Stage Makeup*, one of the few genuinely useful and complete texts in theater literature. Whatever makeup problems I ever came across in production, I found a solution there. However, in recent years, this book has become so expensive that many teachers are shifting to Lee Baygan's *Makeup*.

It is not always easy to get teenaged actors to use makeup properly. Most of them will complain about having to use makeup, especially the boys, but this is generally done only to keep up appearances. Once they learn to use it, they like the sense of protection that makeup gives. When actors wear a good makeup, they lose their sense of self and relax into the otherness of the role that makes acting itself attractive to them. When they look like "someone else," they act more convincingly. As a result, many of my students eventually insisted on wearing makeup even when playing teenaged roles.

Teenage Skin Problems

Teenagers have more skin problems than adults, and makeup can aggravate those problems if used improperly. This means you must invest in the best quality makeup you can afford, a hypoallergenic brand of cake makeup. Greasepaint, the traditional stage makeup, all but disappeared in the 1970s, but in the past decade has been improved and become more popular again. Although greasepaint is somewhat more flexible and works better with latex, it is always harder to clean off than cake, and students are tempted to put it on much more heavily than necessary. So, all in all, water-based cake makeup is better for student use. Whichever type you use, however, don't take anything for granted. Be sure your instructions for cleaning off the makeup are just as precise and complete as the instructions for putting it on. If a student ever develops a new zit on the day after a play, you will have a battle royal to get him or her into makeup again.

Makeup Should Never Be Seen Except On-Stage

This helps to maintain the separateness and specialness of the stage. It also helps avoid social difficulties. This is especially important for boys. Some rock groups go in for flamboyant attire and makeup, but for the overwhelming majority of boys in your school, makeup equals femininity equals homosexuality. Any boy caught outside the building with visible makeup will find himself the object of ridicule, taunting, or worse. It is sad, and it shouldn't happen, but it does. Be sure you show everyone how to get all the makeup off after the show is over.

Makeup Must Fit the Theater

After you get students to put on the makeup, the makeup must still be done well. The books I've recommended will demonstrate how this is done. The one point most books fail to mention is that what you do is ultimately determined by the size of your theater and the intensity of your lighting. After you have followed the directions in the books, or done what you learned in your college makeup class, you still have to modify and adjust to fit the building in which you work. This means that you must do makeup several times before opening night, so that you have time to make modifications. You can't wait until opening night to do it, because you will almost always need modifications.

Hairstyles

The most critical part of any makeup, however, is not the paint but the hairdo. The wrong hairdo, the wrong hairline, can destroy the most meticulous makeup application. No matter how carefully the wrinkles and bags might be applied, no one will accept young actors as middle-aged men and women if they are wearing youthful hairstyles. And please, don't spray gray paint over the student's regular hairdo — no human being ever had hair that looked like that. In many cases, a student needs no significant makeup if the hairstyle is right.

There are limits to what you can demand of students, of course. Hair is a very personal issue in the modern world. You can cut boys' hair some, or get them to let it grow out for a couple of months, but that's about it. This means that you must learn about hair styling. You should also invest in good wigs whenever and wherever you can find them. If you haunt the second-hand clothing stores, you can eventually accumulate a series of wigs that can be used in a number of different ways and still not bankrupt you.

191

Corson gives a marvelous (and cheap) method for making receding hairlines and even complete bald heads with a nylon stocking, soap, and normal makeup. I've used the technique myself, and it works, even when the students do it themselves. I've seen it pass for bald on the street. Hair is an absolutely fundamental part of the makeup; bad hair will destroy the illusion you have spent many weeks preparing. So spend time and, if necessary, money to make it work for you instead of against you.

Students May Become Careless With Makeup

Also, remember that, with students in particular, the first part of the performance to deteriorate is the makeup. It's scary sometimes what students can do to their makeup on the second or third night of the run. I always make students apply their own makeup, for reasons discussed earlier, so I tend to think that when they do it well, they understand what they are doing. And yet, show after show, I find that a student who went out on opening night with a perfectly toned makeup, shadows blended, highlights precisely placed, artificial wrinkles placed with hairline precision, will go out on the third night with grotesque lines scribbled all over the face, almost at random, no highlights, and not the least bit of shading or blending. It is one of the most inexplicable aspects of high school theater. So, although I said you should leave the cast alone before performances, that only applies *after* makeup is finished. You must check in regularly at makeup time to head off the worst disasters.

Aging

Closely related to makeup is the problem of aging the performers. In high school, convincing performances require convincing aging.

No other theater group has this problem. If a professional company or a community theater, or even your local college, wants a performer to play someone who looks fifty or seventy, all they have to do is find an actor who is fifty or seventy. All of your actors are between the ages of fourteen and eighteen.

This leads to two consistent problems. First, no matter how well your cast may perform a show, there will always be critics who say, "Well, yes, but they weren't very convincing old people, were they?" On the other hand, you or the actors can become so obsessed with "playing the age" that you forget to play the action and the characters, which are far, far more important.

As a result, many teachers are tempted to do plays in which their teenaged actors are not required to play anything but teenagers. That is, they do "high school plays." The problem, of course, is that most of the plays that go under this title are terrible plays, from which the actors learn little or nothing about performance except contempt for their audience.

Even more important, a teenaged actor is usually least convincing playing a teenager. In part, this is because such a character is too close to home, which causes young actors either to hold back or to overplay. At the same time, society (as demonstrated regularly on TV sitcoms) has adopted some very strange ideas of what teenagers look and sound like, which often have little to do with reality. Plays about high school teenagers tend to depict people who far more closely resemble junior high school students — young people who have no jobs, no cars, no interest in sex, alcohol, drugs, marriage, politics, suicide, religion, or the terrors of the future, all of which are fundamental to the lives of most teenagers.

You will never silence the complaint about teens "playing the age." Your casts are fourteen to eighteen years old, and they will never convince anyone they are fifty or seventy. But you can convincingly make them seem fifty or seventy in relation to the other members of the cast, which is the only thing that counts.

The Solution

It may seem radical, but it works: Don't worry about aging the performers. Let good costuming, and some very fundamental, but well-done, makeup, take care of the aging. Let the actors concentrate on characterization and acting. It is possible for a well-costumed young actor to play a mature adult convincingly as long as there is no one of the same age actually on-stage at the same time. (This works in reverse, as well. Many a thirty-five-year-old actress has successfully played twenty-year-old ingenues, as long as they made sure no real twenty-year-old women were in the cast with them.)

The critical factor in this deception is to remember that "lines" and "gray hair" are the least important aspects of this deception.

Accurate Costuming Is Fundamental

Convincing aging is convincing costuming. The costumes must be suitable for people of that age. This means that someone has to take a look at real life rather than the simplistic stereotypes of our childhood. Every one of the more than a dozen productions of *Arsenic and Old Lace* that I have seen in the past two decades was done in "modern dress" rather than period 1940s. Yet, every one of them put the two little old ladies in floor-length dresses with lacy shawls and cameos. Seriously, now, when was the last time you saw a sixty-year-old woman in a black high-collared dress? "Sweet little old ladies" in the 1990s wear polyester pantsuits and the dresses, hats, and coats of 1965-75, not of 1900. Their clothes are modeled far more on Jackie Kennedy than on Queen Victoria. Of course the girls playing those roles in such productions looked phony — retirees wearing those costumes would have looked phony.

Costumes Must Fit

Grown-ups buy and wear clothes that fit. The only time clothing might not fit would be a serious plot point. For example, as the families upstairs with Anne Frank stay in their attic, they lose weight, so in the second act when they are fighting over food their clothes should be too large. But when we first see them, the clothes should fit perfectly. It may be hard to convince teenagers after the fashions of the early nineties, but normal clothes for adults fit. This seems so obvious. Yet, one of the most persistent signs of a "high school play" is the boy tripping over his trouser legs while wearing a suit with sleeves that slide over his fingers. This kind of sloppy costuming draws attention to the fact that the actor is just a kid playing a grown-up.

Hair style is perhaps the most important item of all. This is especially true with boys, where even in our free-for-all times, adult men wear their hair differently than do boys. Women's hair styles fluctuate far more than men's, and adult women tend to wear "younger" hair styles just as teenaged girls tend to wear "older" styles to fit fashion and to look sexually attractive. But a good hair style for the age will do more than all the makeup lines on the face.

The Costume May Be Used to Modify the Student's Body

The costume itself can be modified — hips padded, bust line disguised, waists thickened with padding or contracted with corsets, and so on. This is effective because there are general body types associated with general age periods. Increased weight, for example, is associated with middle-aging. Pudgy actors, even when freshmen or sophomores, are often more convincing parents than seniors who are thin and wiry. Old age tends to fall back into a stringy leanness, so very thin teenagers may be effective at weak old age. The exact manner of modification depends on the actor cast and the period of the production.

One thoroughly irrational factor can help produce an effective appearance of age. We tend to associate age with height. Young people are short, growing to full height at maturity and then growing shorter again as we begin to slouch and sag into old age. This is a very generalized scale, and there are many exceptions, particularly in this era of beef-fed teenagers and jogging senior citizens. But it is important to remember the generality. It usually helps, when you have characters of mixed ages, to be sure that the actors playing children are shorter than their parents, or that the little old ladies are shorter than the mature women or men around them.

If you get all these things right, you don't have to worry about making the actors do funny voices and funny walks or have grotesquely painted faces. Remember that the most important part of the performance is a convincing characterization in which every line seems clear, sincere, and "in character." If that happens, and if the costuming and makeup don't draw attention to the fact that the actor is the wrong age, few will notice. Those that do notice won't care. Dress the age, but play the character.

The Kiss

There is perhaps no single piece of business harder for high school actors to perform than the kiss. Unfortunately, there is hardly a play in Western literature that doesn't have at least one kiss in it. Thus, a kiss on-stage will requires some special rehearsal attention.

For most students, problems with the kiss arise from two sources. There are the usual mechanical problems that occur whenever two bodies come in contact on-stage: Who moves first, what hand goes where, how do we avoid tripping over each other or hitting ourselves in the mouths, how do we keep from getting tangled up, and so on? For some of the performers, particularly the younger or shyer boys, there are serious mechanical questions about the kiss itself, due to lack of personal experience.

Far more difficult and disruptive, however, are the psychological problems. This often comes as a surprise, when any teenager can see more than just simple kissing in the school hallways most every day. Even so, it still unnerves teenagers to do a very private thing like a kiss in a very public situation like the stage. They know that there is a very good chance that their friends, or their enemies, will tease or ridicule them afterward (and sometimes during the performance). These concerns are magnified on-stage because the partner to be kissed is almost never a person the actor would choose in real life. You have to kiss whoever got cast. Sally may not want to kiss Tom because he's a jerk, because he ate onions at dinner, because she used to go out with him but broke up months ago, because he's a sophomore and she's a senior, or for any number of other reasons. All of this makes rehearsals and performance awkward.

Seven Basic Steps for Staging a Kiss

1. Before beginning the staging, determine precisely the kind of kiss needed. Is it to be tentative, awkward, passionate, gentle, cursory? As with any other part of rehearsal, you can't stage the action unless you understand its relation to the characters and action of the play.

2. Always do the first rehearsal in private. You and the two persons involved should be the only ones present when the kiss is initially blocked out. Get rid of everyone else, even the stage manager. This is the only way to avoid unnecessary embarrassment about the kiss. If you leave anyone backstage or in the wings, then someone will whistle or hoot or make a joke. Get rid of everyone so you can work with some mature respect and consideration for the actors.

3. Let the actors determine if they want to do a "real" or a "fake" kiss. In a "fake" kiss, the lips don't meet each other, but rather touch the skin as close to the lips as possible. Usually, this means that the male kisses the female in the space just above the lips but below and to one side of the nose. Your staging will be the same, whether they choose to do this or not, but it makes them feel more comfortable and in control if they make this decision themselves. In most of my shows, the couple has usually opted for the fake kiss in the beginning and then switched to the real one after they became comfortable with the scene. Don't let them determine anything else about it. Especially, don't send them off to work out the scene on their own. This will just make them more awkward and self-conscious.

4. Block the kiss backwards. Start work from the position at which the kiss is finished. Then go backwards to find the most comfortable and effective way to work up to that. This is painstaking and meticulous work, during which you must choreograph every single movement. You must decide such things as: Does she stand on her toes to reach him? If so, exactly when can she do this and not lose her balance? Where do his arms go? Where do her arms go? When does each arm move so that it doesn't get caught up in the other person's arms. Who turns first? Who reaches first? Does he bend a knee? And so on. Work backwards until you have worked out all the steps.

5. Once the moves have all been blocked out, go forward several times, always in slow motion. Adjust where necessary, and then repeat until there is no doubt in either person's mind about what to do when. Stay in slow motion until absolutely secure, and concentrate only on mechanics. Don't talk about feeling at all at this time, so that the actors can avoid thinking about any personal aspects of the situation.

6. Rehearse the scene on several other evenings, still alone, and still in slow motion. Gradually increase the speed and then gradually add the rest of the scene leading up to it. Now you can begin to talk about the feelings involved, but always stress the feelings and the relationship of the characters, not of the actors.

7. After the actors are completely secure in the scene, add it into a full, regular rehearsal. By this time, their security and the added rehearsal time during which the rest of the cast has gotten used to playing charac-

ters in a play will eliminate most of the initial discomfort of performing the scene in public.

Comedy and Laughs

For various reasons, most of the plays you stage will be comedies. There is a general tendency among collegiate people to see comedy as somehow beneath other kinds of theater. As a result, it is hard for most directors (after all, we all went to college) to shake the feeling that comedy should have different and lower standards of production than more "serious" work. "The stupider the better" often seems to be the attitude they project to their students, and as a result, when they stage a comedy they accept "anything for a laugh."

The irony is that such productions are rarely very funny.

It is a fundamental paradox of comedic acting that, the more you try to be funny, the less funny you are. We can see this in real life — no one laughs at the kid who desperately tries to make people laugh in order to get attention. Why should they laugh at the same attitude when projected in a performance?

Comic Lines and Funny Business Are Funny Only in Context

There are a few witty epigrams of the Oscar Wilde variety that might be funny wherever and whenever they are spoken, but only a few. Almost all punch lines lose their punch when removed from the proper place in the story. This holds true for any play. The best way to make the lines and business funny in your production is to make a strong context in which they become funny.

This means greater attention to the "reality" of performance. The characters in practically all comedy are involved in what they see as real situations, with real problems, and they usually do not know that they are funny. The director knows, of course, and so do the actors, but the characters do not. The actors must try to accomplish the characters' objectives rather than try to be funny. When they do, they establish the reality of situations and of characters, which makes the comic moments happen "accidentally." This in turn increases the humor of each situation. Comedy actually demands much more detailed, much more "realistic" characterization and performance than more "serious" works might need.

Timing Is Everything in Comedy

A line said too soon, a piece of business done a fraction of a second too late, and the laugh disappears. This is the point at which the director's role as a surrogate audience is especially important. You establish this timing in

197

rehearsal and then maintain it through repetition in rehearsal. However, it is important to remember that, in most cases, you should not discuss timing as such with the actors. Don't say "count to three and then say the line," even when you want the actor to wait three seconds to make the laugh work. The result will be an actor, and a performance, that goes to sleep for three seconds while "waiting." Instead, find an objective that forces the actor to wait for those three seconds but which also keeps concentration and characterization alive.

It is not always easy to remember these points, particularly when we are daily given the examples of TV sitcoms and famous comedians who haven't gotten a laugh in ten years but who are still thought to be great comedians because they were once on *Saturday Night Live*. You don't have a laugh track. You can't pretend your show is funny when it isn't. As a result, your cast has to actually act the comedy. The process of acting doesn't change, just because the show is supposed to be funny. If anything, all the other factors we have discussed in this work become even more important.

Guns, Swords, and Fists

Sooner or later, you are going to have to stage a fight of some kind. This doesn't happen as often as you would expect — playwrights for the most part have avoided scenes that require physical fighting, for some reasons we'll discuss in a moment. There are obvious exceptions, of course. Shakespeare makes battle scenes or duels central to most of the histories and tragedies. Tybalt and Mercutio must duel on-stage, as must Harry and Hotspur. It can be surprising, even with Shakespeare, how often the characters do their yelling on-stage but do the actual fighting in the wings. Most stage fights, as defined in the scripts, consist of little more than a few swipes with the sword or a single slap or punch.

The reason, of course, is that fights are dangerous. Any attempt to do them safely requires extra rehearsal. Most producers don't want to pay actors for extra rehearsals. Until the twentieth century, there was nothing we would recognize as rehearsal for anything. So all stage fights tended to be pretty simple and stereotyped.

Motion Pictures Changed Everything

Moviemakers love fights. They are dramatic, they eat up screen time, they save effort in writing, and they can be easily faked on film. Fights and film are a marriage made in heaven, which is part of the reason we are now debating the social function of violence on screen. Breakaway furniture, sugar bottles that shatter without hurting anyone, stunt men who are substituted into shots to take the actual falls, safety nets, and endless retakes encourage ever more spectacular fights. Roundhouse punches that miss by three feet can be made by careful camera placement to look like they hit square on the jaw. Actors can do scenes in slow motion and have the fight speeded up to normal speed by the editor. Punches that never even touched the opponent can be changed on the sound track to sound like a bomb.

Changed Expectations for Fights On-Stage

Directors and audiences expect fights on-stage to look and sound more like the fights on screen.

The problem is — the stage is not the screen. There are no retakes on-stage, no slo-mo, no stunt men, no pause while the breakaway chair is substituted. Everything you do on-stage is done once, it's done live, and the actors have to go on and say the next line after the fight is over. Actors cannot do it "for real," because they have to get on with the play tonight, and they have to do the play again tomorrow. You don't have a spare costume in case this one gets torn or dirty, and you don't have spare actors to rush on just for the fight, or to come on tomorrow in case this one sprains an ankle or breaks a hand or gets stabbed. You also can't "fake it" the same way they do in the movies, because your audience is watching live. There's no cutting to a different angle on-stage. The blows have to look real, the sounds have to sound real, and yet you cannot do anything for real.

Stage Fights Can Be Dangerous

Even the simplest slap can break a hand or dislocate a jaw. That's the first and last thing you must remember with any kind of fight on-stage. Rule number one is Safety First. Rules number two through ten are: Safety First.

This doesn't mean that you have to resort to the old "you hit my sword three times then I'll hit your sword three times" kind of fight. You can do some pretty spectacular things with young actors. They love this kind of stuff and will work hard at it. It just means you can't make it up as you go, and you certainly can't let the actors make it up for themselves. Every movement has to be planned to simultaneously look effective to the audience and yet to offer absolutely no danger to the people on the stage. Fights of any kind, even a single slap, have to be choreographed like a ballet. Every motion, every step, has to be planned, drilled, and drilled again so that there is no chance of someone forgetting what to do when.

If you have no training in this area, get help. There are some manuals available, and now and then you'll find a good videotape. Best of all is to find a workshop in the summer at a nearby college. There you can get one-to-one instruction. In the past few years, professional fight choreographers have organized, so there are now a number of well-trained teachers who offer training sessions for directors and actors all over the country.

Guns Are a Different Problem

Because of TV, audiences think they are far more knowledgeable about guns now than they were even twenty-five years ago. If you use a gun on-stage, it has to look and sound like an appropriate weapon. You can't just wave around a starter pistol or a kid's cap gun anymore without getting unintentional laughs. But you never want a real gun on-stage. Accidents happen. That's why they are called accidents. One accident with a real gun could leave you with a dead kid.

When I started teaching years ago, there were a number of very realistic cap pistols or BB guns available. After kids began to be shot by others who mistook their toys for the real thing, manufacturers began to make toy guns look more obviously toy-like. So, if you want a gun that looks something like the right kind of gun, you will probably have to resort to plastic models, if you can find those.

Plastic models, of course, can't be fired. If the gun is not just brandished but actually fired, the noise has to come from somewhere else. The oldest, most traditional method is the safest. Turn the gun upstage, so the shooter's back is to most of the audience. Then have the stage manager fire the sound effect from a starter pistol or a very loud cap pistol in the nearest wing. That way, if there is a slight delay between the time the shooter pulls the trigger and the time the shot is heard, the audience is not aware of it (assuming of course that your actors don't give the game away). It's not as viscerally exciting as firing off blanks in the middle of the stage, but it's a lot safer.

Extra Safety

If you feel that you just have to do the shot live on-stage, never fire blanks from a pistol that has not had the barrel plugged. Blanks are real bullets, just without the lead. There is still a powder charge and small bits of wadding in every shell. When the blank is fired, unexploded powder and the wadding are shot out, just like a bullet. If you are close enough, the wadding can penetrate the skin and may even kill you. Not all that long ago, a successful young TV actor was killed when he fired a blank pistol toward his own head. Even from several feet away, tiny flakes of material can damage eyes. Starter pistols, for example, are used safely because the barrel is actually solid; any loose wadding is deflected out the side rather than fired forward.

Whatever you decide to use, always double-check the weapons yourself. You never want to hear yourself saying, "But I thought the gun wasn't loaded." Make sure it's not loaded. Make sure the knives are dulled, the points rounded, the swords properly tipped. This is one thing you can't leave to the stage manager, no matter how much you trust him or her.

CHAPTER NINE
DIRECTING THE MUSICAL

Sooner or later, you're going to be involved in a production of a musical comedy. In almost all schools, it would be impossible to avoid one. Surveys from various sources indicate that one-fourth to one-half of all school plays are musicals. In churches and similar groups where plays are done in part as youth activities, the percentage is much higher.

There is, of course, one very good reason for this — people come to see musicals. Good, bad, or indifferent, a musical comedy brings people through the doors who would otherwise never go near the theater.

This phenomenon is difficult to explain. The traditional musical has all but disappeared from the theater. Yet, amateur theaters and summer stock are overwhelmed by musicals.

Musicals Offer Great Potential

This is because the musical can be the most exciting form of theater in the world. It can be fluid, imaginative, flashy, touching, and joyously unpredictable. With its combination of "acting" with song and dance, spectacle, and music, it can encompass everything that makes the theater worth having. While it can be all of this, it has to be admitted that this doesn't happen very often.

If asked to explain why high school audiences still turn out in droves for *Brigadoon* or *South Pacific*, most serious theater people would be hard pressed to come up with a logical answer. It can't be because they like the music — in the era of rock 'n' roll, most standard musicals might just as well come from another planet. Not only have most of your students (and most of their parents) never heard the songs, they have never heard the instruments that play them. Nor can it be because their plots are so relevant to your teenagers. How many high school students empathize with the difficulties of a middle-aged peasant milkman trying to marry off his daughters or of a middle-aged matchmaker trying to trick a bald fat man into marrying her. And yet, *Fiddler on the Roof* and *Hello, Dolly* do keep packing them in at the local school.

The Musical Offers the High School Drama Program Three Things

First, it has a large cast, which automatically means a larger audience. Secondly, people in that audience feel no threat from seeing their children and friends perform. In our culture, despite our twenty-four-hour entertainment society, we are still very insecure about acting. We simultaneously admire and mistrust actors, and the better they are the more we mistrust them. Acting is, after all, professional lying, and really good acting is really good lying. At the same time, there is always the fear that really good acting is also telling the truth, that if a student actor is convincing in performance, they have exposed something that their parents would rather not have the world know about. But everyone likes to see their friends and family show off a "talent." Singing and dancing are "talents" we all recognize and admire, without any of the confusions associated with acting. So shows that require singing and dancing tend to make parents and friends feel far more comfortable with what they see on-stage. Third, despite the wave of "serious" musicals of the past decade, people think of musicals as "entertainment." More people will come because they figure it won't make any serious demands on them as audience members. There's nothing intimidating about the experience as a whole.

You will notice that all these advantages are audience-oriented, not program- or student-oriented. That's because there are, in fact, very few advantages for the program or the students in the program. Most famous musicals demand a combination of New York star power and enormous budgets. Schools tend to have neither. When schools attack one of the big musicals, they work from their weakest position, as educators and as theater producers.

There Is Enormous Pressure to Do Musicals

Some of this will come from parents, some from students. Even more will come from administrators. Some may even come from you. Before you succumb to that pressure, you should realize that the pressure to do musicals is based on seven myths that are all but universal.

THE SEVEN MYTHS OF MUSICALS

Myth #1: Musicals are fun.

Musicals are fun to watch, especially if they are done well. But then, any show done well is fun to watch. However, musicals are backbreaking labor to produce. You have all the problems of a "normal" production, plus a host of new ones. Just to state the obvious, there will be three times as many people on-stage, and ninety percent of them will have never acted before. They not only have to act but also to sing and dance. This takes two to three times as long to rehearse as even the most complex dialog scenes. If you add in the problems of coordination with conductor, choral director, and choreographer, what you have is a period of constant labor, and often genuine agony, far exceeding anything you have ever experienced as a director.

Myth #2: The musical will make enough money to support the rest of the program.

Musicals do bring in a lot of money. Unfortunately, they also cost a lot of money to produce. With very rare exceptions, the musical will cost well over a thousand dollars for royalty alone. That's more than most schools spend for everything on their non-musicals. After that, you still have to pay for scenery, costumes, props, and publicity. All of these things cost more in a musical. Where a typical school play has one set and one set of costumes for about a dozen actors, a typical musical will have six to ten sets and three or four costumes apiece for thirty to forty performers, usually in period. And everyone expects those sets and costumes to be spectacular as well. You can't just double your audience; you have to increase it by a factor of ten. At best, there is only an even chance of staying in the black; there is almost no chance of making enough profit to pay for non-musical shows, or to pay for other programs.

Myth #3: A musical will bring new students into the drama program.

A musical will bring new people into auditions. In particular, it will bring students from the choir who have not, for the most part, ever auditioned for previous shows. Most of them have never taken drama classes.

Unfortunately, this is the only time you will see them. If they are cast, they will know they were cast because they were good singers and will take more choral classes in hopes of getting a better part in the next show. If they weren't cast, they will know that they should learn to sing better and sign up for choral classes. But almost none of them will sign up for drama classes or audition for non-musical productions. In almost two decades of school productions, I have met only one student who got his first role in a musical and then came back for non-musical productions or took a subsequent drama class. The only schools that I have found that have increased their "drama" enrollment by doing musicals have been those schools that do the musical as a "class project." Generally, a successful musical will increase enrollment in music classes. That's because kids in your acting classes will sign up for choir in order to avoid being left out when the next musical comes along.

Myth #4: The musical will draw new audiences for your program.

This is one of the most persistent myths in school theater. The more that evidence indicates it is a myth, the more people seem to cling to it. You hear it most from directors whose non-musicals draw the smallest audiences. If the musical drew audiences to the rest of their program, the rest of their program would have audiences close to the size of the musical audience. It just doesn't happen that way.

The reason for this is simple. As we discussed earlier, most of the audience for a show comes from people who know cast members, not from people who know the show. In a musical production, you have a much bigger audience because you have a much bigger cast as well as a show that has been the subject of nationwide publicity campaigns. When those people are not in the cast, and when you have no access to such intensely publicized material, those audiences will not come back, no matter how good the productions might be. You can build your audience for nonmusicals only by doing nonmusicals well and by involving a broad cross section of the student body in their production.

You can and should also build your audience for musicals by doing them well and by involving a broad cross section of the student body in their production. But don't expect the audience numbers of one to have any significant effect on the audience numbers for the other.

Myth #5: The shared responsibilities of musical production will lessen the time requirements for the director.

It is true that, for the only time in your career, a musical production will involve other adults. Where you normally have to do everything, now you will have a music director and a choreographer and maybe a few other adults to help out with rehearsals.

This does not cut your work load, however. You will still be responsible for all the things you are usually responsible for. The music director and the choreographer are responsible for *additional* work. You still have to stage the show, teach the cast something about acting, plan the scenery and costumes, supervise the backstage crews, and so on. As we have noted, these are usually far more work, for there is more sets, more costumes, more changes requiring more crew members, and so on.

In addition, the cast will be full of people who have never acted before. They will require far more coaching than usual in other shows where the bulk of the cast will have taken your acting classes, or been in previous shows.

As if this weren't enough, you will also become responsible for all the coordination among the various adults involved. You have to plan rehearsals so that everyone gets enough time to work on their specialized areas; you have to find the extra rehearsal spaces so that the music director can work at the same time as the choreographer. You have to demand and negotiate numerous production meetings at which you hack out agreements among all the staff involved as to the way the show should be planned, rehearsed, and staged. This takes far more time than your preparation work for a typical nonmusical.

This coordination also leads to an area of great psychological stress. Each person who will "share" the responsibility for this production is used to being the final authority for his or her students. This is quite different from the professional situation. There you have clashing egos, of course, but there are clear lines of authority; everyone knows who makes the final decisions. This is not clear at all in a school situation. The choir director is used to telling the choir singers what to do, the dance teacher is used to being the final arbiter on what dances should look like, and so on. Even more importantly, their students are used to listening to them and not to you. And the cast is full of their students, not yours. If you have disagreements with the other teachers involved, the cast will simply ignore you.

This is a worst-case situation, of course, but it does happen. When it does, the students will listen to the people they are used to listening to and who can, at the worst, affect their grades in supposedly unrelated classes. Administrators will always side with the music people, because they are more established, more firmly supported by parents, and have more students in their classes. You must find a way to avoid ever reaching such a point in rehearsals.

This means an enormous amount of time spent in discussion, explanation, preparation, negotiation, and definition of boundaries of authority. The stage director should be in charge, because that's the only way a show can be done. In the school situation, this means far more work, not less, and far more stress.

You cannot do a good show if you just try to split the show three ways: a good musical combines music, dance, and drama, rather than placing them on stage side by side. It's possible to get that combination, and it's possible to establish comfortable and creative cooperation among all the adults and egos involved. It just takes more time and more effort than doing a nonmusical by yourself. One thing you must understand before starting a musical: It will make demands on your time and your psyche that you have never felt in any other kind of production.

Myth #6: Doing a musical is a good experience for your actors.

Doing a musical would be a good experience for your actors, if any of your actors were ever in the musical. The problem, of course, is that they usually aren't cast.

No matter how much you may want to give opportunities to the people who have acted in nonmusicals or taken your acting classes, the fundamental requirement for casting in the school musical is that the people can sing as well as or better than the best singers in the choir. If they can sing that well, they are almost always already in the choral program somewhere.

You can push for the non-singer, but it doesn't help anything. The musical director will simply not accept casting someone who "can't sing" if there are students available who can. In a worst case situation, if the music director doesn't agree to the casting, he or she can take away enough students to make the production impossible. But there is a good practical reason for making singing the most important criterion — it is much easier to teach someone to fake an acting performance than it is to teach someone to fake a singing performance. Sad to say, but nonetheless true, no one in the audience will much care if the acting is pretty poor as long as the performer sings and/or dances well.

Thus, you must cast for musical skill first. You need not cast for musical skill only, for performing ability and experience count a great deal. But they only count after the auditioners have shown a minimum musical competence. It would be a terrible mistake to forget everything we have talked about in casting, for all those criteria still apply in a musical. Still, one of the absolute minimums for almost all roles is the ability to sing in public in an audible and pleasing manner. Singing comes first.

The result, of course, is that the only good experience the "actors" get from a musical is the experience of rejection. This is not a bad thing to teach them, for most of an actor's life consists of rejection. But it is not a foundation on which to build a growing theater program. The best actors will be the ones most upset. You will have to depend on them for almost all your backstage work. If they are genuinely talented young people, they will find the process humiliating. They will stand in the wings and watch the public and the school authorities shower applause and compliments on people who do what they rightly recognize as weak performances. You must be prepared to deal with the frustration and anger that follows from this experience, or the negative attitudes will spread throughout the entire program until you have no drama program.

Myth #7: A good musical production will help the director in the school and in the community at large.

In practice, a good musical helps the choir director's reputation enormously, while a bad one will destroy yours. This happens even if you aren't involved. I have observed a number of schools where relations between music and drama staff deteriorated so much that the choir staged the musical without any participation from the drama department. In one instance, the resulting show was terrible, but it didn't matter. Everyone automatically assumed that the drama director was responsible.

The credit for any good musical production will be given to the choir director, not the drama director. When later as drama director you go to the princpal to ask for more money, the principal will say, "Yes, do more musicals" and increase the music department's budget.

The only drama teachers I have found who have been able to break this pattern were teachers who did nothing but musicals and people who devoted their entire life to self-advertisement. Since neither of these types are teachers or directors in any real sense of the word, they lie outside this discussion. If you expect to do your job as a director and as a teacher and still gain credit and influence from the occasional production of musicals, you must simply outlast everyone else involved. After you've done fifteen to twenty terrific shows with four different music directors and six choreographers, the principal may begin to realize that you might have had something to do with the quality of those productions. Don't plan on anyone giving you your full share of credit for a success, and certainly don't plan on it if you are a relatively new or inexperienced teacher/director.

MUSICALS SHOULD ONLY BE PART OF A TOTAL THEATER PROGRAM

The good musical belongs in a total drama program just as a good play of any period or style. But musicals should not dominate a program.

This may sound as if I'm trying to discourage doing musicals in high schools. I am not suggesting that you refuse to do musicals, nor am I suggesting that there are none worth doing. What I am saying is that the musical should only be a *part* of the high school theater program. Such musicals as are produced should be chosen by exactly the same criteria used to select any other play. When you use such criteria, I think you will be surprised to learn how few worthwhile musicals really exist.

One of the best ways to prevent the overemphasis on musicals is to make sure that you do not unthinkingly accept any of these seven basic myths of musical production.

The musical can be an exciting, educational experience for the director as well as for the students. However, for the director, it is an enormous amount of work, done under unusual and exaggerated pressures, with educationally compromised results. Musicals belong in a well-rounded program, but they must never be allowed to control the program. They should be produced with the same thought, preparation, imagination, and rehearsal as any other play. You should use the same standards in rehearsal and performance. But before you start on one, it's helpful to understand the problems and prepare for them. Then you will not only survive but do a good job.

CHAPTER TEN
BUILDING A
THEATER PROGRAM

You can do a good theatrical production from scratch, reorganizing completely every time you start a new show. That is, after all, how most Broadway shows are done. But, it is better and easier if you have a good production organization to support you. In schools and similar groups, this means that you have to do two jobs at once. No matter how good a director you may become, you must also develop a drama program that goes beyond rehearsal and performance.

In church and community groups, this means that you must develop some kind of regular organization — budgeting, fund-raising, buildings, storage, possibly even a board of some kind. In the school, almost all of these organizational points are provided by the school itself. There, a drama program means that you must develop and teach drama classes. There are numerous sources that can advise you on organizational methods. There are also a large number of sources of advice for the teacher as well as actual textbooks for drama classes. However, there are still some basic points that are rarely if ever dealt with in other sources. These will have a fundamental effect on your success in building a good and self-sustaining program.

A successful drama program is one that allows you to do good theatrical work while your students are actually improving their performance or production skills. Such a program should bring back most of the students you now have and introduce new ones each year. It should also be sufficiently stable that you can assume it will not be canceled at whim by the administrators of your school, church, or community group.

What your program looks like in detail will depend on your organization, your community, your specific talent pool, and your own personality. Specifics can and should vary. But there are some basic principles that will apply no matter what your basic situation.

KEYS TO A SUCCESSFUL DRAMA PROGRAM

Over the years, I have worked in practically every kind of theatrical organization except Broadway. Some of the time it has been in programs I organized and ran, sometimes in programs where I was a guest. I have found many good programs, and many bad ones. All taught me something, if only "what not to do." This experience has gradually boiled down to twelve basic steps toward a good program.

1. **Do good shows.** Nothing else will make any difference if the shows you produce aren't interesting to watch. It's relatively simple to fill an auditorium with students. All you have to do is cast the quarterback, and be sure that at some point he has to wear a dress. Or, you can put a live animal on-stage; the animal will, sooner or later, do what live animals do. This will sell lots of tickets to other students. Always. But that only works for one show.

   More importantly, it won't encourage good students to audition for shows or to take your classes. If the only reason to be in a play is to be ridiculed by other teenagers, teenagers who don't want to be ridiculed will not participate. Likewise, students who want to do well want to be a part of organizations in which doing well is important. Good sports teams attract more participants than bad ones, even though opportunity is obviously greater on a poor team. Good drama productions attract more good people to auditions and to classes for precisely the same reason. Where there is more quality, more and better people want to be involved.

2. **Avoid program incest.** Once you find good students, particularly once you find good actors, you will be tempted to use them over and over again. The danger in this is that other students will believe that you are so committed to your favorites that there will be no room, or more importantly no parts, for newcomers. Once they begin to believe that, you won't have any newcomers.

   Once the program is large enough, this problem will solve itself to some extent. The more shows you have, the more parts there are to go around. The danger point comes in the early stages when you still have a comparatively small number of regulars on whom you can depend. The key is to not cast the same persons in leading roles in any two consecutive shows — that's really all it will take to scare away newcomers.

   It is extremely hard to avoid incestuous casting if you do only two shows a year, and one of them is always a musical. In that case, you have an obligation to cast your nonsinging actors in the only show they can perform in. The result is that a small handful of people are associated with the drama program, and that small handful stays small.

3. **Watch your budget.** Don't waste money. Never buy or build anything that you can't re-use. You may have to put it away and reuse it in two or three years, but always plan on a second use for anything you build or buy.

This also gives you a reputation for fiscal responsibility. It's amazing in this modern world how many outmoded clichés dominate the thinking of professional administrators. One of those clichés is that people in the arts don't know how to handle money and therefore can never be trusted with it. Build yourself a reputation as a person who can be trusted with money, and it will be easier to get money to be trusted with. Not easy, mind you, but at least easier.

4. **Make the program visible.** Perhaps the greatest problem in getting students interested in taking theater classes or trying out for plays is making the students aware that such an option is available. This is why the bulk of your new students will be friends and acquaintances of your old students.

Simply doing plays well is not enough. If you do good plays, the students who go to plays will be impressed, and some of them will decide to sign up and participate. That will have no effect whatsoever on the bulk of your organization's teenagers who don't go to the plays to begin with.

I made that breakthrough in my most successful school program by accident. I had an advanced acting class that was not responding well to classroom scene study. So I set up a program of one-act play performances done for English classes. As a result, students who never thought about coming to evening, public performances saw a wide variety of theatrical productions and realized that the drama program actually existed. This may not be the best method for you or your school, but you must do something that makes the program visible and attractive to the general student body. Without that, your program will always be limited to the one or two sub-groups of the school population from which you draw your very first set of performers.

In churches and community groups, this is even more difficult. Most people struggle to make the program visible to adults; that is, they focus all their publicity on trying to draw an audience to the plays themselves. Somewhere along the way, you have to find a way to attract student-aged people as participants. It's not enough just to announce auditions.

5. **Get parents involved.** Administrators respond to pressure, not to reason. Most successful programs for teens anywhere are successful because the parents insist that the school, church, or city government support them. If the parents don't care enough to nag administrators about a program, then administrators will neglect the program in favor of the ones supported by the parents who do nag.

Hence, a parent support group is essential to getting budget and administrative support. This is an area in which I was never very successful, so

I haven't a great deal of practical advice to offer. It is very difficult to find time to build booster clubs for drama, since production takes so much of your time already. It is also difficult to sustain such clubs, because parent interest is directly related to student participation. A student in the choir is in the choir all year, while a student in a play is only in that one play and may not participate in anything else all year long. As a result, parents of choir students tend to support the choir all year long, while parents of actors tend to lose interest after a particular show closes.

Many directors in programs with teenagers are very leery of parental involvement, for good reason. For the most part, parents want to see their own children do well. In drama programs, this means they want their kids to be stars. No parents are more obnoxious than stage parents. Life is just a lot easier without having such parents around. However, most of your students' parents are not stage parents. If anything, they're not quite sure that they want their kids involved in drama to begin with. These are the parents you want on your side, because they will be most enthusiastic when they start seeing the positive effect your program is having on their own teenager.

If you can't make supporters of your parents, then at the very least, do not make enemies of them. Always keep them informed about rules, responsibilities, and schedules. Answer questions when they have them. Stick to your schedule in rehearsals. Angry parents will do you an incredible amount of harm, and they can do it very quickly. Administrators will automatically side with parents over teachers or staff. If you can't organize the parents, or cultivate the parents, then at the very least, do not give them any grounds for complaint.

6. **Develop a program with easy entrance but difficult advancement.**
   You must have high standards of performance. You must also remember that students are not born with the skills you want, nor can you quickly spot the most productive performers. One of my most dependable actors started as a freshman who could barely hold his head up in public. I cast him in a tiny part only because I ran out of bodies. He was in every public show we did thereafter, because he got better in every show. We couldn't have done some of the shows without him. This doesn't begin to mention the tremendous personal impact he had on the other students in the program who saw this "average nice guy" succeeding. Had I not let him in that first show, I would never have seen him again. The chances are very good that I would never have seen a half-dozen other (and quite talented) boys that he brought along in the next year or so.

   You must find a way to let practically anyone in at the beginning levels of the program, and then weed out the people who don't work hard and

214

improve. I did this with open auditions for all public plays, and open enrollment in all beginning courses. But I let no one advance to intermediate or advanced classes without teacher consent. Everyone was welcome to see if they liked drama, but no one was promoted automatically in classes, and no one was cast automatically in productions.

7. **Get out of the English classroom.** For directors in schools, this may ultimately be the most important organizational advice I can offer. Good shows take teacher time, and English teachers have no time. If you make one writing assignment per week in English, and have the usual 150 students, even at a minimum of five minutes per paper, you'll spend 12.5 hours grading them. That's almost your whole rehearsal time, right there. That doesn't begin to count the time spent reading material, preparing lesson plans, dealing with the committees forced upon you, and so on. In addition, every new idea in education that comes along always gets dumped on the English teachers first. This means that English teachers are expected to revise their curriculum almost annually. In spite of what other teachers will claim, no one else in the school has that kind of workload. If you are a good English teacher, you won't have the proper time to devote to the drama productions. If you are a bad one, it won't matter because your reputation among the students will be that of a bad teacher.

The best thing, of course, is to teach drama classes. These take a lot of preparation time but have the advantage that they are completely under your control and don't have the paper grading demands of the English class. Naturally, you can't teach these until they exist, and you have to survive the early years when the program has not yet been built.

Until you get your drama classes, teach practically anything else but English. You can even be a counselor. It will be a shock to most people, who think of drama as part of literature and therefore obviously part of English, but remember, one of the values of drama is that it uses all of human experience. There's no reason why you must be a specialist in literary analysis.

To considerable extent, of course, this advice is pointless. Almost all drama teachers are hired to be English teachers first. No school administrators would even think of looking for a drama teacher who could also teach math. What you must concentrate on from the first day you walk through the door is a way to get any drama classes and drama budget items shifted out of the English department. No department in the contemporary school gets less support from administrators than the English department. As long as your program is thought of as an extension of the English program, you will have no status, no administrative support, and no budget. Try to get a separate drama or drama-speech department, if

215

speech still exists in your school. That probably won't work, at least not initially, but it's worth a try. At the very least, get into the arts department with the choir and band. You'll still be a second-class citizen there, but that's better than being the fifth-class citizen in the English department.

8. **Teach good classes.** This is really hard, much harder than directing good productions. For the most part, I would recommend throwing out anything and everything you ever learned in college about teaching or about acting and starting over from scratch. College education teachers think drama is a set of games you can use for personal therapy. College drama teachers think high school teachers are beneath their notice and wouldn't offer any useful training even if they knew any. Many textbook publishers think the field is too small to worry about and in general just try to rewrite college texts. Even when publishers try to be more useful and practical, they are severely limited by the fact that textbooks are selected by committees of "educators," not by the teachers themselves, and so they have to include much of the standard educationese of the day.

Most teachers ultimately deal with this by trying to reteach the classes they took in college, or even high school. For the most part, this doesn't work. High school teenagers simply do not have the same attention span, concentration, or sense of responsibility as college students, even in this era of declining college standards. You have to adjust to that quickly, or you won't survive. Most people quickly turn to theater games and improvisation, because they keep the class occupied. That's fine; I recommend it, if the games and improvisations are focused on learning to act rather than on personal therapy. But when you begin to use these games and improvs, it is absolutely critical that you still do written work, tests, homework, memorization, theater history, theater literature, and even the occasional lecture. When you do only theater games and/or improvisation, students tend to forget that there is real work involved in drama productions. Then they rebel when you suddenly demand it in rehearsals. Don't let the ease with which theater games in particular occupy class time deceive you into relying on them alone.

There is a second danger in heavy reliance on games and improv. A program that students associate with the playing of games is a program that will lose students who think their time is too valuable for game playing. Those will almost always be your best students. You have to provide some real challenge for the smarter or more experienced students as well as nurse along the beginners and the "average."

Whatever content you may offer in your classes, always remember that you are working with teenagers. Whenever possible, do at least two different things in class every day. Attention span is twenty minutes at the maximum. If you send groups into corners to work on scenes, don't leave them there all period long. If you do games, stop the games half-way through and switch to something else.

9. **Don't rehearse big, public shows in class.** A number of schools have production classes in which a show is rehearsed for the semester and then performed. While this does save extracurricular time for the teachers involved, it most often closes down the program itself. First, it limits your casting to the people who are able to schedule a particular period of the day. Second, it limits your casting to the people you already know, for how else are they to know they should sign up for the class? Third, it wastes an inordinate amount of student time. How can you justify to yourself, much less to parents, the idea that a student should take an entire semester course in order to say one line in a play? Fourth, the students who can't find room in their schedule are usually the best potential performers — the kids who are taking a full academic load of college prep courses and can't afford to drop an advanced math class or a language class *just* to be in a play. Fifth, it encourages outsiders to believe they are not wanted, with the result that they never try to get in.

10. **Establish a technical class.** This is important for several reasons:

First, it takes some pressure from your time schedule. It allows you to move the bulk of your technical work to class time rather than extracurricular time. It gives you a dependable work force for that technical work.

Second, it augments the program — gets those all-important enrollment figures up, gets you out of another English class, and gets people from a broader segment of the student body in the program.

Third, it provides a pressure-free entrance into the drama program. I established mine because I thought I could attract some boys who, once they saw we would not emasculate them, could be lured into acting. As it happened, the classes drew just as many girls who wanted to learn about tools and electricity and such things but were afraid of taking regular shop and mechanics classes. Almost all were people who had no particular interest in theater before taking the class.

Many people offer a similar class but keep it tightly restricted to five or six boys who "take care of the auditorium." I went the opposite direction and sold the class to my principal on the grounds that I would use technical production as a means to teach "life skills," such as making measurements, following directions, fulfilling responsibilities, meeting deadlines, and so on. I invented a grading system built completely on points "paid" for successfully fulfilling "contracts." Students knocked down the doors. The first semester there were twenty-five in the class, and the second semester we turned away that many. The next year we had two classes of thirty, and by the third year I could have filled a third class, but I simply didn't have the funds or the productions to keep them busy.

You, of course, will adapt things to your own needs. In an era of fewer electives, there will be fewer kids with the flexibility to try such a class. The point is, you can tap a vast body of "average" students with these classes, teach them something useful, and perhaps get them interested in a cultural program that they would avoid like the plague if you tried to sell it as culture. The existence of the tech classes can make everything else possible.

11. **Do all musicals, or do almost none.** You can't build drama classes if the bulk of your play choices encourage students to take music classes. There must be significantly more roles for non-singers than for singers, or there will be no reasons why students should take any acting classes.

You should do musicals, as discussed in the previous chapter. If you want a big program, however, you must either do them rarely, or do them all the time. Anything in between will harm more than it will help. The balance that seems to work best is one musical every two to three years.

12. **Stay out of personality reclamation.** This is one of the hardest bits of advice to offer, and one of the hardest to follow.

Drama is a craft and a discipline. It is not therapy. It never has been, and it never will be.

You are not a psychiatrist. If students come in with personal problems, you have no obligation to solve those problems for them. If they learn to meet your standards — if they work hard, do good work, make real progress, and become better actors or more skilled and responsible technical workers, then there should always be room for them in the program. If they don't, you have a much greater obligation to those who do.

This is a serious point, for how you deal with these "problem" students will determine how you are perceived by the rest of the school. If drama is a good place for students with problems to go, then drama will be full of students with problems. Pretty soon, they will crowd out all other students, and you will have nothing but problem students. Once this happens, you are dead. No average or good students will want to be associated with a program that is full of "losers" and "jerks." No one on the faculty or in the administration will take you seriously as a teacher or as a director. The shows will turn bad, because students with personality problems don't make good student actors and don't take on responsibility well. If you welcome the dregs of school society, you will soon get nothing but the dregs of school society, because no other students in the school want to be associated with these people. Harden your heart just a bit, and let someone else save them. Otherwise, you will soon need someone to save you.

There will be a lot of pressure on you to "save" these kids. Since the words drama and class were first combined, counselors and administrators have used those classes as dumping grounds for students no one else wants. Resist. The arts are not "someplace to put the kids no one else wants."

Two groups in particular must be kept out of your classes and productions at any cost. One group consists of what used to be called "head cases." These are the kids with serious psychological problems, who need real counseling. Counselors try to put them into drama classes for the same reason that institutions offer handicraft classes — they believe the classes have no standards. Give a few Fs and the counselors will stop doing this. Send them back to the counselors and let them do the job they're supposed to do.

Second are the "druggies." In the contemporary world, the majority of your students have probably experimented with drugs of some kind, so you can hardly eliminate anyone who ever came into contact with drugs. The druggies are different — drugs are their culture, the central focus of their daily life. For some reason, since the 1950s, the general public has come to believe that drugs and art are somehow interconnected. They're not; theater is hard work, and you don't do it better under the influence. Resist any attempts to dump these kids in your classes, no matter how much you need the enrollment.

In a practical sense, kids from these two groups are no real problem. Most of the time, they don't bother to come to class at all. They will rarely bother to audition for shows, so you don't often need to reject them. The problem is that kids in the middle, the kids who are wavering, don't want people to think that they're head cases or druggies. They'll drop out of your classes, and stop coming to auditions. And those kids in the middle are precisely the kids you can do something to "save."

This doesn't mean you should only take perfect students. For one thing, there aren't any. There are still lots of students you can "save." But they are the "average" kids who haven't yet found their way. They may be about to give up but are still hesitating. Some of these may be unpopular, most are just ignored. Nobody pays much attention to them, one way or another. For them, success in any school program can be wonderful. In a play in front of the public, it can be earth-shattering. There are hundreds of these in every school. Every now and then, you will find a kid with great talent whom everyone likes and who has no problems. Every now and then you will find a kid with great talent who has lots of problems. But these are special cases, and very rare. You can't build a program around them. Look for the untapped talent in the kids no one pays much attention to. That's the core of your program, and the ultimate secret of your success as a teacher as well as a director. Make room for kids who are on the edge — always, whenever and wherever you can. When they've gone over the edge, leave them to the counselors and psychiatrists.

CASE HISTORY ILLUSTRATION

Many teachers allow themselves to start thinking like their community. They begin to believe that you can only have successful drama programs at the rich schools, the suburban schools, or even worse, the "white" schools. This is simply not true. To illustrate this, permit me to tell of my own experience.

In 1971, I came to teach in a high school with a single drama class of twenty-one students. The high school was average or below average in every conceivable way. The student population of about 1,700 invariably scored around the fiftieth percentile in national tests, the student body for all the time I taught there was about thirty percent minority students, and the drop-out rate from freshman to senior year always exceeded forty percent. The parents in the district were lower-middle-class — clerks, secretaries, mechanics, truck drivers, oil field workers, salesmen, etc. It was in a community known for its lack of interest in arts or culture. The school had no special funding for "the arts."

The previous year, the school produced fall and spring plays that had drawn average student attendance of less than fifty per play. By 1975, we had 200 students a year in drama-related classes. We added a second drama teacher to the staff, produced four public productions a year that averaged about 300 students in the audience per show (plus the usual parents and relatives). In addition, we presented ten to twelve one-acts each year to classroom audiences as part of a drama curriculum for English classes, complete with annual themes and lesson plans. That enrollment and output sustained itself with some fluctuations for ten years or more.

It was a dream program in a place where it was supposed to be impossible. My story is repeated in some form in hundreds of schools and community groups across the nation daily. It can be your story, too. You *can* do a good program, just as you can do good play productions, in "average" schools and with "average" students in "average" communities. You need only have faith in yourself, believe you can do it, and be willing to dig in to get the job done.

FESTIVALS

At some point, you will be invited to participate in a play festival. When it comes, be careful.

In theory, festivals, like musicals, are a good idea. They bring together a number of different plays from a number of different organizations. You can exchange ideas with other teachers and directors, and your students can see plays and meet other students. The plays are observed by visiting experts who critique performances, giving students a chance to receive outside evaluation from persons who have participated in the larger world of theatrical experience. The festival situation gives new publicity and status to the theater programs in all the schools. In theory, this should be wonderful for all concerned.

Unfortunately, like musicals, festivals in practice are often quite different from the theory.

Festival Awards — Winners and Losers

Almost all festivals give awards of some kind. No matter how carefully the sponsors emphasize that these awards are merely recognitions of excellence, it always turns into winners and losers. There is no way to avoid this — if you go to a festival without awards, your principal will want to know why you're wasting the school's money and time. It is nice to be recognized, and it is especially good for students who are talented but who receive little or no support from the school administration. Still, theater is not a contest. The purpose of a race or a game is to beat your opponents. The purpose of a play production is to make sense of the script and to entertain the audience. No matter how much festival sponsors try to downplay the idea, festivals by their nature will encourage the idea that the purpose of theatrical production is to compete with other producers of theater and beat them.

You can deal with this syndrome only by setting a good example to your students. Stress that the purpose of the festival is to see and to be seen, not "to win." It won't remove that sense of competitive exultation when your students win prizes, or eliminate the self-doubt and depression when they don't. But it will lessen the intensity of such feelings. That's all you really can do.

Festival Adjudication Is Sometimes Inconsistent and Arbitrary

The other point to remember is that everything about the festivals depends on the persons adjudicating. Even in the best of circumstances, there is no general agreement on judging criteria. Festivals are rarely the best of circumstances. Sometimes, the judges will be very knowledgeable but have no experience at transferring their knowledge to students. Sometimes they will be very knowledgeable and see things you have never noticed (which is one of the reasons for going to a festival, after all). Sometimes they will be very knowledgeable but use very different criteria from those that you use. Often, however, they may not be very knowledgeable at all. They will reward what they like and give low evaluations to what they don't like, regardless of the criteria that are announced.

Sometimes, they are just plain perverse. I once attended the finals of a festival in which I had no show competing and had no stake in the awards. There were four shows, two of which were very strong in some aspects of production, but weak in other ways. One was okay, meaning that there was nothing particularly inadequate about it, but nothing particularly outstanding. The fourth was wretched — the male principal did not know his lines and was obviously reading them off the backs of props, in which he would occasionally lose his place. Other cast members were making up pointless jokes to fill in the spaces while he looked for his lines. Nothing intended to be funny got any laughs, and the whole production was so poorly staged and rehearsed that we in the audience didn't know when it was over. So, as we waited for awards, the general audience discussed the relative merits of the two obvious leaders and tried to figure out how the terrible production had made it into the finals to begin with. The teachers among us hoped that the third, competent show would get some kind of consolation award to recognize its competence and preparation. It would be hard to imagine our surprise when the fourth show won the bulk of the awards.

As it happened, I knew one of the judges, and later met him and asked him how they had come to that decision. After enumerating the many obvious failings of the show I had seen, he agreed with me that all those faults were there in that show and not present in any of the others. "Then how," I asked, "could it be the best performance?" Absolutely straight-faced, he answered, "The show was so weak and the male lead was so bad that the rest of the cast must have been great or they'd never have made it to the end of the show." I didn't have the nerve or energy left to ask him how, then, the male lead who was reading his lines from the back of the props had been given the best actor award.

Festivals May Not Help to Support the Goals of Your Program

Not every festival will be judged by people who have different criteria of excellence than yours. You cannot depend on them to encourage what you want to encourage, to recognize what you hope will be recognized, to correct what you know needs correcting, or to say what needs to be said. You cannot psych them out and prepare a show especially to win awards, because the judges vary from festival to festival. You can only do the best you can do, stage the shows well, prepare the actors for their roles, and also prepare the actors for the good and the bad aspects of the festival experience.

Costumes Often Influence the Judging Unfairly

Festival rules always say: "Shows will be judged solely on the quality of performance. Technical aspects will not count in the judging." At the same time, I have rarely been to a festival at which the show with the prettiest costumes didn't win the best show award. Not necessarily the best costuming, but always the prettiest, most attractive costuming, usually in period. Sometimes this was a result of good costuming, where good costuming supported good performances. In many others, it was simply pretty costumes that disguised the parts of the production the judges were supposed to be evaluating. This often hurt shows that were well-costumed for their characters and situations, but happened to be contemporary or lower-class and thus not very pretty or fancy or "costumey." It always hurt shows where the director had been naive enough to bring a good show in "rehearsal clothes" or "suggested costumes."

I don't want to suggest that you should throw over all your principles in order to win festival prizes. At the same time, I think you'll find that this observation is accurate at most festivals you will attend. Until you find a festival that requires everyone to perform in T-shirts and jeans, you will find that the awards given are directly related to the flashiness of the costumes.

VIDEO

Nothing has ever affected theater the way the camera has. Theories, religion, and censorship have all had an effect, but the camera remade our conception of the actor. Stanislavski started theorizing about "natural" acting just before movies were invented, but it took decades for his ideas to travel from Russia. By that time, the camera in movies had already made naturalness an ideal. The introduction of sound to film and the use of microphones soon made it a necessity.

For the most part, this didn't really bother teachers and directors in the schools. We had to use what we had, and what we had was a stage. Until the late sixties, it was a gigantic stage, in a gigantic auditorium. Good teachers encouraged their students to be natural, but it was a heightened naturalness, something that could project to the back of a thousand-seat house. However, television and changing urban patterns cut down the size of our audiences. We moved to smaller stages and experimented with unusual shapes, like the arena.

Television Redefined Everything in the Sixties and Seventies

Television began permeating our lives. It changed everything for the teacher/director. Drama became what it was on TV, and acting became the kind of acting that worked on TV. Even during the golden age of Hollywood movies, the stage was a legitimate equal. After TV, the stage became a by-way, a quaint minority interest. The glamour was in Hollywood, the regular jobs were on TV. Most actors began to use their stage jobs purely as a means to audition for the casting agents who choose actors for TV and films. This idea has now permeated almost all of our work in the schools. The only acting your students know, and in most communities, the only acting the teachers know, comes from what we see on the screen. Students still learn on the stage, but only because the stage is a cheaper place to learn.

Everything Changed Again in the Eighties With Video Cameras

Another technological change came to redefine the world of drama. Video cameras got small enough and cheap enough to be ubiquitous. When I began teaching in the late 1960s, only a handful of very wealthy schools had a video camera. It was usually a clunky, heavy thing on a tripod that no one knew how to use. It recorded in dirty grays on reel-to-reel tape on a machine so heavy it couldn't be moved out of the A-V room. It was useless for anything but talking heads. People in other fields were always talking about how great this would be for drama, but drama teachers soon realized that it was pointless to even try to use it. Now, in any classroom in even poor school districts you will find a dozen or more students who have handheld video cameras that shoot in color at near professional standard. Many also have editing machines that allow them to intercut scenes, add titles, sound-tracks, and animation. There is no practical reason why you cannot do everything in class for the camera.

The Video Camera Cannot Be Ignored

You are a stage director. You would like to concentrate on teaching how to act on-stage and on staging plays well. I have a strong emotional belief in the theater as a living entity. Where film from the past or from other cultures somehow seems to turn merely quaint and cute after a few years, plays from the past or from other cultures almost always seem alive and current on-stage. Actors and crew members working together on-stage get a completely different experience from the one they get working for a camera. Stage work is interpersonal work, while camera work is impersonal at best. In simplistic terms, you can make a living from drama on camera, but you can have a life on-stage.

But the camera is everywhere. It's cheap. Students expect it. Parents expect it. Administrators expect it. In the back of our own minds, we teachers and directors also expect it. You're going to have to use the camera in some way. How you use it will depend ultimately on your own personality and your own situation. It will also depend on technology. Things have moved so fast in video electronics and computer technology that I don't want to try to advise anyone in a field that depends completely on predictions. However, I would like to mention some pitfalls that have been common in the past and will probably continue to be common in the future.

Videotaping Exercises Can Be Self-Defeating

One of the most obvious ways to use the camera is to record classroom exercises and scenes so that students can see and evaluate their own work. This is an obvious use of the technology, and it is the use most administrators described when they justified buying the cameras to begin with. In practice, this doesn't work as well as theory says it should. First and foremost, actors in general are insecure, and teenagers are the most insecure actors of all. To take pictures of their faults magnifies their faults. No matter how positive your verbal criticism might be, there's no way to disguise the fact that you are taping a scene or a monolog to show the student what is "wrong" with it. Thus, students who are already self-conscious grow even more self-conscious.

Over the years, I simply stopped doing this. Actors were *always* worse after they saw video of their own work. Instead of thinking about the *Now* of Performance, they were thinking about "how they looked." The last thing you want any actor thinking about is "how they look." Even at the most successful levels, actors try to avoid seeing themselves. When people are making movies, every day the director looks at the film that just got back from the lab, to make sure there is no need to retake a scene. Most actors go out of their way to avoid watching these "dailies." Many big stars tell interviewers that they don't even watch the movies or TV shows after they are completely finished. They have learned over the years that it makes them too self-conscious, and that it often interferes with rather than helps their acting. If even established, secure stars feel that way, imagine how beginning students full of teenaged anxiety will feel. Be very careful with this. It has a tendency to backfire and produce exactly the opposite effect from what you intended.

Videotaping Is an Inefficient Use of Time

There is also a practical problem with this particular use of the camera. If you tape a person in class, then you must show the tape of that person in order to criticize the tape. You may even need to rerun it a couple of times to make clear what you mean. Unfortunately, you have twenty-five to thirty-five other people in that class, who are doing nothing while this is going on. It can take three or four days just to have everyone in class do a monolog; with video taping, the assignment could take two weeks. And that's assuming that the tape recorder, the VCR, and the TV monitor all work perfectly every time, which is a pretty big assumption with school equipment. That's enough time to completely lose your entire class for the semester.

Videotaping Performances of Copyrighted Plays Is Illegal

The second major use of video is to tape performances. This always has several problems. First and foremost, it is illegal. Period. Always, in every situation. You are breaking the law. If the play is still in copyright, every playscript and every royalty bill will state that you have the rights to perform only on-stage and only a fixed number of performances. Video rights must be negotiated separately. This applies to all video rights. You may think that the law doesn't apply to schools, but it does. As far as the law is concerned there is no difference between a tape of your high school or church production of a play and a pirate video made with a hidden camera at a Broadway production.

This hasn't stopped very many from making tapes of shows. The parents will run their cameras no matter what you do. Often you may feel you need to make a tape available to all just to keep the noise of the mini-cams from drowning out the actors' voices. Most people assume that, since the tape is made only for the purpose of a "record" of the program, it is somehow exempt from the law. At the very least, they think that none of the copyright holders will bother about one little school a thousand miles away from New York. In the past, that was probably true, but that was before the VHS cassette. Now there are lots of companies who have paid for video rights to plays and films, and who expect to sell or rent them to schools and libraries. They see your tape as competition. And they will prosecute. Not everyone, of course, and not every time, but the risk is real. Schools have been prosecuted and fined.

Videotapes Can Be Counterproductive to Your Total Theater Program

If you do make a tape, you will soon find that it is always a disap-pointment. We expect plays on tape to look like TV shows. Even if you are recording live, you need at least three cameras. You need good microphones arranged to cover all the stage. You need a plan, to know when each camera goes into closeup and when it stays in long shot. Suddenly you realize that you're no longer directing a play, you're spending all your valuable time planning a videotape production.

Finally, regular taping of shows may ultimately destroy your audience. For reasons I can't explain, once students believe a tape will be made, they assume that it will be shown in class somewhere, probably an English class. So why should they come see it, when they'll just see it in class anyway? It doesn't matter that you have no intention of showing it in English classes. They'll think it anyway, as soon as they hear rumors of plans to make an "official" tape.

The one really valid educational use of the camera in the theater program is to make productions directly for the camera. You design and plan the production to be taped. You rehearse and shoot it as if it were a video production. Students get the experience of "making a movie." It doesn't interfere with or skew the experience of a stage production or the daily life of the classroom. It may be debatable whether it is still a theater program, but it is at least practical.

As with my comments on musicals, I have stressed the negatives, because most people automatically think there are only positives. The camera is a fact of life. But it is not an unmixed blessing. Be careful and think long and hard before you make it a central part of your program.

APPENDIX

Books Related to Staging, Directing, Costuming, and Rehearsal

Anderson, Barbara and Cletus. *Costume Design*. Holt, 1984.
Attractive, well-illustrated, and wide-ranging, probably the best single textbook for costume designers.

Baygan, Lee. *Makeup for Theatre, Film, and Television: A Step-by-Step Photographic Guide*. Drama Books, 1982.
Affordable, practical, and very useful — black-and-white photos — with specific problems illustrated step by step and with careful attention to the needs of minority actors and actresses.

Benedetti, Robert. *The Actor at Work*, 6th ed. Prentice-Hall, 1994.
The most widely used acting text of the seventies and eighties, with tendencies toward the touchy-feely kind of exercises and attitudes.

Berry, Cicely. *Voice and the Actor*. Macmillan, 1973.
Vocal coach at the RSC with a ground-breaking and now widely imitated approach aimed at using the voice you have better rather than trying to change it into some standardized stage voice.

Bland, Joellen. *Playing Scenes From Classic Literature*. Meriwether Publishing Ltd., 1996.
Excellent rehearsal and audition dialogs. Gives students a chance to act from classic literary scenes.

Boleslavski, Richard. *Acting: The First Six Lessons*. Theatre Arts, 1933.
The book from which Americans learned — and mis-learned — about Stanislavski, written in a cutesy tone that will drive you nuts, but nonetheless absolutely essential to anyone connected with theatrical production.

Boucher, Francois. *20,000 Years of Fashion*. Abrams, 1987.
The best single-volume survey of costume history.

Brockett, Oscar G. *History of the Theatre*. 7th ed. Allyn and Bacon, 1995.
The standard college text in the field.

Burris-Meyer, Harold and Cole, Edward C. *Scenery for the Theatre,* rev. ed. Little, Brown, 1971.
The bible for scenery designers and TDs; everything you need to know

about everything related to construction, painting, shop organization, safety, and materials. Detailed and expensive.

Cassady, Marsh. *Characters in Action.* Meriwether Publishing Ltd., 1995. The basics of playwriting. A helpful book for play selection and considerations for adaptations.

_____. *Theatre and You, The.* Meriwether Publishing Ltd., 1992. An introductory text on all aspects of participating in a stage production.

Clurman, Harold. *On Directing.* Macmillan, 1972. A classic in the field, from one of the most respected professional directors from the Golden Age on Broadway.

Cohen, Robert. *Acting Professionally: Raw Facts About Careers in Acting,* 4th ed. Mayfield, 1990. Advice for aspiring actors, which can give you insight on what is expected of you as director and/or teacher of aspiring actors.

Corson, Richard. *Fashions in Hair.* Prentice-Hall, 1965. Hundreds of illustrations and discussions of period hair styles and their significance in characterization and costume.

_____. *Stage Makeup,* 8th ed. Prentice-Hall, 1989. I've never met a makeup problem that I couldn't find a solution for in here. Unfortunately, recent editions have grown terribly expensive, and the concentration on latex prosthetics which amateurs cannot afford has caused some of the most valuable material to be dropped as "outdated," so you might find used earlier editions more helpful in your situation.

Dean, Alexander and Carra, Lawrence. *Fundamentals of Play Directing,* 5th ed. Harcourt Brace College, 1989. The most practical of the traditional college texts; each new edition seems to be simpler and less practical, so you may want to look for older versions.

Dearing, Shirley. *Elegantly Frugal Costumes.* Meriwether Publishing Ltd., 1992. A practical, do-it-yourself costume maker's guide. Excellent special effects costumes.

Dryden, Deborah. *Fabric Painting and Dyeing for the Theatre.* Drama Books, 1981. Techniques for many situations, including many simple and cheap methods to turn those cast-offs into something very useful and attractive.

Ellis, Roger. *Scenes and Monologs From the Best New Plays.* Meriwether Publishing Ltd., 1992.

An anthology of new scenes from contemporary American plays. Excellent for acting practice.

Gibson, William. *Shakespeare's Game*. Atheneum, 1978.
Using Shakespeare as his source, the best book ever written about playwriting; insights that will help your dramatic sense at every turn.

Goldman, William. *The Season*. Limelight, 1984.
A classic you should read, even if it wasn't so helpful. Goldman follows the complete 1967-68 season on Broadway both as critic and reporter backstage, producing an invaluable guide to How-Not-to-Do-It.

Green, Michael. *The Art of Coarse Acting*. Drama Books, 1981.
The funniest book ever written about play production; a step-by-step guide on how to guarantee that everyone will think you are amateurish and incompetent.

Grote, David. *Script Analysis*. Wadsworth, 1985.
Detailed practical advise about what to look for and how to find it in a playscript.

Hodge, Francis. *Play Directing*, 4th ed. Prentice-Hall, 1994.
The most intellectual of the standard college texts.

Ingham, Rosemary and Covey, Liz. *The Costume Designer's Handbook*, 2nd ed. Prentice-Hall, 1992.
Extremely valuable guide to the practical process of costume design, organization, and construction.

King, Nancy. *Theatre Movement: The Actor and His Space*. Drama Books, 1971.
One of the earliest textbooks for movement, so it tends to be simplistic, but in many ways her layout and annotations are still the most valuable help for a field that is almost impossible to put on paper.

Lee, Robert L. *Everything About Theatre!* Meriwether Publishing Ltd., 1996.
A guidebook of theatre fundamentals, it is an overview of all aspects of dramatic production.

Litherland, Janet and McAnally, Sue. *Broadway Costumes on a Budget*. Meriwether Publishing Ltd., 1996.
How high schools can improvise costumes for name Broadway shows. Lists over 100 famous musicals categorized by costume style.

Lord, William H. *Stagecraft I*. Meriwether Publishing Ltd., 1991.
A complete guide to backstage work. This book will help your students learn the tools and language of backstage work. Loaded with photographs and illustrations.

Markus, Tom. *An Actor Behaves*. Samuel French, 1992.

A revision of his earlier *The Professional Actor*, and the name change says it all. A guide to the behavior you want to train your students in, and a reminder that you are not alone — professionals now share many of the same problems you do.

Marshall, Henry. *Stage Swordplay, or "So You Want to Be Errol Flynn."* Marymount College, 1977.
Detailed guide to dramatic and safe stage sword fights.

Martinez, J. D. *Combat Mime: A Non-Violent Approach to Stage Violence.* Nelson-Hall, 1982.
Excellent, well-illustrated introduction to the problems, with strong emphasis on safety, falls, and blows, but not as helpful on swordplay.

McGaw, Charles J. and Blake, Gary. *Acting Is Believing: A Basic Method,* 5th ed. Harcourt Brace College, 1992.
One of the first college texts, still widely used; Method in approach.

Miller, James Hull. *Self-Supporting Scenery for Children's Theatre...and Grown-Ups' Too,* 5th ed. Meriwether Publishing Ltd., 1986.
A classic by the man who developed the concept of scenery that can march on and off the stage platform. Illustrated throughout.

_____. *Stage Lighting in the Boondocks,* 4th ed. Meriwether Publishing Ltd., 1995.
Lighting for people who have little or no modern equipment — that is, almost every school or church group.

Parker, W. Oren and Wolf, R. Craig. *Stage Design and Stage Lighting,* 6th ed. Harcourt Brace College, 1990.
Popular and widely used college text, with lots of information that is well organized.

Rosenthal, Jean and Wertenbaker, Lael. *The Magic of Light.* Little, Brown, 1972.
Not a practical textbook, but its numerous photos are the best available introduction to all the things lighting can do for you.

Spolin, Viola. *Improvisation for the Theatre.* Northwestern University Press, 1963.
Arguably the most influential book in American theater, certainly the most significant in theater education. A bountiful supply of ideas for acting class, sometimes also useful for specific problem areas in rehearsal.

Stanislavski, Konstantin. *An Actor Prepares,* trans. by Elizabeth Hapgood. Theatre Arts, 1948.

_____. *Building a Character,* trans. by Elizabeth Hapgood. Theatre Arts, 1949.

_____. *Creating a Role*, trans. by Elizabeth Hapgood. Theatre Arts, 1961.
If you're going to deal with modern acting theory, get it from the source.

Stern, Lawrence. *Stage Management*, 5th ed. Allyn and Bacon, 1995.
Aimed primarily at the stage manager, the most detailed book on the process of organizing and operating all aspects of rehearsals and backstage during performance.

Tompkins, Julia. *Stage Costumes and How to Make Them.* Plays, Inc., 1969.
Out of print and often hard to find, but easily the best simple introduction to the problems and solutions of pattern making for period costumes (or any others).

Welker, David. *Theatrical Direction.* Allyn and Bacon, 1971.
A middle ground between Hodge and Dean/Carra.

ABOUT THE AUTHOR

Since he organized his own theater company in Wichita Falls, Texas, at age eighteen, David Grote has directed more than 150 productions. He headed an independent student company at the University of Texas. He later taught and directed theater programs in high schools in Bakersfield, California, for eleven years before moving to Scripps College in Claremont, California. Since the mid-eighties, he has been a free-lance director based in San Francisco, but he has continued to work regularly with high school and college student actors in workshops, summer programs, and as a guest artist. He is the artistic director of the Classic Theater Project in San Francisco and has been a regular artist-in-residence at the San Francisco School of the Arts. He is the author of many books and critical studies dealing with a wide variety of subjects concerning theater production. Eleven of his plays have been produced. His seven one-act published plays are used in high school competitions nationwide.

ORDER FORM

MERIWETHER PUBLISHING LTD.
P.O. BOX 7710
COLORADO SPRINGS, CO 80933
TELEPHONE: (719) 594-4422

Please send me the following books:

_____ **Play Directing in the School #TT-B214** $15.95
by David Grote
A drama director's survival guide

_____ **Directing for the Stage #TT-B169** $16.95
by Terry John Converse
A workshop guide of creative exercises and projects

_____ **Everything About Theatre! #TT-B200** $16.95
by Robert L. Lee
The guidebook of theatre fundamentals

_____ **Theatre Games for Young Performers** $12.95
#TT-B188
by Maria C. Novelly
Improvisations and exercises for developing acting skills

_____ **Acting Games — Improvisations and** $12.95
Exercises #TT-B168
by Marsh Cassady
A textbook of theatre games and improvisations

_____ **The Theatre and You #TT-B115** $15.95
by Marsh Cassady
An introductory text on all aspects of theatre

_____ **Theatre Alive! #TT-B178** $24.95
by Dr. Norman A. Bert
An introductory anthology of world drama

These and other fine Meriwether Publishing books are available at your local bookstore or direct from the publisher. Use the handy order form on this page.

NAME: _____

ORGANIZATION NAME: _____

ADDRESS: _____

CITY: _____ STATE: _____

ZIP: _____ PHONE: _____

  ❑ **Check Enclosed**
  ❑ **Visa or MasterCard #** _____

Signature: _____ *Expiration*
                                          Date: _____
      (required for Visa/MasterCard orders)

COLORADO RESIDENTS: Please add 3% sales tax.
SHIPPING: Include $2.75 for the first book and 50¢ for each additional book ordered.

  ❑ *Please send me a copy of your complete catalog of books and plays.*